Distributed Intelligent Systems

T0137774

Abdellah Bedrouni • Ranjeev Mittu
Abdeslem Boukhtouta • Jean Berger

Distributed Intelligent Systems

A Coordination Perspective

 Springer

Abdellah Bedrouni
Department of Mechanical &
Industrial Engineering
Concordia University
1455 de Maisonneuve
Boulevard W.
Montreal, QC H3G 1M8
Canada

Ranjeev Mittu
Head, Intelligent Decision Support
Section (Code 5584)
Information Technology Division
U.S. Naval Research Laboratory
4555 Overlook Avenue, SW
Washington, DC 20375
USA

Abdeslem Boukhtouta
Defence Research & Development
Canada - Valcartier
Decision Support Technology Section
2459 Pie-XI Blvd. North
Val-Belair, QC G3J 1X5
Canada

Jean Berger
Defence Research & Development
Canada - Valcartier
Decision Support Technology Section
2459 Pie-XI Blvd. North
Val-Belair, QC G3J 1X5
Canada

ISBN 978-1-4899-8305-3   ISBN 978-0-387-77702-3 (eBook)
DOI 10.1007/978-0-387-77702-3
Springer Dordrecht Heidelberg London New York

Printed on acid-free paper

Springer is part of Springer Science+Business Media (www.springer.com)

Preface

It is commonly acknowledged that the number of deployed multi-agent system based applications is still surprisingly limited, despite intense and innovative research being conducted in this community. Practical commercial and industrial applications that are deployed are very few, and those that are in-use, are typically characterized as closed systems incorporating pre-defined communication and interaction protocols. Thus, it is likely that future research in the area of agent-based systems will be directed towards bridging the gap between academic promises and reality.

Emerging application domains such as Ambient Intelligence, Grid Computing, Electronic Business, Semantic Web, Bioinformatics, and Computational Biology will certainly influence the direction of future agent-oriented research and technologies. Over the next decade, it is thus expected that real-world problems will impose the emergence of truly-open, fully-scalable agent-oriented systems, spanning across different domains, and incorporating heterogeneous entities capable of reasoning and learning, as well as adopting adequate protocols of communication and interaction.

Among all emerging issues associated with building such sophisticated applications, none is more fundamental, challenging, and complex than the need to dynamically ensure adequate management of activities attributed to a large number of heterogeneous entities. Thus, "coordination" will remain a central issue in agent-oriented engineering research. In this context, the agent research community will likely continue to strive for establishing appropriate coordination models and frameworks, devising novel strategies, and building adequate protocols and mechanisms.

This book covers issues and comprehensively answers commonly asked questions about coordination in agent-oriented systems. It is dedicated to providing a broad overview of current coordination models, strategies, techniques and mechanisms. Progress achieved in addressing multi-agent systems coordination highlights the need to develop "unifying" models and frameworks in order to better understand the coordination process, and clearly shows that researchers are indeed moving in that direction. However, it is apparent that the research community can gain tremendous knowledge through a formal and systematic documentation of "best practices" pertaining to the use, under realistic operational environments, of pre-existing as well as new coordination models and techniques. Such procedures would be susceptible of leading to further opportunities to bring new approaches in multi-agent coordination into the mainstream application domains. Lastly, based on current practical deployed applications and future opportunities, this book identifies and examines current trends, emerging issues and challenges, and future agent-oriented research directions.

Contents

Chapter 1 Coordination

Abstract Coordination is a central issue in agent-oriented distributed systems. Coordinating adequately the activities attributed to a large number of heterogeneous entities in agent-oriented engineering research remains a fundamental, challenging, and complex issue. This Chapter strongly suggests that coordination is central to distributed systems. It explores the interdisciplinary nature of this concept, reviews the definition of various forms of interaction, highlights the need for a universal or a unified definition, and finally examines key fundamental aspects related to the coordination function.

1.1 Introduction

Creative and innovative ideas are unmasked through a "synergy of knowledge" resulting from the interaction among research areas that were once considered distinct disciplines. Indeed, Cognitive Science has recently emerged at the interface of several disciplines, in particular neurobiology, psychology, Artificial Intelligence (AI) and epistemology. Chaos Theory has found applications in such diverse disciplines as mathematics, physics, economics, and psychology. In the same way, Distributed Artificial Intelligence (DAI) is an exciting and fruitful domain of scientific research that "brings together and draws on results, concepts and ideas from different fields such as computer science (including AI), sociology, economics, organization and management science and philosophy" [1].

Confusion, discomfort or disquiet often accompanies the use of multiple methods, concepts, and approaches using theoretical frameworks from different disciplines. Much interdisciplinary and cross-disciplinary research has not yet produced a synthesis which would go beyond disciplinary boundaries, and hence produce innovative solutions to deal with and solve real world problems. The development and implementation of feedback loops which can link researchers and experts of different disciplines would promote understanding and eliminate confusion. It is thus believed that the current practice of using multiple methods, techniques and technologies in the area of DAI should be grounded in a comprehensive and pragmatic framework, if results are to be integrated and interpreted in a meaningful way.

Indeed, research in the area of DAI appears to be only concerned with the transfer of tools and methods across disciplines in response to specific problems. Based on an instrumental view of knowledge, DAI thus lacks a disciplinary ap-

A. Bedrouni et al., *Distributed Intelligent Systems: A Coordination Perspective*,
DOI: 10.1007/978-0-387-77702-3_1, © Springer Science + Business Media, LLC 2009

proach that would introduce order and control required to ensure that knowledge produced is legitimate and reliable. In this respect, there have been relatively few or no attempts to reconstitute the past, shape the future, clarify the objectives, carefully set up rules, and establish reasonably identifiable boundaries of this emergent research and application field. We will discuss in this chapter the challenging issue related to the coordination theory and we will explain the ill defined concept related to coordination.

1.2 Coordination, a Challenging Issue

Among all presently identified issues inherent in DAI, none is more fundamental, challenging, and complex than the need to adequately manage inter-agent activities. Thus, coordination has emerged as a central issue in agent-oriented engineering research. Hence, DAI focuses primarily on designing coordination protocols and mechanisms to manage activities of artificial, intelligent, and autonomous entities.

Indeed, there is a growing interest in questions regarding how activities of autonomous entities in complex systems are, or can be, adequately coordinated? Scientific research focuses on coordination in parallel and distributed systems, in human systems, in organizations, and in complex systems involving human-computer interactions. On the other hand, research regarding collective activities in insect societies has long discovered that insects, relatively simple natural agents, form a society with a very high-level of coordination. Coordination is thus the subject of interdisciplinary research in a variety of different disciplines including computer science, sociology, economics, organizational theory, management science, biology, etc.

Present in every activity in human society, coordination remains an elusive concept. Almost everybody has an intuitive sense of what the term coordination means. While good coordination is often invisible, a lack of coordination is obviously highly noticeable. In attempting to investigate and characterize this area of research, it becomes necessary to have a clear and more precise definition of the term coordination. However, due to its multi-disciplinary nature, the coordination concept has generated a diversity of definitions.

Over the last three decades, the particular area of DAI has witnessed intense research activities regarding problems associated with inter-agent processes. In this respect, efforts directed towards developing practical agent-oriented application systems have brought a considerable progress, ranging from the establishment of coordination models to the design and development of coordination protocols and mechanisms.

Indeed, different application contexts exhibit different needs with respect to coordination, and the choice of a coordination model or mechanism can have a great impact on the design of multi-component applications. Research on coordination languages and models provided the ability to evaluate and compare the impact of different classes of coordination models and languages. On the other hand, research addressing coordination strategies in agent-based systems led to different techniques, protocols and mechanisms, ranging from the simple but effective Contract Net protocol to more sophisticated market mechanisms. More recently, formal dialogue games have found application as a foundation for interaction protocols between autonomous agents. Thus, dialogue game protocols have been proposed for agent team formation, negotiation, consumer purchase interactions, and joint deliberation.

Finally, research activities are currently focusing on achieving a smooth transition from existing closed agent-based applications to interconnected automated and scattered systems in large and open environments – AgentCities, Grid[1] computing, Semantic Web, etc. Building and deploying such ubiquitous, open, and scalable applications will certainly pose a major challenge in terms of providing adequate and specifically adapted coordination models and protocols.

1.3 Coordination, an Ill-defined Concept

Presented as an inherently interdisciplinary concept, coordination thus becomes diverse enough to accommodate a broad spectrum of definitions. As Coates et al. point out [2], this concept still remains ill-defined despite the significant amount of research devoted to developing a wide range of approaches, models, strategies, and mechanisms. Differences in the definitions of coordination can indeed represent a contributing factor to the reigning confusion in the area of coordination. At first sight, these differences appear to stem from the perception and conception that scientists, experts, and researchers from different disciplines have on the functional role ascribed to coordination.

A rough examination of the literature provides the ability to highlight at firsthand the absence of a single operational definition of the term coordination which is acceptable to all. In seeking to identify the differences that experts use to define coordination, it may be at least possible to help promote the idea that a consensus or a common understanding would enhance communication between researchers from different disciplines and thus pave the way for a larger cooperation in the area of coordination. Indeed, the literature provides a number of alternative definitions of the concept of coordination. The purpose is to address the question regarding the meaning of this term, further attempt to outline the differences, examine whether these differences in meanings are complementary or contradictory and finally seek to identify a common thread that could be used by researchers and experts from various disciplines as a basis for communication and research.

---

[1] A software environment that makes it possible to share disparate, loosely coupled IT resources across organizations and different geographic zones.

First recorded in 1605, the term coordination generally means *"orderly combination"*[2]. Without changing the basic traditional meaning that prevails over centuries, contemporary English brought fresh insights into the meaning and usage of the term coordination. Thus, literally, the term coordination is generally increasingly associated with harmonious functioning of different parts. In the American Heritage Dictionary of the English Language[3], coordination is defined as *"harmonious adjustment or interaction"*. The Hyperdictionary[4] describes coordination as *"the regulation of diverse elements into an integrated and harmonious operation"*. Furthermore, the Oxford Advanced Learner's Dictionary proposes an entry for the word coordination which is defined as *"the act of making parts of something, groups of people, etc. work together in an efficient and organized way"*. Finally, the Web-based AllWords.com[5] offers a number of other words that can be used as synonyms of the term coordinate: organize, harmonize, integrate, synchronize, correlate, match, relate, arrange, codify, grade, and graduate.

Indeed, Ossowski et al. draw attention to the differences in how the research issue pertaining to coordination is addressed in different disciplines [3]. While referring to research addressing coordination in Social Sciences as primarily *analytic*, the authors identify coordination-related interest in the area of Distributed Artificial Intelligence as *constructive*. In this respect, Ossowski et al. argue that a scientist in a Social Sciences discipline "observes the outside world and builds a model of how human agents mutually adapt their activities as part of societies or organizations". On the other hand, research in Distributed Artificial Intelligence is primarily concerned with the design and implementation of appropriate and adequate coordination mechanisms in accordance with known requirements and anticipated operating conditions of groups of artificial agents. More precisely, a central designer in the sub-area of Distributed Problem-solving constructs interaction patterns among benevolent agents, so as to enable these entities to efficiently achieve a common goal. In addition, a researcher in Multi-agent Systems is concerned with how to install desired global properties into "heterogeneous groups of autonomous agents that pursue partially conflicting goals in an autonomous fashion". On the other hand, Ossowski also points out that research in the area of economics is focused on the structure and dynamics of the market as a particular coordination mechanism [4]. As noted, in organizational theory, the emphasis is, however, placed on "predicting future behavior and performance of an organization, assuming that a certain coordination mechanism is valid".

Carriero and Gelernter advocate making a clear distinction between computation and coordination to provide the ability to build a complete programming model [5]. Such separation provides the advantage of both facilitating the reuse of the components of a program and allowing the identification of coordination pat-

---

2 The Barnhart Concise Dictionary of Etymology, 1994

3 The American Heritage Dictionary of the English Language, 4th Edition, 2000

4 http://www.hyperdictionary.com/dictionary/

5 http://allwords.com

terns that could be applied in similar situations [6]. Based on these considerations, coordination is specifically defined as "*the process of building programs by gluing together active pieces*" [7]. Within the framework of this research, the term *coordination* is thus used to refer to the process of *gluing together* independent active pieces to build programs whose pieces – i.e. a process, a task, etc. - can effectively communicate and synchronize with each other [7].

According to Van de Ven et al. [8], organizational theory is based on the premise that all organizations need coordination. As noted, coordination of organizations is achieved either through a programming approach or a feedback approach. In this context, three predominant modes are thus identified to be frequently used to coordinate work activities within an organization. While the programming approach is said to be exercised through an *impersonal mode*, the feedback approach, also known as mutual adjustments, is described as a method of coordination that occurs either through *personal channels* or *group meetings*. Whatever approach or mode is however used, Van de Ven et al. define the coordination of work activities within an organization as a process of "*integrating or linking together different part of an organization to accomplish a collective set of tasks*".

In a paper entitled "*A note on Hierarchy and Coordination: An Aspect of decentralization*" [9], Kochen and Deutsch focus on the costs and benefits associated with coordination and attempt to define in operational terms the concept of coordination. In this context, the authors ask the question of what is logically intended by the term coordination, while recalling that in popular usage it means "*harmonious functioning of several actors*". Then, Kochen and Deutsch put forward the 'managerial-based view' that coordination is "a task involving planning and execution of how two or more jobs should be synchronized in time and space". From this point of view, the coordination concept is thus defined as "*a means of directing the operation of functional units so that their joint behavior attains a specific goal with a higher probability and/or at a lower cost*". In this respect, the authors draw attention to the fact that in case the functional units are human, a common expectation of reward is usually also required. In tackling the question of the operational meaning of "coordination", Kochen and Deutsch observe that in case several activities are required for obtaining a joint reward, coordination then "consists in bringing about a deployment in time and space of the combined activities such as to increase the expected reward".

While recalling research efforts pertaining to coordination in diverse disciplines, Nwana et al. note that systems – even biological systems – appear to be coordinated through "*individual cells or agents acting independently and in a seemingly non-purposeful fashion*" [9]. In this context, the authors further argue that human brains exhibit coordinated behavior from apparently 'random' behaviors of very simple neurons. Apparently based on these arguments, Nwana et al. state that coordination is essentially "*a process in which agents engage in order to ensure a community of individual agents' acts in a coherent manner*".

1.4 Coordination, Objective or Subjective?

A critical challenge to providing the foundation of an organized DAI discipline is to capture, classify and evaluate knowledge regarding the concept of coordination so as to facilitate the transfer of information and foster the development of new concepts and strategies. Indeed, coordination in DAI is fundamentally an interdisciplinary topic with research efforts scattered across disparate communities. Coordination concepts, techniques and technologies developed in one area are not easily transmitted to researchers and practitioners in other disciplines.

Given the confusion that characterizes the area of DAI, it would seem impossible for experts and researchers to correlate, categorize, analyze and act on the unstructured information, concepts, results and data hidden in reports and published literature. Despite significant difficulties, many attempts gave rise to a series of empirical coordination-related studies and surveys in order to organize ideas, assess knowledge, evaluate progress, track down trends, and shape future research.

Based on the widely accepted framework introduced by Malone and Crowston, coordination in Multi-Agent Systems (MAS) is indeed viewed as the art of managing dependencies [11]. Within this framework, Schumacher recently proposed to distinguish between objective and subjective dependencies as a way *"to define an original and comprehensive framework for modeling, designing, and implementing interactions in complex MAS"*.

Indeed, *objective dependencies* are referred to as inter-agent dependencies, or in other words, the configuration of a system in terms of the basic interaction means, agent generation/destruction and organization of the environment. On the other hand, *subjective dependencies* are described as intra-agent dependencies often involving "mentalistic" categories. Correspondingly, Schumacher classifies coordination into two categories:

- *Objective coordination:* refers to the management of the objective dependencies that are external to the agents and essentially concerned with inter-agent aspects.
- *Subjective coordination:* refers to the management of intra-agents dependencies towards other agents.

The author argues that a failure to differentiate between these two levels of coordination would complicate the design and subsequent implementation of MAS, since it leads to using intra-agent aspects for describing system configurations. He gives the example of a multi-agent system that is intended for modeling the hierarchy in an organization but would model this hierarchy within each agent through knowledge representation, instead of describing it by establishing communication flows that represent it. He finally notes that this confusion between subjective and objective aspects is typically present in MAS composed of mental agents that use Agent Communication Languages (ACLs) in order to communicate.

According to Schumacher, subjective coordination is dependent on objective coordination, as the first is based on and supposes the existence of the second. Thus, adequate mechanisms specifically designed and implemented to ensure subjective coordination in MAS must have access to mechanisms associated with objective coordination. Otherwise, no subjective coordination can be possible.

1.4.1 Objective Coordination

Objective coordination is, as already stated, mainly associated with the organization of "the world of a multi-agent system". This type of coordination is indeed achieved through:

1. *A description of how the environment of a multi-agent system is organized.* In this respect, M. Schumacher introduces the notions of implicit and explicit organizations. An organization given or imposed by the underlying logical structure on which a MAS evolves is identified as the implicit organization, since it does not explicitly model the environment. However, the explicit organization establishes a model of an environment that does not necessarily reflect the intended logical structure.

2. *Proper handling of the agents' interactions.* Handling agent interactions implies the need to describe the interactions between an agent and its environment, and the interactions between the agents evolving in that environment. Through its perception, an agent establishes a relation with its environment. It can also influence this environment through specific actions.

In this respect, it is argued that the interaction with the environment can be understood by a given agent and thus used to communicate. Since all information is transmitted within the environment, communication thus becomes an action that influences the agent's milieu. To explain this view, the author cites the case of a robot spreading or diffusing information like an insect that spreads pheromone in its environment. Another robot can then sense this information and certainly notice the presence of the source in the same way an insect can detect the trace of another roaming insect.

However, interactions between agents are based on specific communication means. As shown in Figure 1.1, Schumacher classifies these communication means into four basic paradigms [12]:

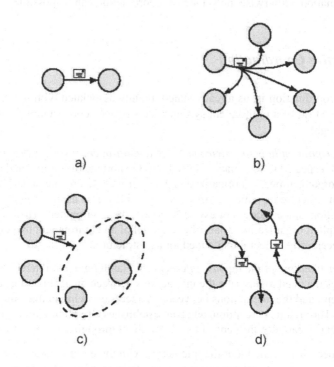

a. Peer-to-peer communication

b. Broadcast communication

c. Group or multi-cast communication

d. Generative communication

Figure 1.1: Basic communication paradigms [12]

- *Peer-to-peer communication.* – This form of communication is characterized by messages sent directly to specific agents. Agents usually identify their partners through, for instance, email-like addresses. It is however possible that an intermediate channel is used to ensure this form of communication and takes charge of the transmission of data.

- *Broadcast Communication.* – In this form of communication, a message is sent to all agents. In this context, agents are offered the opportunity to evaluate or ignore the transmitted and received data.
- *Group communication.* – A group communication is achieved when a message is sent to a specific group of agents.
- *Generative communication.* – Generative communication is a particular form of communication between agents realized through a blackboard, where agents generate persistent messages which can be read by other agents. Access to messages in the blackboard is achieved independently of the time a message is provided. This form of communication is thus uncoupled.

Schumacher further distinguishes between *identified* and *anonymous communication*. He identifies *identified communication* as a form of communication requiring an identity of a partner. *Anonymous communication* is, on the other hand, described as a form of communication where the agent producing the message ignores the recipient, and vice-versa.

1.4.2 Subjective Coordination

Based on how the management of dependencies is handled, subjective coordination has been divided into two categories:

1. **Explicit subjective coordination.** Schumacher notes that the research in DAI has induced the development of several coordination techniques that are designed to tackle explicit subjective coordination. Quoting Jennings, the author clearly identifies these techniques as approaches that typically consider coordination as "*the process by which an agent reasons about its local action and the (anticipated) actions of others to try and ensure the community acts in a coherent manner*". According to him, these techniques are considered as subjective coordination because of a common tendency to resolve subjective dependencies by means of intra-agent structures. He notes that the latter often involves high-level "mentalistic" notions and appropriate protocols.

Characterized as explicit because of their explicit handling of coordination, the techniques identified above are further divided into three categories in accordance with Ossowski's classification [13]:

- *Multi-agent Planning techniques* – Multi-agent planning techniques can indeed be centralized or decentralized. Using these techniques, agents establish and commit to behave according to a plan. The latter contains and describes all actions required for agents to appropriately achieve their respective goals.
- *Negotiation techniques* – According to Schumacher, negotiation techniques represent the most significant part of DAI coordination-related research. Bor-

rowed from Bussmann and Mueller [13], he proposes a definition where negotiation is described as *"the communication process of a group of agents in order to reach a mutually accepted agreement on some matter"*. He finally notes
that the negotiation process which starts from contradictory demands generates
agreements that can be later re-negotiated.

- *Organization techniques* – Schumacher observes that these techniques support
  a-priori organization patterns by defining *roles* for each agent. He explains that
  a role determines the expectations about the agent's individual behaviour by
  describing its responsibilities, capabilities and authorities within a MAS. He
  adds that the agent then consults its organizational knowledge and the role devoted to him and acts accordingly.

According to Schumacher [12], the purpose of organization is associated with
objective coordination, while the notion of role refers to a subjective dependency
towards other roles in a MAS. This argument is indeed used to label organization
techniques as methods belonging to subjective coordination. The author finally
notes that organization methods generally suffer from a lack of dynamicity in the
structure of a given organization, since roles are considered as long-term relationships.

2. **Implicit subjective coordination.** – In collective robotics, different methods and
   approaches of using autonomous robot teams are implemented to efficiently
   fulfill predefined missions. The use of multiple mobile robots offers significant
   advantages over the use of a single robot: the possibility of distributed sensing,
   distributed action, task dependent "reconfigurability", and system reliability
   through redundancy. Multiple robots sharing a common environment organize
   their actions based on the result associated with the actions attributed to other
   robots. Locally perceived through distributed sensors, this result provides the
   ability to resolve subjective dependencies, namely the necessity to sense specific information in order to act. This type of coordination, commonly known
   as *"stigmergic coordination"* allows indirect communication between autonomous entities through sensing and modification of the local environment. It literally means *"an incitement to work by the product of the work"*. Using research on coordination in the area of collective robotics as an example,
   Schumacher outlines how agents may also coordinate themselves implicitly,
   without having explicit mechanisms of coordination.

The Storms and Grant paper [15] gives a short description of the Explicit and
Implicit coordination. This paper gives also a short taxonomy of the coordination
properties and the agent coordination mechanisms for network enabled capabilities.

References

1. Gerhard Weiss, "Multiagent Systems and Distributed Artificial Intelligence", In Multiagent Systems – A Modern Approach to Distributed Artificial Intelligence", Gerhard Weiss, Editor, the MIT Press, Cambridge, Massachusetts, 1999.
2. Coates, R. I. Whitfield, A. H. B. Duffy, and B. Hills, "Coordination Approaches and Systems – Part II: an Operational Perspective", Research in Engineering Design, Vol. 12, pp. 73-89, 2000.
3. Sascha Ossowski and Ana García-Serrano, "Social Co-ordination among Autonomous Problem-solving Agents", In Agents and Multi-Agent Systems: Formalisms, Methodologies, and Applications, W. Wobcke, M. Pagnucco, C. Zhang, Editors, Vol. 1441, pp. 134-148, January 1998.
4. Sascha Ossowski, "Coordination", In Coordination in Artificial Agent Societies, LNAI 1535, pp. 15-30, Springer-Verlag Berlin Heidelberg, 1999.
5. N. Carriero and D. Gelernter, "Coordination Languages and Their Significance", Communications of the ACM, Vol. 35, No 2, pp. 97–107, February 1992.
6. B. Freisleben and T. Kielmann, "Coordination Patterns for Parallel Computing", In Proceedings of the Second International Conference on Coordination Models, Languages and Applications, LNCS, Springer Verlag, September 1997.
7. N. Carriero and D. Gelernter, "How to Write Parallel Programs", A First Course, MIT Press, 1992.
8. Andrew H. Van de Ven, André L. Delbecq, and Richard Koenig, JR, "Determinants of Coordination Modes within Organization", In American Sociological Review, Vol. 14, pp. 322-338, April 1976.
9. Manfred Kochen and Karl W. Deutsch, "A note on Hierarchy and Coordination: An Aspect of decentralization", In Management Science, Theory Series, Vol. 21, Issue 1, pp. 106-114, Sept. 1974.
10. H. S. Nwana and L. C. Lee and N. R. Jennings, "Coordination in Software Agent Systems", In the British Telecom Technical Journal, Vol. 14, No 4, pp. 79-88, 1996.
11. M. Schumacher, "Objective Coordination in Multi-agent Systems Engineering: Design and Implementation", Lecture Notes in Artificial Intelligence, Vol. 2039, Springer Verlag, Heidelberg, Germany, April 2001.
12. M. Schumacher, "Multi-agent Systems", In Objective Coordination in Multi-agent Systems Engineering: Design and Implementation, M. Schumacher, Editor, Lecture Notes in Artificial Intelligence, Vol. 2039, Springer Verlag, Heidelberg, Germany, April 2001.
13. S. Ossowski, "Co-ordination in Artificial Agent Societies" In Social Structure and Its Implications for Autonomous Problem-Solving Agents, Vol. 1202, LNAI, Springer Verlag, 1999.
14. S. Bussmann and J. Mueller, "A Negotiation Framework for Co-operating Agents", In Proceedings of CKBS-SIG, S. M. Deen, editor, pages 1–17, Dake Centre, University of Keele, 1992.
15. P.P.A Storms and T.J. Grant, Agent Coordination Mechanisms for Multi-National Network Enabled Capabilities, 11th ICCRTS Cambridge, UK, 2006

Chapter 2 Coordination in Distributed Problem Solving and Planning

Abstract Coordination in distributed problem-solving and planning systems presents multiple dimensions to be notionally characterized. This chapter first introduces distributed problem-solving properties and motivations through various applications. It then explores fundamental notions, problems and issues associated to task and result -sharing as well as characterizing the salient features of distributed planning. Different distributed planning categories are discussed: distributed planning for distributed plans, distributed planning for centralized plans and distributed planning for distributed plans.

2.1 Introduction

The concepts and algorithms that establish the foundations of Distributed Problem Solving (DPS) and planning are addressed by Durfee in [1]. In this respect, the author devotes a great deal of effort to outline, through practical examples, how protocols of interaction can be used to ensure that appropriate information is conveyed to the right agents to adequately accomplish problem solving and planning. Durfee refers to distributed problem solving as a subfield of distributed AI where efforts are directed towards "getting agents to work together well to solve problems that require collective effort". While underlying the inherent distribution of resources such as knowledge, capability, information, and expertise among agents in a DPS system, the author argues that an agent incorporated in such environments is unable to accomplish its own tasks alone, or at least can accomplish its tasks through collective action. Indeed, solving distributed problems requires coherence – a common property of multiple agents associated with the incentive to work together - and competence – an attribute of multiple agents describing their ability to work together well.

Durfee points out that group coherence is hard to realize among individually-motivated agents, and essential for multiple agents to solve a problem in a distributed way [1]. Considering that agents are designed to work together in distributed problem solving, Durfee further notes that a fair degree of coherence is thus already present in such environments. In addition, he attributes this coherence either to the implementation of some sort of stimulating payoffs to self-interested agents that are only accrued via collective efforts or to the introduction of disincentives for agent individualism. Finally, Durfee thus concludes that distributed problem solving concentrates on competence to provide the ability to tackle problems that need to be solved so as to meet expectations about what constitutes viable solutions.

In "Trends in Cooperative Distributed Problem Solving", Durfee et al. compare the problem of designing a DPS system to the problem of building a house [1]. This process obviously involves several expert agents – each expert in a different area: one agent may be an expert in the strength of materials, another in the required space for different types of rooms, the next in plumbing, the other in electrical wiring, etc. As this task is beyond the individual capability of agents, building the house requires that agents cooperate.

In this respect, partial results have to be exchanged – the architect passes the blueprint to a construction company, tasks may be delegated from one agent to another – the construction company engages subcontractors, information related to the state of the problem-solving process has to be exchanged – the plumber will start his only when the building-workers notify to have finished the required task, and, finally, unforeseen conflicts have to be solved – the same plumber may have to negotiate with a building worker on how to solve a given conflict. Indeed, the house-building example highlights the boundary delimitation between DPS and ordinary distributed systems. According to Ossowski, an ordinary distributed system is designed to solve "*well-defined problems in the frame of fixed control structures and rigid problem decomposition*" [3]. As stated, this type of system is mainly adapted to, or concerned with, issues such as "synchronization and technical aspects of communication". On the other hand, DPS tackles complex tasks where diverse aspects cannot be totally anticipated beforehand. In this type of system, the focus lies on aspects of cooperation within a dynamic problem-solving process. In this context, Ossowski observes that DPS tackles the issue of how the problem-solving activities of agents can be coordinated to successfully deal with the overall task. This issue includes many topics and questions related to finding and designating suitable agents to perform a given task, defining the appropriate partial results to be exchanged, and determining the right time for communication to take place.

2.2 Properties of Distributed Problem Solving systems

In "*Distributed Artificial Intelligence*" [3], Ossowski points to the problem of using the vaguely defined term "*cooperation*" when tackling aspects related to DPS. In this respect, he reports that various attempts have recently been made to characterize the area of DPS without the need to refer to the ambiguous notion of cooperation. However, Durfee and Rosenschein define and propose various properties designed to enable the identification of DPS systems [4]. Defined in the form of assumptions likely to be made with respect to DPS systems, the main properties are described below.

2.2.1. The benevolent assumption

This assumption implies that the agents in the system are benevolent – *the agents help each other whenever they are requested to do so.* While Ossowski notes that benevolent agents slavishly "do what they are told" [3], Durfee and Rosenschein clarify the meaning of benevolence by clearly stating that benevolent agents help each other whenever possible [4]. In groups of benevolent agents, any one entity might request others to do something without having to put forward the possibility of a reward or any kind of compensation. As a result, the benevolent assumption does not imply the existence or the necessity to implement a sort of authority structure or any other kind of organization between agents.

When using the Contract Net Protocol [5], an agent first determines whether the task it should perform can be subdivided into subtasks, then announces the resulting tasks that could be transferred and requests bids from agents that could perform any of these subtasks. In this context, tasks are allocated based on suitability and availability of individual entities, without any sense of an agent asking whether it wants, or has, to perform a task for this or the other agent. Upon hearing the task announcement, an eligible agent will make an honest bid with a reference to its ability to perform this task. In the end, the agent making the best bid will be awarded the task. As already stated, in the absence of any sense of reward, agents do not need to be bribed or otherwise persuaded to undertake tasks that other agents want them to perform.

However, Durfee and Rosenschein argue that the benevolent assumption is not a guarantee to cooperation and coherent coordination [4]. Even with agents willing to help each other, difficulties associated with timing and local perspectives can, as stated, lead to uncooperative and uncoordinated activities. To support this view, the authors provide the example of the Contract Net protocol where, according to them, important tasks could go unclaimed when suitable agents are busy with tasks that others could have performed. While referring to the Contract Net protocol, Durfee and Rosenschein also put forward the argument of a more general case where tasks could be improperly assigned so as to result in redundant or incompatible agents' activities.

2.2.2. The common goals assumption

Pursuing a common goal represents indeed a motivation for benevolence among agents sharing a common environment. Engaged in a group activity, these agents will thus attempt, in whatever way it is possible, to maximize "the same global utility measure". In this context, conflicts between agents are, according to Ossowski, essentially subjective [3]. Indeed, rather than arising from objective contradictory interests, such conflicts are due to "*incomplete or incorrect view of the state of the world*".

On the other hand, the common goals assumption is considered to lie at the heart of the Contract Net protocol [4]. As argued, this assumption is also at the core of cooperation in inherently distributed tasks where agents value "the development of a global result". Indeed, the Distributed Vehicle Monitoring Testbed (DVMT) simulates a number of geographically distributed sensor nodes that share the system wide goal of integrating the nodes associated local maps into a global map of vehicle movements [6]. In working together to achieve the convergence of the distributed system towards the global solution, each node is indeed helping the others make "good local interpretations as quickly as possible".

However, as Durfee and Rosenschein point out, local views on the problem to be solved – such as the above DVMT example – may indeed lead to globally incoherent local decisions [4]. Thus, in the absence of strict guidelines about responsibilities or interests, agents can "inundate each other with superfluous information". A more negative aspect lies in the fact that agents can, through information they send, distract other entities into pursuing unimportant tasks.

Finally, Durfee and Rosenschein highlight the absence of clarity regarding the level at which goals should be common so that a given system can be considered a DPS system [4]. In this respect, the authors imagine an environment where agents are meeting to hold a competition. Within this environment, the agents might, as explained, share a high-level goal of holding the competition, while having opposing goals regarding which agent is supposed to win the competition. Indeed, the PERSUADER system provides an interesting example of a distributed environment where agents, representing opposing sides in a labor contract, share a goal of reaching an agreement while having diverse preferences in rating candidate contracts [7]. As far as the PERSUADER system is concerned, the question is raised as to whether this system falls within the DPS category [4].

2.2.3. The centralized designer assumption

This assumption refers to whether a DPS system is a system with a centralized designer. In reference to concerns about getting all of the parts of a system to perform effectively as a whole, the central designer would likely design and implement agents that have the required characteristic of benevolence. With the task of building a DPS system, the central designer would thus calibrate the preferences associated with the agents and standardize the mechanisms required to express and act on these preferences.

As in the case of the common goals assumption, Durfee and Rosenschein raise the open question regarding the detail to which the common designer must specify each agent's design so as to incorporate all the agents into a DPS system [4]. Finally, the authors argue that the approach which consists in categorizing systems will likely remain arbitrary until aspects of agents that need to be dictated by a central designer to make an environment a true DPS system are exactly defined.

However, Ossowski refers to the third property as the *homogeneous agent's assumption* [3]. In this particular context, homogeneity is defined through the absence of "unnecessary" conflict or incongruity between agents. According to Ossowski, homogeneous agents would thus use compatible representation and communication languages, without pursuing conflicting goals.

2.3 Distributed Problem Solving, applications and motivations

Durfee identifies various technical motivations that stimulate and induce the development of both distributed problem solving and distributed planning [1]. At the same time, he enumerates examples of the kinds of applications through which these motivating factors can be clearly recognized and understood.

According to Durfee, an obvious motivation lies in the need to use distributed resources concurrently to allow a speedup of problem solving, thanks to the advantages conferred by parallelism. As noted, any possible improvements that can be achieved through parallelism obviously depend on the degree of parallelism inherent to the problem.

In this context, the *Tower of Hanoi* (ToH) puzzle is, as shown in Figure 2.1, described by Durfee as a classical toy problem that allows a large amount of parallelism during planning. The author reports that the puzzle is well known to students, since it appears in virtually any introductory AI course. He then explains that the ToH consists of a board supporting three pegs and n disks of different sizes initially placed on one peg with the largest one on the bottom and the other disks following in order of size. Under the condition that the disks must be moved one at a time, without ever placing a larger disk on top of a smaller disk, the problem, then, is to find an appropriate sequence of moves that will achieve the goal state: move the disks from the start peg to another peg.

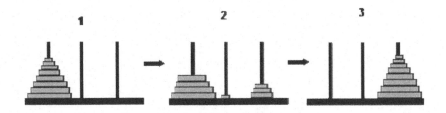

Figure 2.1: The Tower of Hanoi

According to Durfee, expertise or other problem-solving abilities may be inherently distributed to provide a motivation for distributed problem solving and planning. In this respect, he provides a practical example of a problem pertaining to concurrent engineering where a team of specialized agents could be involved in the design and manufacture of an artefact such as a car. As stated, this problem is characterized by the need to allow the agents to individually formulate components and processes, and combine these into a collective solution.

On the other hand, Durfee mentions other examples of applications where different problem-solving abilities are inherently distributed, such as supervisory systems for air-traffic control, factory automation, or crisis management. He explains that these applications can involve an interaction between tasks pertaining to event monitoring, situation assessment, diagnosis, prioritization, and response generation. Associated with these kinds of systems is, according to him, the need to employ diverse capabilities to solve both large and multi-faceted problems. However, Durfee prefers to use an application problem commonly known as *Distributed Sensor Network Establishment* (DSNE) – an application designed to provide the ability to monitor a large area for vehicle movements – as an example to further address strategies employed in the area of distributed problem solving and planning. The author then argues that the overall monitoring task cannot be accomplished through a central location, since a large area cannot be sensed from a single location. Thus, the problem in DSNE consists, according to him, in decomposing the large monitoring task into subtasks that can be appropriately allocated to geographically distributed agents.

Another motivation introduced by Durfee is based on the fact that beliefs and other data can be distributed. In this respect, the author further provides an example of an application where the problem is to actually conduct *distributed vehicle monitoring* (DVM) through a centralized mechanism. He points out that the procedure could be designed to allow each of the distributed sensor agents to transmit raw data to a central site to be interpreted into a global view. However, this centralized mechanism could, according to him, involve unnecessary communication compared to a strategy where separate sensor agents could formulate local interpretations that could then be transmitted selectively.

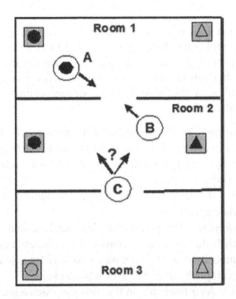

Figure 2.2: Distributed delivery example

A last motivation is considered and presented by Durfee as a possible case where the results of problem solving and planning might be distributed to be acted on by multiple agents. This possibility is then detailed through an example of a *Distributed Delivery* (DD) system (Figure 2.2), where agents can act in parallel to conduct the delivery of objects between locations. In this context, Durfee suggests that plan development could either be undertaken at a centralized site through a dispatcher or involve distributed problem-solving among agents. According to the author, features of the environment that unexpectedly change or were unknown earlier during planning can, during the execution phase, trigger changes in what the agents are supposed to do. In this respect, Durfee observes that all these decisions could be routed through a central coordinator. He further explains that it could be preferable for a variety of reasons that agents modify their plans unilaterally or with limited inter-agent communication.

Following the identification and brief description of the motivations underlying the development of applications in distributed problem solving and planning, various classes of distributed problem-solving strategies are then addressed by Durfee in a detailed and very structured and helpful way.

2.4 Task sharing

Task sharing, also known in the literature as *task passing*, represents the first class of distributed problem-solving strategies that Durfee considers. As reported, the idea behind this strategy consists in allowing an agent that has many tasks to enlist the help of other entities that have few or no tasks. The task sharing strategy is indeed presented as a four-step process: decomposition, allocation, accomplishment, and result synthesis.

1. **Task decomposition** – This is the initial step characterized by the need to generate a set of tasks susceptible of being attributed to other agents. In general, it consists in decomposing large and complex tasks into subtasks that could be undertaken by different agents.
2. **Task allocation** – This crucial step in the process consists in assigning the subtasks to appropriate agents.
3. **Task accomplishment** – The purpose of this step is to allow the agents to adequately accomplish the allocated subtasks. This process could eventually lead to further decomposition of the subtasks into smaller subtasks so as to allow each agent to accomplish alone the tasks it is handed.
4. **Result synthesis** – As a final step in this process, each agent that accomplishes its subtask is instructed to pass the result to the appropriate agent. The latter is usually the original agent which is behind the decomposition process and is thus likely to effectively and adequately compose the results into a complete overall solution.

In conclusion, Durfee notes that different steps might, under different circumstances, be more or less difficult. In this respect, he gives the example of an overburdened agent that begins with a bundle of separate tasks, making the decomposition of tasks into subtasks an unnecessary step. He also mentions the effect on the allocation process resulting from the case of the agent that passes tasks off to any of a number of identical agents. He finally points out that accomplishing the tasks does not always yield results that need to be synthesized in any complex way.

2.4.1 Task sharing among homogeneous agents

Durfee uses the example of the ToH problem described above in order to highlight the possibilities of task sharing. Concomitantly, he provides a thorough understanding of how this strategy can be implemented among homogeneous agents. Considering the task-sharing four-step process outlined above, the author describes how this very simple puzzle can be solved. We describe below the task-sharing steps for the ToH.

1. *Task decomposition* – Tackling the first step of the process through means-ends analysis leads to a recursive decomposition. It first amounts to solving the problem of getting to the state where the largest disk can be moved, and once it is moved, the next approach is to eventually determine how to get from this intermediary state to the goal state. Resulting from the ToH puzzle are thus a collection of sub-problems that can indeed be further decomposed into problems corresponding to the need to move the second largest disk to the middle peg so as to get it out of the way, etc.
2. *Task allocation* – Assuming an indefinite number of identical idle agents having enough skills and knowledge to solve the ToH problem, the allocation is thus reduced to a simple process of randomly assigning a task to one of these idle agents. On the other hand, the recursive decomposition terminates if the decomposed problems are such that the start and goal states are the same.
3. *Task accomplishment* – In general, using means-ends analysis, an agent can find the most significant difference between the start and goal states for which it is responsible. It can further decompose the problem based on this analysis.
4. *Results synthesis* – Once an agent has solved a problem, it then proceeds to pass the solutions back on up. In addition, the agent that has received solutions to all of the sub-problems it passed down can subsequently compose these into a single solution corresponding to a more comprehensive sequence of moves. This sequence is then passed up by the agent as its own solution.

Due to its hierarchical nature, the ToH problem represents, as stated, an ideal case for demonstrating the possibilities of distributed problem solving. However, it is worthwhile noting that most frequently encountered problems are more complicated than the ToH problem. In "Distributed Problem Solving and Planning" [8], Durfee enumerates the reasons for which most real-world problems are more complicated:

1. As the solution of one problem can affect the solution of others, problems will often "require backtracking upward in the abstraction hierarchy".
2. Rather than scaling up the number of agents with the problem size, the number of available agents is generally maintained at a fixed level.
3. In various domains problems are decomposed into qualitatively different sub-problems that require different expertise. As a result, problems to be solved cannot usually be decomposed into equal-sized sub-problems.
4. Substantial time is often required to conduct the process of decomposing problems, distributing sub-problems, and collecting results.

2.4.2 Task sharing in heterogeneous systems

In the ToH problem tackled above, the resulting sub-problems require agents with identical skills and knowledge – competencies. As a result, the decisions regarding the assignment of tasks and sub-problems are "extremely simple". However, the distribution of sub-problems becomes a complicated process in case the global problem is decomposed into sub-tasks that require different capabilities from agents having different expertise.

Indeed, it is difficult to train humans or build artificial entities that can handle every possible task. In this respect, Durfee points out [8] that building or training an omni-expert agent would result in an obvious waste of most of its capabilities. As in human-based systems, the strategy adopted in many distributed problem-solving systems consists in bringing together on demand combinations of experts from different areas [1,8]. These agents can thus combine their skills and knowledge in order to collectively solve problems that are beyond their individual capabilities.

Having a "table" designed to allow the identification of the agents' skills and knowledge – i.e. capabilities, an agent can indeed simply select a suitable agent to which it can also assign and send an appropriate sub-problem. However, Durfee notes that the decisions regarding the distribution of tasks are usually based on more "dynamic information" [1,8]. He further provides a typical example of a problem that may arise when an agent attempts to assign and distribute sub-problems to several other candidate agents. In this respect, Durfee raises the question of how this agent can discover which entities among the candidate agents that are capable of solving the sub-problem are already committed to other tasks.

According to Durfee, one way of discovering which candidate agents are already committed to other sub-problems is to use the *Contract Net protocol* with *directed contracts* or *focused addressing* [1, 8]. Based on the table of capabilities mentioned above, the agent – *called the manager in the Contract Net protocol* – announces a sub-problem to a specific agent – *in directed contracts* – or to a subset of other agents – *in focused addressing* – and requests that bids highlight acceptance and/or availability. Based on the collected returned bids, the manager can then award the sub-problem to the most favourable bid – either to the directed contractor or to one of the focused available contractors. However, it may happen that none of the agents is available to respond to the announcement as requested. In this context, the manager has various available options described below [1, 8].

- *Broadcasting contracting* – In an open environment, a manager using the Contract Net protocol is unlikely to be familiar with all of the possible contractors. In case first attempts to find an available agent through directed contracts or focused addressing fail, the manager may desire to extend its area of activity and update its knowledge regarding eligible contractors. In this respect, broadcasting the announcement remains the most commonly considered mode of operation in the Contract Net protocol available to the manager in order to reach those agents whose existence and / or capabilities may be unknown.

- *Retry* – Another simple strategy available to the manager is to retry the announcement. Assuming that a contractor can eventually free up, the manager can retry the announcement periodically at appropriate intervals. While quick retries may cause the network to bog down with messages, slow retries prevent agents from efficiently using each other. However, the Contract Net protocol can be reversed in order to overcome this problem. In other words, potential contractors can use the protocol to announce availability and managers can, instead of announcing sub-problems and collecting bids, respond to the announcements through bids of pending tasks.

- *Announcement revision* – Indeed, the eligibility specifications that can be examined by every potential contractor are contained in the announcement message. In case no contractors respond to an announcement, the manager may have been "too exclusive in whom it would entertain bids from". In this respect, another option offered to the manager is to relax the eligibility requirements until it begins to receive bids. Hence, the revision of the announcement can indeed be an iterative process.

However, the eligibility specifications could well reflect certain preferences over the quality of services that different contractors can provide. In this case, the manager will otherwise handle the lack of bids by taking a decision concerning "the relative importance of having a preferred contractor eventually pursue the sub-problem compared to finding a sub-optimal contractor sooner". According to Durfee, these preferences and trade-offs between them can, in many cases, be captured using economic representations [1,8].

- *Alternative decomposition* – In response to the lack of available contractors, another procedure consists in decomposing the overall problem so as to obtain a set of alternative sub-problems. As pointed out, the relationship between the problem decomposition process and the allocation of tasks is, in general, extremely complex [1,8]. While sometimes the space of decompositions can be very restrictive, the manager should, in other times, first determine the space of alternative contractors so as it can later focus on problem decomposition. In addition, the manager has to make appropriate decisions regarding the number of problems to decompose into sub-problems and the granularity of the resulting tasks. According to Durfee, these decisions depend on other features relating to the application environment [1,8].

2.4.3 Task sharing for distributed sensor net establishment

In *"Negotiation as a Metaphor for Distributed Problem Solving"* [9], Davis and Smith examine the concept of distributed problem solving and explore the use of the Contract Net framework of communication and control to demonstrate the solution of a simulated problem in area surveillance – *ship or air traffic control*. In this context, the authors discuss the mode of operation of a distributed sensing system – the Distributed Sensor Net Establishment (DSNE), a network of nodes scattered throughout a relatively large geographic area. Although the distributed sensor system may have several functions, ranging from passive analysis to active control over vehicle courses and speeds, the authors focus on the analysis function. While the task involves detection, classification, and tracking of vehicles, the solution of the problem is, as stated, to provide a dynamic map of traffic in the area.

2.4.4 Task sharing for interdependent tasks

Durfee has also looked into the question regarding task-sharing in problems characterized by the presence of interdependent tasks [1,8]. Indeed, problems similar to the ToH are widely acknowledged to generate tasks that can be accomplished independently. In other words, the sequence of actions required to get from the initial state to an intermediate state can be determined completely separately from the sequence required to move from that intermediate state to the goal state. As noted by Durfee, the sub-problems resulting from the task decomposition process can thus be successfully accomplished in any order or concurrently. Furthermore, the synthesis – the act of passing the result to the appropriate agent – need "only wait to complete until all the subtasks are carried out".

However, it is obvious that often tasks or subtasks contracted by eligible agents are interdependent. In this respect, Durfee puts forward the example of a concurrent engineering application where *"process planning subtasks usually need to wait until product design tasks have progressed beyond a certain point"* [1,8]. Consequently, a manager in charge of coordinating the execution of the subtasks can initiate a given subtask based on the progress of another, or, as noted, by communicating to contractors interim results that are required to accomplish other interdependent subtasks.

On the other hand, Durfee recalls the complexity associated with the process of solving assigned interdependent sub-problems [1,8]. Rather than being *a-priori* defined through the process of problem decomposition, aspects related to subtasks interdependencies might, more generally, only become apparent during the course of problem solving. Indeed, the task-sharing strategy can, as discussed above, be implemented through the Contract Net framework to establish, for example, a distributed sensor network. However, an important and challenging question arises on how to discover and exploit existing interrelationships between different classes of tasks allocated through the task-sharing strategy. While it can effectively be used to establish a distributed sensor network, this strategy does not provide sufficient basis for using the network, since "the runtime relationships between what is being monitored in different areas is as variable as the possible movements of vehicles through the areas". In this respect, it is interesting to note that the most appropriate approach is to generate and share tentative results so as to be able to accomplish interdependent tasks.

2.5 Result sharing

Given the same task, different problem solvers sharing a distributed environment will separately and independently (likely) derive different solutions – like students that are often given the same homework problem. Derived within the context of each problem solver, the results of the same problem-solving task performed by different problem solvers could thus well differ. Incentives that effectively motivate problem solvers to share results in order to enhance group performance include:

1. Confidence – Problem solvers can independently accomplish the same task from which results are separately derived. These results obtained independently can indeed help corroborate and/or clarify individual approaches and used to achieve and provide a collective solution with a higher level of confidence.
2. Completeness – Results emanating from each problem solver are assembled so that altogether can form a more complete portion of the overall task.
3. Precision – Results formulated independently by a set of problem solvers can be used by any agent in order to refine its own solution.
4. Timeliness – Solving subtasks in parallel offers the ability to optimize the time required to achieve an overall solution, though in principle an agent could solve a large sub-problem alone.

In a distributed problem-solving environment, agents obviously need, in some cases, to share results in order to accomplish subtasks. However, the process of sharing results is not as simple as it may at first sight appear. Emerging from this discussion is an important question on how a particular agent should assimilate shared results into its own solution. In response to this question, Durfee highlights the need for agents "to first know what to do with shared results" [1,8]. On the other hand, the author points to the need for agents to also practice a selective exchange of results. Indeed, communicating large volumes of results can obviously be costly, and managing a large volume of assimilated results "incurs overhead".

2.5.1 Functionally accurate cooperation

In various conventional applications – such as the ToH, problem-solving agents operate separately and independently without the need of exchanging results. In such applications, the problem-solving process amounts to the decomposition of the global task in such a way that each subtask can be performed completely by a single agent, without the need for this particular agent to see the intermediate results associated with the activities of other agents. Indeed, having all information and a complete specification regarding the subtasks assigned to them, these agents are "completely accurate in their computations".

Naturally well suited to distributed implementation, a number of other applications - such as sensor networks, tasks involving mobile robots, automotive and air-traffic control, etc. – lack the task decomposition characteristics of conventional distributed applications. In these applications, the lack of information makes it difficult to partition the data required to achieve a solution in such a way that an agent can locally complete a subtask without having to examine "the intermediate state of processing" elsewhere in the network. Apparently ill-suited to conventional approaches, such applications are indeed characterized by the lack of information and, hence, uncertainty and errors.

As suggested, an alternative approach is for the processing agents to engage in a different style of problem-solving characterized by highly cooperative interactions. Agents may thus formulate and exchange tentative results with one another. Initially proposed by Lesser and Corkill [10], this approach is commonly known as *functionally-accurate cooperation*. In the presence of uncertainty, the functionally-accurate cooperation paradigm provides an alternative model for task decomposition and agent interaction in distributed problem-solving architectures.

In *"A Retrospective view of FA/C Distributed Problem Solving"* [11], Lesser examines again the paradigm of the functionally-accurate cooperation, traces the development of a series of increasingly sophisticated cooperative control mechanisms for coordinating agents, and presents ongoing and new research directions in functionally-accurate cooperative (FA/C) systems. In this context, the author raises the key question of how to structure cooperative interactions among agents in order to limit costs associated with communication and still generate an acceptable answer with a reasonable amount of time.

In response, Lesser notes that the FA/C paradigm is designed to provide the answer to this question when an application can be structured in such a way that agents produce more complete partial results, handle solution uncertainty, detect inconsistencies and can speed-up local problem solving in a constrained problem space. According to the author, errors introduced as a result of incomplete, inconsistent and out-of-date local information are, in this way, resolved as an integral part of the asynchronous, co-routine exchange of tentative, high-level partial results among agents. In general, the objective behind FA/C distributed problem-solving is to allow agents to cooperate effectively in the presence of limited and inconsistent information related to the activities of other agents, different criteria regarding the most appropriate activities to perform, contradictory raw information and *"conflicting long-term problem-solving knowledge"*.

On the other hand, Durfee reports that the functionally-accurate cooperation approach has been extensively used in distributed problem-solving application where agents *"only discover the details of how their sub-problem results interrelate through tentative formulation and iterative exchange"* [1,8]. This author notes that participating agents need to consider the partial results that are formulated and received as tentative.

Furthermore, it is interesting to note that exchanging tentative partial solutions can impact completeness, precision and confidence. However, the iterative exchange of partial results is, eventually, expected to lead to agents accumulating enough information *"to keep moving the overall problem-solving forward"*. On the other hand, FA/C based problem solving could obviously incur dramatic communication overhead and wasted time, a problem that could be tackled through some control decisions. Another phenomenon known as **distraction** may well arise as a result of agents sharing too many results.

2.5.2 Shared repositories and negotiation search

The adverse side effects of increased communication associated with the functionally-accurate cooperation approach has already been outlined above. A common strategy designed to reduce the "potential flurry of multicast messages" is to instead concentrate and store tentative partial results from agents sharing the same environment in a single, shared repository. Indeed, the blackboard architecture is a commonly known strategy designed to allow *"cooperating knowledge sources to exchange and use results by communicating through a common, structured blackboard"*.

Using a shared repository in a design application would allow agents with different design criteria to search through alternative designs and critique these alternatives [12]. While it differs from traditional formulations, the search process amounts, in many ways, to a distributed constraint satisfaction problem [1,8]. In attempting to highlight the important differences, Durfee notes that agents are first not *"assumed to know whose constraints might be affected by their design choices"*. Since agents would not know whom to notify of their decisions, a shared repository is thus highly recommended. On the other hand, Durfee adds that these entities can also *"relax constraints in a pinch"*. Agents might, at any given time, need to choose between improving solutions, rejecting solutions, or relaxing expectations. In this context, heuristics to control the distributed search are also highly needed.

Negotiated search is applicable to diverse application areas and problem-solving environments [13]. As stated, the approach requires only basic search operators and allows maximum flexibility in the distribution of these operators. *Initiate-solution* represents the basic operator that proposes an initial state for searching a solution. *Critique-solution* is the operator that provides an evaluation of the solution in the form of feedback analysis together (when necessary) with information regarding detected conflicts. *Extend-solution* is applied "*to extend and evaluate a partially specified composite solution*". This operator is required in domains where solutions include interacting components, each developed by an agent. *Relax-solution-requirement* represents the operator that allows agents to change local requirements to reach mutual acceptability. At any given time, an operator can be invoked by an agent. According to Durfee, the problem domains for negotiated search are complex enough to require heuristic guidance [1,8]. Indeed, heuristic measures designed to guide an agent in its approach to invoke an operator – such as the *relax-solution-requirement* – are generally application-specific.

2.5.3 Distributed constrained heuristic search

Problems associated with contention for resources can frequently arise in distributed environments. The idea that these problems, commonly known as constraint satisfaction problems, can be solved by searching a space of states has been extensively explored. Instead of using a shared repository, a search strategy can thus be implemented as a way of associating an "agent" with each resource and then bringing that agent to process "the contending demands for the resource".

Indeed, *market-oriented programming* provides the ability to associate auctions with resources to support the search for "equilibria" in which resources are allocated efficiently [14]. Another strategy consists in allowing resources to compute their associated demands that competing agents can take into account as they attempt to solve their constraint-satisfaction problems.

Sycara et al. propose a decentralized problem solving model known as distributed constrained heuristic search that allows the use of aggregate demand to guide asynchronous distributed search [15]. In this respect, Durfee observes that more informed search decisions are susceptible of decreasing wasted backtracking effort. He adds that constraint satisfaction heuristics such as variable and value ordering can be beneficially employed in a distributed environment.

2.5.4 Organizational structuring

In distributed problem solving, a shared repository cannot be systematically supported. In this case, exploiting the structure of task decomposition can be a suitable alternative strategy for reducing communication. In an attempt to explain this strategy, Durfee puts forward an example of a distributed design problem [1,8]. In this respect, he argues that it is naturally reasonable that designers working on components that must "connect" communicate more frequently with each other rather than with designers working on more remote parts. The idea behind this example is that agents can make appropriate decisions based on knowledge about general roles each agent has to play in the collective effort.

This idea can be explicitly implemented in an organizational structure that defines roles, responsibilities, and preferences that in turn determine the control and communication patterns between agents. In addition, the organizational structure indicates capabilities associated with each agent and usually provides a prioritization of such capabilities. Through the prioritization of capabilities, the structure permits overlapping responsibilities that can increase probability of success.

In the organizational structure, it is important to have mechanisms through which an agent can learn about partial results that affect its assigned task. However, it is even more important not to communicate to agents results that are not susceptible of affecting their respective actions. As a result, the organizational structure provides adequate mechanisms designed to allow the identification of agents or the agent that may be potentially interested in a partial result.

2.6 Distributed planning

A distributed planning architecture consists of a group of computational agents that interact, share resources, and coordinate activities in order to achieve an overall common goal: design and integrate individual plans to yield a final global plan. Assuming that the task of designing and accomplishing the global plan is a problem assigned to these computational agents, distributed planning can thus, in many respects, be considered as a branch of distributed problem solving. Specifically characterized by particular features, planning problems are addressed through particularly suitable techniques.

In this respect, Durfee highlights the ambiguity that lies behind the term "distributed planning" [1,8]. In his view, it is unclear exactly what is "distributed" in distributed planning. However, the author admits the existence of various explanations on the use of the term "distributed planning". Indeed, as a consequence of planning, the formulated plan could be distributed among a variety of execution systems. On the other hand, whether the resulting plan(s) is/are distributed or not, the planning process could alternatively be distributed. Finally, another possible issue regarding distributed planning is that both the planning process and the resulting plan(s) could be distributed.

2.6.1 Centralized planning for distributed plans

Consider a partial order planner that is used to generate desired plans where there is no need for strict ordering between some actions, except the fact that these actions can be executed in parallel. One can thus imagine an agent acting as a centralized coordinator that takes the resulting plan and breaks it into separate threads. Using task-passing techniques, the resulting separate pieces of the plan are then passed to other agents and executed locally. Based on the assumption that the world is predictable and the knowledge is correct, the agents operating in parallel will, in the end, achieve "a state of the world consistent with the goals of the plan".

While the actions of the plan are, as required, locally executed in a distributed manner, the formulation of the plan is nonetheless achieved centrally. Durfee examines algorithmically the issue of centralized planning for distributed plans [1,8]. As presented, this process involves the following actions:

1. **Generate** a partial order plan based on a set of operators and a description of both the goal and the initial state. It is better to have a plan characterized by few ordering constraints among its steps.
2. **Decompose** the plan into sub-plans. The decomposition task should be conducted so as to minimize ordering relationships between steps contained in the same sub-plan, as suggested by Lansky [16].
3. **Define** and **introduce** synchronization actions into the resulting sub-plans.
4. **Allocate** these sub-plans to the appropriate operators or agents through adequate task-passing mechanisms. Following a successful allocation, an additional action is to insert remaining bindings into sub-plans – such as binding names of agents to send synchronization message. However, in case of failure, the previous steps should be reviewed in order to provide a different decomposition of the plan, or generate a different partial order plan, etc.
5. **Initiate** the execution of the plan, and conduct monitoring activities (optional) in order to ensure, for example, a complete plan execution.

A close examination of the algorithm described above offers the opportunity to understand the nature and impact of the specific issues of decomposition and allocation. In planning, the decomposition and allocation steps essentially amount to the objective of finding, among all the possible plans susceptible of accomplishing a given goal, the most appropriate plan that can be effectively decomposed and distributed. This statement raises the question of the availability of appropriate agents to execute the sub-plans resulting from the decomposition process. It is obviously not totally certain that the plan considered "the most decomposable and distributable" can be allocated in any context [1,8]. Indeed, the availability of agents to locally execute sub-tasks is naturally difficult to determine without first having decomposed the plan.

Another question worth pondering concerns the impact of the communication infrastructure on the degree to which plans should be decomposed and distributed. While the distributed sub-plans may require synchronization, the communication channels could at the same be slow or undependable. In this extreme case, it is suggested to form "a more efficient centralized plan" and take into account the monetary and/or time costs associated with distributing and synchronizing plans [1,8].

2.6.2 Distributed planning for centralized plans

In various areas, such as manufacturing, the planning process is too complex to be conducted through a single agent. As a result, the tedious planning function could well be distributed among a group of agents. In this context, each agent is assigned the task of contributing pieces to the plan, until a more acceptable or overarching plan is formulated. Similar to generating a solution to a complex problem, creating a complex plan might indeed impose collaboration among a number of cooperative planning experts.

Durfee appropriately highlights existing parallels between task-sharing and result-sharing strategies used in DPS, on the one hand, and distributed planning for centralized plans, on the other hand [1,8]. According to this author, the overall problem-formulation task can be thought of as being decomposed and distributed among a group of planning experts, which individually proceed to generate their contribution to the plan. These distributed planning-related activities raise the crucial issue regarding the interactions among the planning experts.

Indeed, many real-world planning problems, such as planning in manufacturing [17], unmanned vehicles control [18] or logistics domain [19], involve interactions between planning experts through the exchange of a partially-specified plan. In an attempt to highlight the use of this model in various domains, Durfee [1,8] refers to an investigation regarding the implementation of a hybrid model that utilizes "*a set of specialist to complement the overall expressiveness and reasoning power of a traditional hierarchical planner*" [17]. Used in the manufacturing domain, the approach consists in coupling a general-purpose planner with specialist planners for geometric reasoning and "fixturing". As mentioned, the planner is a hierarchical non-linear planner similar to NONLIN [20]. While the geometric specialist augments the specification of the problem, as seen by the planner, and detects interactions that the planner itself cannot detect, the fixturing specialist utilizes the generated plan to make its own further commitments. In this respect, the geometric specialist uses solid models of the part and features to detect a variety of geometric interactions that may affect the machining or fixturing of parts. Finally, the geometric specialist generates an abstract plan as an ordering over the geometric feature to put into the part and constructs or updates the interaction graph. Specific ordering constraints are then conveyed to the planner via the interaction graph. The hierarchical general-purpose planner uses these ordering constraints to plan the required machining operations. The resulting augmented plan is then passed on to the fixturing specialist. The task of the fixturing specialist is finally achieved in two phases: the first phase consists in proposing adequate set-ups and the second phase amounts to testing these set-ups.

In contrast, a result-sharing approach would impose on each planning agent the necessity to individually generate a partial plan in parallel and then share and merge these plans to "converge on a complete plan in a negotiated search mode". Indeed, mechanisms based on this approach have been developed and implemented to solve problems in the domain of communication networks [21]. In this class of problems, known as distributed constraints satisfaction problems, the satisfaction of each goal requires a coordinated set of actions distributed over a sub-set of nodes for completion. The mechanisms are thus designed to allow agents, each of which has incomplete knowledge about system resources and awareness of only partial solutions of system problems, to cooperate in solving complex dis-tributed constraint satisfaction problems. Using a result-sharing strategy amount-ing to a distributed constraint satisfaction problem, localized agents can, in sum, "*tentatively allocate network connections to particular circuits and share these tentative allocations with neighbours*". However, in the case inconsistent alloca-tions are detected, other allocations are tried without the interruption of the proc-ess until a consistent set of allocations are determined.

2.6.3 Distributed planning for distributed plans

Indeed, the distributed planning for distributed plans represents the most chal-lenging issue of distributed planning. While both the planning process and the re-sults are distributed, it is not however necessary and required to have a complete global plan available locally at each node. To avoid conflicts, the distributed pieces of the global plan should be compatible to allow agents to effectively exe-cute the plans or at least rationally help each other achieve their respective plan-ning task.

Research regarding distributed planning for distributed plans is relatively "*rich and varied*". As a result, various techniques for managing agent-related planning activities have been proposed in the literature. In "*Distributed Problem Solving and Planning*" [1,8], Durfee covers extensively some useful techniques:

2.6.3.1 Plan Merging – A question that may quite normally arise in this area con-cerns the challenge related to the need to identify and resolve potential conflicts. Having to individually formulate plans for themselves, a group of agents are con-sidered to be consequently faced with the problem of ensuring that the resulting separate plans can be executed without any conflict. In this context, it is thus as-sumed that the assignment of goals is either systematic – the application domain is inherently distributive – or has been conducted through task-sharing based tech-niques.

A potential approach that that may allow agents to avoid conflicts is to use a centralized plan coordination technique. Thus, the solution consists in appointing an agent to collect together the individual plans, analyze these plans to identify the sequences of actions that may lead to conflicts, and consequently remove these conflicts through a plan modification procedure. Given a set of possible initial states and a set of action sequences that can be executed asynchronously, the prob-lem amounts to the task of enumerating "all possible states of the world that can be reached". In conducting this task, the agent can then determine the subset of worlds that should be avoided so as to be able to eliminate them through insertion of adequate constraints on the sequences.

However, the task which consists in enumerating the reachable state space is a difficult process. Appropriate strategies are thus required to deal with the complexity of this search. In *"Distributed Problem Solving and Planning"* [1,8], Durfee provides an extensive discussion on a search easing method adapted from the work of Georgeff [22].

Given the plans of several agents, the merging method is first implemented to provide the ability to analyze interaction between pairs of actions to be taken by different agents. From this analysis, unsafe situations are thus identified. Actions that commute with all others can thus be dropped to "reduce the agents' plans to relatively short sequences". Given the simplified sequences, the merging process can enable the identification of the space of unsafe interactions by "considering the number of interleavings". Since the unsafe interactions are discovered, the synchronization of actions can finally be added to the plans to allow agents to avoid conflicts with ongoing actions.

Other alternative methods are also available to adequately deal with more complex forms of the search problem. A look-ahead coordination based mechanism to maximize expected performance and to make forecasts regarding future activities have indeed been introduced to tackle problems related to uncertainties about the time required to conduct tasks or the possibility of new emerging tasks [23]. On the other hand, the issue about how agents should decide which plans to combine to maximize their global performance in the absence schedules has also been addressed [24]. Finally, Petri-net based mechanisms and other techniques based on model-checking have also been explored and proposed as a way to coordinate more complex representations of reactive plans [25,26].

2.6.3.2 Iterative Plan Formation. – The plan merging approach presented above is considered to be a powerful technique to achieve increased parallelism in both the planning process and execution. However, locally made decisions are sometimes tightly dependent on decisions attributed to other agents. Such a scenario offers a great challenge to researchers faced with the problem of how to manage the *"degree to which local plans should be formulated"* without ignoring the presence of other planning agents that impose the necessity to look into all aspects related to coordination.

Rather than allowing each agent to propose a single specific plan, agents should, in this respect, search through larger spaces of plans as a way of *"tempering proposed local plans based on global constraints"*. Using this approach, each agent would thus establish a set of all feasible plans that allow it to accomplish its own goal. Hence, the distributed planning process would then amount to a search through generated plans to determine the subsets that can adequately fit together.

In *"Divide and Conquer in Multi-agent Planning"* [27], Ephrati and Rosenschein propose a *plan combination search* approach to deal with this type of search problem. This approach emphasizes on starting with the inclusion of sets of possible plans and the refinement of these plans to achieve a desired convergence on a "nearly optimal subset".

Designed to perform *distributed hierarchical planning*, an alternative approach consists in exploiting the hierarchical structure of a plan space. According to Durfee [1,8], this approach presents substantial advantages – exemplified in the ToH problem – in that "some interactions can be worked out in more abstract plan spaces". It results in pruning away "large portions of the more detailed spaces".

Known as the *hierarchical behaviour-space search* approach, a variation of the distributed hierarchical planning approach is to allow each agent to represent its associated local behaviours at multiple levels of abstraction. Durfee characterizes this approach as a search through hierarchical behaviour space [28], since, he explains, the plans at various levels dictate the behaviours of agents to a particular degree.

2.6.3.3 Negotiation in Distributed Planning. – In various cases, determining which agent should wait for another is, as Durfee explains, both fairly random and arbitrary [1,8]. This issue has been examined through a large amount of work in the area of negotiation.

In a work conducted in the air-traffic control domain, Steeb et al. focus on determining which of the various aircraft should alter direction in order to reduce *"potentially dangerous congestion"* [29]. While the agents exchange descriptions regarding their flexibility, the system is designed such that the agent that has the greatest number of options is asked to alter its plan. In this case, the selection of the agent susceptible of revising its local plan is based on *"models of the possibilities open to agents"*.

Designed to resolve goals, these and other negotiation mechanisms presume, as Durfee points out, that agents are honest about the importance characterizing their goals and the options of how to achieve them [1,8]. The literature pertaining to this area shows that issues regarding how to incite self-interested agents to be honest have been covered. While recognizing that the space of possible conflicts between agents is large, Durfee argues that the space of possible cooperative activities can be even larger, and introduces a variety of utility assessments [1,8]. According to this author, cooperation is "better", but the degree to which agents benefit might not outweigh the efforts required in finding cooperative opportunities. Finally, in *"Coordinating Plans of Autonomous Agents"*, von Martial focuses on strategies that agents can exploit to achieve particular goals based on *"favor relations"* [30]. While it can pursue its specific goal, an agent may, as a result, be able to achieve or accomplish a goal for another agent.

References

1. Edmund H. Durfee, *"Distributed Problem Solving and Planning"*, In Multiagent Systems – A Modern Approach to Distributed Artificial Intelligence, the MIT Press, Cambridge, Massachusetts, 1999.
2. Edmund H. Durfee, Victor R. Lesser, Daniel D. Corkill, "Trends in Cooperative Distributed Problem Solving", IEEE Transactions on Knowledge and Data Engineering, 1995.
3. Sascha Ossowski, "Distributed Artificial Intelligence", In Coordination in Artificial Agent Societies, LNAI 1535, pp. 31-63, Springer-Verlag Berlin Heidelberg, 1999.
4. Edmund H. Durfee and Jeffrey S. Rosenschein. *"Distributed Problem Solving and Multi-Agent Systems: Comparisons and Examples"* In Proceedings of the Thirteenth International Distributed Artificial Intelligence Workshop, pp. 94-104, July 1994.

5. R. G. Smith, "the Contract Net Protocol: High-Level Communication and Control in a Distributed Problem Solver", In IEEE Transactions on Computers, Vol. 29, No 12, December 1980.
6. V. Lesser and D. Corkill, "the Distributed Vehicle Monitoring Testbed: a Tool for Investigating Distributed Problem-Solving Networks", In Artificial Intelligence Magazine, Vol. 4, No 3, pp 15—33, 1983.
7. Katia Sycara-Cyranski, "Arguments of persuasion in labor mediation", In Proceedings of the Ninth International Joint Conference on Artificial Intelligence, pp. 294--296, Los Angeles, California, August 1985.
8. Edmund H. Durfee, "Distributed Problem Solving and Planning", In LNAI 2086, ACAI 2001, M. Luck, Editor, pp. 118-149, Springer-Verlag Berlin Heidelberg, 2001.
9. R. Davis and R. G. Smith, "Negotiation as a Metaphor for Distributed Problem Solving", In Artificial Intelligence, No 20, pp. 63-109, 1983. – Reprinted in Communications in Multi-agent Systems, LNAI 2650, M.-P. Huget, Editor, pp. 51-97, 2003.
10. Victor R. Lesser and Daniel D. Corkill, "Functionally Accurate, Cooperative Distributed Systems", In IEEE Transactions on Systems, Man, and Cybernetics, Vol. 11, No 1, pp. 81-96, January 1981.
11. Victor R. Lesser, "A Retrospective view of FA/C Distributed Problem Solving", In IEEE Transactions on Systems, Man, and Cybernetics, Vol. 21, No. 6, pp. 1347–1362, Nov/Dec 1991.
12. Keith J. Werkman, "Multiple Agent Cooperative Design Evaluation using Negotiation", In Proceedings of the Second International Conference on Artificial Intelligence in Design, Pittsburgh PA, June 1992.
13. Susan E. Lander and Victor R. Lesser, "Understanding the role of negotiation in distributed search among heterogeneous agents", In Proceedings of the Thirteenth International Joint Conference on Artificial Intelligence (IJCAI-93), pp. 438–444, August 1993.
14. Wellman M., "A Market-oriented Programming Environment and its Application to Distributed Multicommodity Flow Problems", Journal of Artificial Intelligence Research, Vol. 1, pp. 1–23, 1993.
15. Katia Sycara, Steven Roth, Norman Sadeh, and Mark Fox, "Distributed constrained heuristic search", IEEE Transactions on Systems, Man, and Cybernetics, SMC-21(6):1446–1461.
16. Amy L. Lansky, "Localized Search for Controlling Automated Reasoning", In Proceedings of the DARPA Workshop on Innovative Approaches to Planning, Scheduling, and Control, pp. 115–125, November 1990.
17. Subbarao Kambhampati, Mark Cutkosky, Marty Tenenbaum, and Soo Hong Lee", "Combining Specialized Reasoners and General Purpose Planners: a Case Study", In Proceedings of the Ninth National Conference on Artificial Intelligence, pp. 199–205, July 1991.
18. Edmund H. Durfee, Victor R. Lesser, and Daniel D. Corkill, "Cooperation Through Communication in a Distributed Problem-Solving Network", In Cognition, Computing, and Cooperation, pp. 159-186, 1990.
19. D.E. Wilkins and K.L. Myers, "A Common Knowledge Representation for Plan Generation and Reactive Execution", Journal of Logic and Computation, Vol. 5, No. 6, pp. 731–761, 1995.
20. Austin Tate, "Generating Project Networks", In Proceedings of the 5th IJCAI, 1977.
21. Susan E. Conry, Kazuhiro Kuwabara, Victor R. Lesser, and Robert A. Meyer, "Multistage Negotiation for Distributed Constraint Satisfaction", IEEE Transactions on Systems, Man, and Cybernetics, SMC-21(6), pp. 1462–1477, Nov. 1991.
22. M. P. Georgeff, "Communication and Interaction in Multi-agent Planning", In Readings in Distributed Artificial Intelligence, Alan H. Bond and Les Gasser, Editors, Morgan Kaufmann Publishers, Inc., San Mateo, California, 1988.
23. Jyi-Shane Liu and Katia P. Sycara, "Multiagent coordination in tightly coupled task scheduling", In Proceedings of the Second International Conference on Multi-Agent Systems (ICMAS-96), pp. 181–188, December 1996.

24. Eithan Ephrati, Martha E. Pollack, and Jeffrey S. Rosenschein, "a Tractable Heuristic that Maximizes Global Utility through Local Plan Combination", In Proceedings of the First International Conference on Multi-Agent Systems (ICMAS-95), pp. 94–101, June 1995.

25. Jaeho Lee, "an Explicit Semantics for Coordinated Multiagent Plan Execution, PhD dissertation, University of Michigan, 1997.

26. Amal El Fallah Seghrouchni and Serge Haddad, "a Recursive Model for Distributed Planning", In Proceedings of the Second International Conference on Multi-Agent Systems (ICMAS-96), pp. 307–314, December 1996.

27. Eithan Ephrati and Jeffrey S. Rosenschein, "Divide and Conquer in Multi-agent Planning", In Proceedings of the Twelfth National Conference on Artificial Intelligence (AAAI-94), pp. 375–380, July 1994.

28. Edmund H. Durfee and Thomas A. Montgomery, "Coordination as Distributed Search in a Hierarchical Behavior Space", IEEE Transactions on Systems, Man, and Cybernetics, Special Issue on Distributed Artificial Intelligence, SMC-21(6):1363–1378, November 1991.

29. Steeb, R., Cammarata, S., Hayes-Roth, F. A., Thorndyke, P. W., and Wesson, R. B. Architectures for Distributed Intelligence for Air Fleet Control. TR R-2728-ARPA, Rand Corp., Santa Monica CA, 1981.

30. Frank von Martial, "Coordinating Plans of Autonomous Agents", Lecture Notes in Artificial Intelligence, Springer-Verlag, 1992.

Chapter 3 Scalability and Performance Evaluation for the Coordination of Distributed Systems

Abstract This chapter investigates emerging challenges related to the coordination of large-scale distributed systems. It highlights two key design factors that must be considered when building practical and robust distributed systems, namely scalability and performance. Hence, the present chapter is devoted to the discussion of scalability and performance analysis of distributed multi-agent systems in the context of the coordination space. It also presents a critical description of the factors that affect scalability, and further describes existing standards and metrics for performance evaluation and analysis.

3.1 Coordination and scalability

Scalability is a problem for many intelligent distributed systems. The dimensionality of the search space grows significantly with the number of agents involved, the complexity of agent behaviors, and the size of the network based on interactions between agents.

Research dealing specifically with scalability in multi-agent systems is relatively scarce. Increasing demand for large-scale agent based environments brought a limited number of researchers and experts to look into different aspects related to this issue. A review of the literature regarding scalability of multi-agent systems provides the ability to broadly categorize research in this area into several categories:

1. Definition, delimitation and further clarification of issues regarding scalability in agent-based environments.
2. Development of metrics and other adequate methods and procedures that offer the ability to conduct formal, theoretical and experimental analysis of scalability of existing mechanisms and protocols designed to allow interaction and resource allocation and distribution.
3. Development and implementation of tools to allow the prediction of agent-based systems performance and scalability.
4. Development of appropriate, scalable mechanisms and protocols.
5. Construction of scalable applications.
6. Development of algorithms and methods designed to increase the scalability of a multi-agent system through a change of the environment.

A. Bedrouni et al., *Distributed Intelligent Systems: A Coordination Perspective*,
DOI: 10.1007/978-0-387-77702-3_3, © Springer Science + Business Media, LLC 2009

In "*Reflections on the Nature of Multi-Agent Coordination and its Implications for an Agent Architecture*" [1], Lesser examines key challenges facing the multi-agent community in addressing the issue regarding the development of next generation multi-agent systems consisting of large number of agents operating in open environments. In this respect, the author raises the fundamental question of what are the basic functions and interaction patterns required to support the realization of open, large, complex, and robust systems and offers specific strategies and recommendations. In focusing on major problems associated with the design of an agent architecture that has to operate in an open and large-scale multi-agent environment, Victor R. Lesser outlines the importance of effective coordination strategies and the corresponding need for more sophisticated coordination mechanisms.

Roughly at the same time, Lee et al. highlight the lack of sufficient attention devoted to issues regarding non-functional properties of multi-agent systems such as scalability, stability and performance [2]. From this point of view, the authors explore the meaning of the term "scalability" of multi-agent systems and then attempt to demonstrate how this property can be properly analyzed. Thus, Lee et al. introduce a model of a multi-agent system, and describe a procedure that was used to analyze its performance and scalability. The objective behind this approach is to show that different designs of multi-agent systems need to be investigated in order to optimize these important non-functional requirements that underpin the quality of service. In a quite similar connection, Burness et al. recognize the significance of issues pertaining to the non-functional aspects of a complex multi-agent system [3]. According to these authors, it is quite hard to detect and correct many scalability problems through testing procedures, particularly if these problems are intimately related to the design of the system. From the analysis of a high-level design, Burness et al. demonstrate the ability to identify potential scalability problems embedded in a multi-agent system.

In an interesting paper entitled "*What is Scalability in Multi-agent Systems*", Rana and Stout first report that most agent-based systems built so far involve interactions between relatively small numbers of agents [4]. Having in mind the growing trend towards building large scale systems, the authors note that the contribution of this work is to propose a performance modeling scheme that can be combined with an agent-oriented design methodology in order to build large agent-based applications. While recalling that scalability, in its most general form, is defined as "*the ability of a solution to a problem to work when the size of the problem increases*", Rana and Stout state that multi-agent systems will, in the context of multi agent communities, need to scale in a number of different dimensions. These dimensions include an increase in:

1. The total number of agents involved on a given platform,
2. The total number of agents involved across multiple systems or platforms,
3. The size of rules-based data on/with which agents operate,
4. The diversity among agents.

In case the total number of agents increases – scenarios 1 and 2, the authors suggest using metrics associated with a particular platform or operating environment "*to determine the total agent density and the resulting effect on system performance*". As noted, memory usage, scheduling/swapping overheads for active agents, cloning or dispatching an agent to a remote site are the only metrics reported in the literature pertaining to agent performance and scalability [5,6].

On the other hand, Rana and Stout [4] provide an extensive discussion regarding the potential case where the agent density is increased as more agents will have to be necessarily added in response to an increase in the size of a particular problem. As noted, scalability in this scenario measures "*the overall effect of parallel processing overheads on performance when the system and problem size scale up*".

In addition, the authors point to another case regarding the increase in the diversity of agents and the corresponding effects on agent density. In this particular case, scalability management is, according to them, related to methodologies pertaining to agent analysis and design. In this respect, Rana and Stout highlight the need for "*software engineering approaches for developing agent communities which extend beyond existing approaches based on object oriented modeling techniques or knowledge engineering*". They also outline the need for other methods that have been implemented to build large complex systems based on interacting entities. Motivated by A-Life research, these methods are, according to these authors, based on the premise that societies of simple agents are capable of complex problem solving behavior, while processing limited individual capabilities. Referring to A-Life research [7,8,9] Rana and Stout highlight the absence of a central coordination of activity in such societies. It is some kind of "*social coherence*" that is, as reported, used to guide agents to work together towards a global objective. In this context, inter-agent communication is generally local and conducted through "time dependent signals" in such a way that no single agent is aware of the global state.

On the other hand, scalability can, according to Rana and Stout, also be stated in terms of "*coordination policies in agent communities*". It can thus be stated in terms of the total number of message exchanges to converge on a solution. Hence, a first approach is to group agents in order to limit message exchanges. Another approach consists in specifying a global utility function. Implemented in the COIN system [10,11], this approach is inspired by game theoretic methods applied to economic markets. In these methods, the emphasized necessity to converge to a global optimum has indeed an impact on performance, and correspondingly on scalability

Finally, Rana and Stout point to another set of approaches that provide the ability to manage scalability. As noted, these approaches are related to modeling agent systems to predict performance. Based on the concept of a *messenger* paradigm, various approaches are mainly aimed at mobile agents. It is explained that messenger systems view agents as systems which involve mobile threads of execution without a central control. Modeling interactions in a messenger system can, as stated, be divided into: process algebras, actors and actor related formalisms, Petri nets, coordination languages, temporal logic, category theory and others. According to Rana and Stout, Petri net extensions – *Mobile Petri nets* [12] and *Communicative and Cooperative Nets* [13] – are proposed to handle mobility and dynamicity.

3.1.1 Scalability and coordination strategies

Aware of the fact that multi-agent systems have already moved out from research laboratories to commercial application environments, Buckle et al. have investigated the scalability issue [14]. In this paper, the authors propose a revision or rather a further clarification regarding the meaning of the term scalability. In addition, they describe a new model of scalability, which is also investigated through a discussion of qualitative as well as quantitative issues. According to these authors, scalability in a multi-agent system is not just a factor determined through counting the number of agents' resident on a platform within any particular environment. Phil Buckle et al. claim that other qualitative issues are also crucially important. They further suggest the development or extension of a methodology in order to identify benefits and losses associated with agent behavior when deploying larger numbers of agents within a multi-agent system.

Extensively described later, the Contract Net protocol is indeed a coordination mechanism widely used in multi-agent systems. While commonly considered as a simple and dynamic scheme, this protocol is however communication intensive due to "broadcast of task announcements". In "Learning in Multi-agent Systems" [15], Sen and Gerhard Weiss address the problem of reducing communication in multi-agent environments. In this context, the authors consider the Contract Net protocol and highlight various disadvantages associated with this approach. While noting that the Contract Net based approach operates quite well in small problem environments, Sen and Weiss assert that the protocol runs into problems as the number of communicating agents and the number of tasks announced – problem size – increases. In this respect, the authors advocate the development of adequate mechanisms designed to reduce the communication load resulting from broadcasting in more complex environments. Sen and Weiss then refer to various solutions – *focused addressing* and *direct contracting* – proposed by Smith [16] in the form of mechanisms designed to substitute point-to-point communication for broadcasting. However, these mechanisms present the disadvantage of imposing that a system designer must in advance know direct communication paths. Therefore, the resulting communication patterns may be too inflexible in dynamic environments. Based on this analysis, Sen and Weiss propose and describe an alternative and more flexible learning-based mechanism known as *addressee learning*. As explained, the primary idea behind this approach consists in reducing the communication efforts associated with task announcement through a procedure that enables individual agents to acquire and refine knowledge regarding task abilities of other agents. Hence, using this knowledge, tasks can thus be directly assigned without the need to broadcast announcements to all agents. Referring to various research papers [17,18], Sen and Weiss report that case-based reasoning is indeed used as an experience-based mechanism to acquire and refine knowledge.

Similarly, Deshpande et al. have examined and extensively investigated the scalability problems related to the Contract Net protocol [19,20]. In *"Adaptive Fault Tolerant Hospital Resource Scheduling"* [20], the Contract Net protocol is used as a coordination mechanism in a distributed hospital to provide the ability to share resources across nodes. In using this protocol, Deshpande et al realize that at high task arrival rates, many tasks cannot be completed within deadlines and the average task waiting time of the multi-agent system increases. In response to these scalability-related problems, an *Instance Based Learning* mechanism is used to improve the performance of the Contract Net protocol [19]. While similar to the *addressee learning* method described above, this mechanism is designed to use *"the history of subtask migrations in order to choose a target node for a new subtask"*. In this respect, Deshpande et al. explain that the history of subtask migrations contains instances, which consists of both the system state and the target node selected by the coordination mechanism at that state. Thus, using the Instance Based Learning mechanism, the appropriate target node is decided whenever a task is close to the deadline.

Inserted into the Instance Based Learning mechanism is the k-Nearest Neighbor algorithm used as a technique to determine the k instances that are close to the current system state. As noted, using this technique provides the ability to both save valuable time - the bidding process is avoided through local computations – and reduce the communication load on the channels. Thus, incorporated into the coordination mechanism to allow resource sharing, the Instance Based Learning approach contributes appreciably to improving the performance of the simulated distributed hospital system. On the other hand, results are provided to outline the ability of this approach to improve the overall scalability with respect to the number of tasks. Indeed, Deshpande et al. report that, even at high loads, a greater number of tasks complete within the required deadlines, and the average task waiting time improves considerably.

In *"Scalability Analysis of the Contract Net Protocol"* [21], Juhasz and Prasenjit also present early results of a study designed to investigate the performance and scalability of agent coordination protocols. Using the JADE environment, the authors implemented a test-bed system in order to measure the length of task execution under varying experimental conditions. The results provided show that the performance of the Contract Net mechanism depends largely on the number of agents and the load attributed to each entity. Under heavy load, the protocol often has to be performed repeatedly, while under light load, the delay is linear in the number of agents. Finally, Juhasz and Prasenjit report that this investigation re-

garding the scalability of coordination mechanisms will be extended to other protocols and approaches.

Turner and Jennings [22] examined various aspects related to agent-based systems deployment in distributed large-scale, open and dynamic environments. In
[22], the authors raise the common question regarding the significant increase in
the number of agents and address the corresponding challenging problem of scalability. In this respect, Turner and Jennings suggest that multi-agent systems are
required to be *self-building* and *adaptive* in order to cope with the prominent adverse effects resulting in large-scale environments. While a self-building agent-
based system could, at runtime, independently determine its most suitable organizational structure, an adaptive system would, on the other hand, modify this structure as the environment undergoes any change. According to the authors, agents
that are able to build and maintain their own organizational structure are required
a-priori to be able to independently determine the importance of acquaintances
and decide on tasks to be shared, delegated, or individually pursued. Since changing the organizational structure is a collective process, agents complying with the
above requirements must be both aware and able to:

- Meta-reason about their individual internal efficiency and goals,
- Infer or question the goals of the system as a whole and the abilities and goals
  of their acquaintances,
- Create and annihilate other agents,
- Delegate and surrender tasks and information,
- Modify and influence their own operation,
- Influence the operation and activities of other agents.

In order to evaluate these hypotheses, Turner and Jennings implemented a self-
building and adaptive multi-agent system. Applied to the domain of automated
trading, the results show that adaptation and self-organization enhance the ability
of a multi-agent system to cope with large numbers of agents. Despite the confirmation of the self-building and adaptive hypotheses, the authors believe that the
experimental tests should be extended to several domains of application.

Similar approaches have also been proposed to address the issue of scalability
through algorithms and techniques designed to deal with dynamic changes to the
organizational structure of agent-based environments. Christian Gerber dedicated
an extensive work – a Ph.D. thesis – to methods designed to allow agents to adapt
themselves to any application scale and nature in order to achieve and maintain efficiency and scalability in multi-agent societies [23]. In this context, the author
presents GRAIL – *G*eneric *R*esource *A*llocation & *I*ntegration a*L*gorithm – a self-
adaptive scheme designed for a society of benevolent agents. In this work, the
concept of a *bounded-rational agent society* is introduced as an extension of a
bounded-rational agent. According to the author, agents in such a society *"optimize their behavior to their individual resource"*. Implemented through special
monitor agents, control instances optimize the allocation of societal resources.

The resource concept is thus extended to the multi-agent case where an abstract resource describes *"an entity of the environment of an agent society, which expresses interdependencies"* among members of this society. As noted, the task which consists in organizing such a society of agents is conceived as an optimization problem through a procedure designed to characterize a multi-dimensional *search space* and an *objective function*. The objective function denotes the performance of the system, while the search space describes the set of possible configurations of this system.

According to Christian Gerber, the theoretical foundations discussed above are implemented and used in the SIF – Social Interaction Framework – system which supports rapid prototyping of multi-agent scenarios. As an extension of the SIF system, another system called the SIFIRA – *Social Interaction Framework for Integrated Resource Adaptation* – is conceived to provide the ability to conveniently design self-adapting agent societies. Christian Gerber reports that the GRAIL approach makes only few assumptions on the nature of agents in a society. He explains that the autonomy of agents is in particular modified as little as possible. However, the author notes that if the autonomy of members of a group, or even all society members, can be changed more significantly, the GRAIL approach can be refined to a *holonic* agent society. In a holonic society, agents give up part of their autonomy and unite to a *holon*, which is seen by the outside world as one single entity.

Furthermore, Brooks et al. explored the area of large-scale multi-agent systems and attempt to tackle the complexity resulting from interactions of a significantly large number of agents [24,25,26]. The authors recall that agents in a large-scale multi-agent system are faced with *"a combinatorially explosive number of potential interactions"* [24]. Brooks et al. argue that one approach for agents to deal with this complexity is to form *congregations*. The idea behind this approach lies in the fact that most agents in a multi-agent system would rather interact with a subset of agents, instead of interacting with every other agent. As noted, this subset would ideally form a group of agents having complementary needs, goals, or preferences. Christopher H. Brooks et al. point to the idea that agents would tend to group together with agents that share some important features and obviously avoid interacting with incompatible agents.

Referred to as congregation, this grouping together represents a common phenomenon in human societies. Indeed, congregations that exist in a society – such as clubs – make it much easier for humans to find people with complementary interest or capabilities. From this behavior, the idea thus put forward is how to emulate such congregations within a computational framework. In [24], Brooks et al. implemented the idea regarding the formation of congregations in a particular domain peculiar to information economy. As stated, an economy is an example of a multi-agent system in which congregations naturally occur, typically in the form of markets. Moreover, artificial agents may in this context represent producers and consumers in an information economy. Hence, Brooks et al. [26] addressed a particular type of congregation formation regarding the need to group together consumers and producers of information goods in such a way as to produce a desirable global state. In this respect, the authors propose two classes of strategies pertaining to the formation of desirable congregations. While the first class consists in using external mechanisms, such as taxes, the second class is about the introduction of learning to members of the agent population. The results are finally analyzed to provide a better insight into the problems associated with the formation of desirable congregations.

Later, Brooks et al. conducted further research on congregating in multi-agent systems to explain and predict the behavior of self-interested agents that search for other agents in an attempt to interact with them [25]. Experimental and analytical results are provided to highlight the difficulty of the congregating problem. Indeed, this problem becomes exponentially more complex as the number of agents increases. In this respect, Christopher H. Brooks et al. report how the complexity of the problem regarding the formation of congregations is reduced through the introduction of basic coordination mechanisms such as labelers. As noted, labelers are agents that "*assign a description to a congregation in order to reduce agents' search problem*". While highlighting the similarity between labelers and focal points [27], the authors explain that labelers allow agents to coordinate by "*providing an external mechanism for synchronizing behavior*".

In a more recent follow-on research work [26], Brooks et al. show how a structured label space can be exploited to simplify the labeler related decision problem and reduce the congregation problem to linear in the number of labelers. However, experimental evidence is also presented to demonstrate that the formation of congregations among agents can reduce search costs, thereby allowing the system to scale up.

In focusing attention entirely on agent coordination strategies, Durfee dedicates a whole research paper to the issue of scalability of agent-based systems and applications [28]. While noting that advances in agent-oriented software engineering provide the ability to develop complex, distributed systems, the author highlights the importance of building agents that are able to act and interact flexibly. In this context, Durfee argues that coordination has indeed emerged as a central concern of intelligent agency. Based on this analysis, the author puts forward the idea that an effective coordination strategy should scale and respond well to being stressed along various dimensions. According to him, any attempt in understanding the capabilities and limitations of coordination strategies that are designed to support flexible component agent interaction would thus require the characterization of agents' properties as well as their task environment and collective behavior.

3.1.2 Agent dimensions impacting the scalability

Durfee devotes an extensive discussion to various dimensions that are identified to allow mapping of the space of potential coordination approaches. In tackling properties associated with agent population, the author emphasizes the need to handle more agents as a challenge in scaling any coordination strategy. Thus, *Quantity* is identified as an important dimension of coordination stress. As pointed out, this property infers the absolute necessity to avoid using a centralized coordinator in order to direct the efforts of other agents. On the other hand, *heterogeneity* and *complexity* are mentioned as the two other agent population related dimensions that impact the scalability of proposed coordination strategies and mechanisms. While complexity refers to the difficulty associated with predicting the activity and reaction of a given agent, heterogeneity reveals the presence of different kind of agents having different goals, beliefs, or expertise and using various communication languages, ontologies, or internal architectures.

Furthermore, Durfee provides a set of task-environment properties that can also be considered in order to anticipate the performance, effectiveness, and suitability of a given coordination strategy. These properties include the *degree of interaction*, *dynamics*, and *distributivity*. As stated, the *degree of interaction* grows as *"the number of agents concerned with the same issues"* increases and as *"more issues become a concern to each agent"*. On the other hand, the *dynamics* property may indeed characterize a multi-agent setting where each member of a group of agents monitoring only portions of the environment can change its own perception about what goals to pursue and how to pursue them. Finally, a central feature of current multi-agent environments lies in the way both agents and tasks are distributed. In various task environments, inherently distributed tasks are often allocated to highly distributed agents. As a property of such environments, distributivity obviously impacts coordination, since it contributes to increasing uncertainty about the presence - which agents are currently sharing the task environment – and activities of individual agents.

Durfee notes that coordination strategies are still required to yield satisfactory solutions. In this respect, the author suggests the idea of making solution criteria more stringent along dimensions that include *quality, robustness*, and *overhead limitations*. As proposed, the quality of a solution can be expressed in terms of some standards regarding the coordination of agent interactions, the use of agent resources, and the ability to settle issues. While lower quality may express a mere satisfactory level of coordination, a high quality standard may, as noted, correspond to "near optimal" coordination. Given the uncertainty and dynamic behavior characterizing a task environment, robustness of a solution may express the ability of the coordination strategy in anticipating *"the range of conditions under which the solution it provides will be followed"*. Durfee then observes that costs associated with a given coordination strategy could include computation requirements, communication overhead, time spent, etc. He finally raises the question on *"whether a coordination strategy can scale well to environments that impose stringent limits to the costs the strategy incurs"*. However, scaling along combinations of the above dimensions would, as Durfee points out, induce even greater challenges.

3.2 Coordination Performance Evaluation

Traditionally, a designer of a system involving multiple agents analyzes the task domain of interest and, based on this analysis, imposes upon the agents rules that constrain them into interacting and communicating according to patterns deemed desirable. The idea is to provide agents with ready-to-use knowledge in order to allow these entities to share a common environment, effectively interact, and achieve a set of desirable properties: load balancing, conflict avoidance, stability, and fairness. This approach has guided research into coordination techniques and often led to prescriptions for a variety of methods: task-sharing protocols [29], negotiation conventions [30], rules for interaction, social laws [31], etc.

On the other hand, another alternative approach is based on the argument that agents should, in the absence of common pre-established protocols or conventions, be able to make decisions regarding interactions within a shared environment. The idea does not imply any obligation to restrict agents from interacting through protocols, so long as these entities are not however restricted from deliberating about what to do. Without relying on protocols or conventions, an agent should be able to use knowledge regarding the environment and the capabilities, desires, and beliefs of other agents in order to rationally act, interact, and coordinate in a multi-agent setting. This conception of agents' coordination has, on the other hand, given rise to a number of methods such as the techniques based on the normative decision-theoretic paradigm of rational decision-making under uncertainty [32].

As already described in the previous sections, a wide variety of mechanisms and protocols have been proposed to address the challenging issue of coordination in DAI. Having different properties and characteristics, these mechanisms are obviously suited to different types of tasks and environments. As coordination techniques are not equally effective, as each protocol or mechanism has its benefits and limitations, another proposed strategy consists in providing agents with a range of tools with varying properties so that any appropriate mechanism or protocol can be selected to handle a coordination episode [33,34].

Whatever approach described above is deemed the most effective; a fundamental and legitimate question can then be raised on how to evaluate this entire panoply of coordination protocols and mechanisms. In the absence of a standard methodology, an analysis of the literature reveals a substantial inadequacy of research focused on the development of methods and tools to evaluate coordination mechanisms and protocols in comparison to the efforts dedicated to the coordination issue.

Over the last two decades, research in the area of DAI has, among other things, focused on the design of agent-based architectures providing the ability to dynamically modify agent organizational structures. The approach is based on the idea that a single specific organizational structure cannot handle many different situations pertaining to a dynamic environment. Just as a single organizational structure is not suited to every situation, there is not either a single coordination technique that can well handle all organizations. In response, agents are thus offered, as mentioned above, the ability to operate using a variety of coordination mechanisms. In *"Coordinating Distributed Decision Making Using Reusable Interaction Specifications"* [35], Barber et al. investigate the issues involved in enhancing the flexibility of agents in terms of coordination capabilities. In this paper, the authors describe an approach – a representation of coordination strategies based on "designed to assist" agents, for evaluating and dynamically selecting alternative coordination strategies. Based upon object oriented concepts such as encapsulation and polymorphism, the approach consists of a representation of coordination strategies, which also offers the ability to compare coordination techniques through a constant framework and other techniques. As coordination strategies are treated in an abstract manner, agents have the ability to change strategies and incorporate newly developed strategies.

According to Barber et al., strategic decision-making, whether performed online or off-line by a designer, must be made with regard to which strategies are appropriate for the given problem. In this respect, the authors recommend the analysis of the coordination strategies in terms of domain dependent and independent characteristics [35]:

- *Strategy related requirements*. A given strategy may impose constraints on an agent's reasoning capabilities. This strategy may (or may not) require inter-agent communication and only partially make use of agent's abilities.
- *Cost of strategy execution*. When executed, each strategy uses part of the resources attributed to an agent. On the other hand, a strategy may, for instance, require a larger number of messages or a longer time. In this case, it is important to consider these factors to better deal with all aspects related to deadlines or limited agent resources.
- *Solution quality*. Indeed, using different strategies may lead to solutions with differing quality. Furthermore, agents may need longer deliberation to generate a better a solution. Depending on the time available, an agent may perform trade-off analysis between the expected quality of a solution and the cost associated with the execution of a strategy.
- *Domain requirements*. Strategies may or may not be able to satisfy requirements associated with an application domain.

Furthermore, Barber et al. mention the existence of multiple approaches that are *"applicable to the manner in which agents consider the above characteristics and select the most appropriate strategy"*. While it is recognized as difficult to manage, trade-off reasoning between multiple objectives is roughly classified into two categories: utility-based dynamic decision-making and ranking relations.

Furthermore, Bourne et al. have also tackled the problem resulting from the design of complex applications where autonomous agents are required to behave rationally in response to uncertain and unpredictable events [36]. In a similar way, the authors thus explored the idea of building systems where agents are fitted with the ability to coordinate their activities in accordance with demands and needs of prevailing circumstances. Instead of implementing a detailed coordination plan in which actions associated with each participant are rigidly prescribed, a more appropriate approach implies, according to Rachel A. Bourne et al., the necessity to adopt much looser coordination policies enabling agents to reason and select, at run-time, the method best suited to their current situation. As reported, such flexibility can thus be achieved through an adequate framework where agents, given a set of varied coordination mechanisms with different properties and characteristics, are offered the ability to assess the likely benefit of adopting an available mechanism deemed appropriate in the prevailing circumstances.

Based on this analysis, Bourne et al. propose a decision-theoretic model offering the ability to evaluate and select between competing coordination mechanisms. In this context, the authors identify a number of potentially differentiating features that are specifically common to a wide range of coordination mechanisms. Then, Bourne et al. show that agents can effectively evaluate and decide which mechanism to use, depending on the prevailing operating conditions. Referring to contingency theory [36], the authors observe that coordination mechanisms that are guaranteed to succeed typically have high set up and maintenance costs, whereas mechanisms that have lower set up costs are more likely to fail [34]. In this respect, Bourne et al. propose a framework to provide agents with the ability to select appropriate coordination mechanisms through set up costs and probability of success.

3.2.1 Criteria for the evaluation of coordination

In "*Criteria for the Analysis of Coordination in Multi-agent Applications*" [37], Frozza and Alvares highlight the importance of having tools designed to evaluate coordination in a society of agents. Such tools would help design more efficient and robust multi-agent systems and offer designers the opportunity to discuss the quality of coordinated actions executed by agents. In an attempt to provide a conceptual framework that can be used to conduct performance analysis of coordination mechanisms, Frozza and Alvares propose a set of criteria offering the ability to characterize various elements related to agents' coordination:

- *Predictivity*. The predictivity of a coordination mechanism represents its ability to determine the future status of both agents and the environment.
- *Adaptability*. The adaptability represents the ability of a coordination approach to deal successfully with new situations or unexpected events.
- *Action control*. The action control can be either centralized or distributed. While a centralized action control is characterized by the use of a single agent that holds the knowledge of a given problem and assigns tasks to other agents, a distributed control supposes that any agent can establish rules based on its knowledge.
- *Communication mode*. Communication between agents can be achieved through interaction, perception, or direct communication. Coordination can also be conducted without communication.
- *Conflicts*. Depending on the nature of conflicts, some coordination mechanisms are unable to avoid conflicts, while others demonstrate a great ability to approach and resolve conflicts.
- *Information exchange*. Coordination is also achieved through handling and exchange of information.
- *Agents*. Agents involved in a coordination scheme demonstrate both characteristics – homogeneous or heterogeneous – and capabilities.
- *Applications*. Applications are either suited to specific domains or adaptable to any domain.
- *Advantages*. Qualities that make a coordination method more successful.
- *Disadvantages*. Negative aspects associated with a coordination approach.

Based on these criteria, the authors provide a table of comparison of different coordination approaches. The objective behind this comparison is to demonstrate the effectiveness and applicability of such criteria.

Finally, in the area of negotiation, Sandholm suggests the use of various criteria or properties for evaluating negotiation protocols or mechanisms [38]. Listed below, these criteria include:

- *Negotiation time* – Assuming that a delay in reaching an agreement induces an increase in the cost of communication and computational time, negotiations conducted without delay are thus preferred over time-consuming negotiations.
- *Guaranteed success* – In case a protocol ensures that an agreement is, eventually, certain to be reached, it guarantees a successful negotiation outcome.
- *Maximizing social welfare* – In a given solution, social welfare is the sum of all agents' payoffs or utilities. It can be used as a property or criteria for comparing alternative mechanisms. Hence, a protocol maximizes social welfare if the resulting solution maximizes the sum of the utilities of negotiation participants.
- *Efficiency and Pareto efficiency* – An efficient outcome is preferred since it increases the number of agents that will be satisfied by the negotiation results. Pareto efficiency represents another property or criteria for evaluating a solution that a negotiation mechanism can lead to. A solution or negotiation out-

come is said to be Pareto efficient – i.e. Pareto optimal – "if there is no other outcome that will make at least one agent better off without making at least one another agent worst off". Similarly, a negotiation solution which is not Pareto efficient is characterized by the existence of another outcome that "will make at least one agent happier while keeping everyone at least as happy".

- *Individual rationality* – An individually rational mechanism supposes that participation in negotiations is individually rational for all agents. In other words, it is in the best interests of all agents to participate in negotiations through a mechanism that is individually rational. Thus, in the absence of individually rational protocols, agents lack incentive to engage in negotiations. Hence, an agent participating in an individually rational negotiation will get a payoff in a solution that is no less than the payoff it would have by not taking part in the negotiation process.

- *Stability* – Where agents are self-interested, mechanisms or protocols should be designed to be stable so as to motivate each entity to behave in a desirable way. Indeed, a self-interested agent tends to behave in some other way than desired if it is better off. A stable protocol is defined as a protocol that "provides all agents with an incentive to behave in a particular way". According to him, the best-known kind of stability is *Nash equilibrium.*

- *Simplicity* – A simple protocol makes the appropriate strategy "obvious" for a negotiation participating agent. He adds that a participant using a simple negotiation mechanism can easily determine the optimal strategy. Indeed, simple and efficient protocols are better than complex mechanisms.

- *Distribution* – A protocol should be designed so as to avoid the presence of a single point of failure, such as a single arbitrator, and minimize communication between agents.

- *Money transfer* – Money transfer may be used to resolve conflicts. In this respect, a server may, for instance, "sell" a data item to another server when relocating this item. Such procedure requires the necessity to provide agents with a monetary system and a mechanism designed to secure payments. Finally, negotiation protocols that do not require money transfers are indeed preferred, since maintaining such systems requires both resources and efforts.

References

1. Victor R. Lesser, "Reflections on the Nature of Multi-Agent Coordination and Its Implications for an Agent Architecture", In Autonomous Agents and Multi-Agent Systems, Vol. 1, pp. 89-111, 1998.
2. L. C. Lee, H. S. Nwana, D. T. Ndumu and P. De Wilde, "The Stability, Scalability and Performance of Multi-agent Systems", BT Technology Journal, Vol. 16, No 3, July 1998
3. Anne-Louise Burness, Richard Titmuss, Caroline Lebre, Katie Brown and Alan Brookland, "Scalability Evaluation of a Distributed Agent System", In Distributed Systems Engineering, Vol. 6, pp. 129-134, December 1999.
4. Omer F. Rana and Kate Stout, "What is Scalability in Multi-Agent Systems?", In Proceedings of the 4th International Conference on Autonomous Agents, pp. 56-63, June 2000.
5. M. Stasser, J. Baumann, and F. Hohl, "Mole - A Java Based Mobile Agent System", 2nd ECOOP Workshop: Mobile Object Systems, 1996.

6. Yamamoto and Y. Nakamura, "Architecture and Performance Evaluation of a Massive Multi-Agent System", In Proceedings of the third annual conference on Autonomous Agents, May 1999.
7. N. R. Franks, "Army Ants", In Scientific American, vol. 77, 1989.
8. Holldobler and E. Wilson, "Journey to the Ants", Bellknap Press/Harvard University Press, 1994.
9. M. M. Millonas, "Swarms, Phase Transitions and Collective Intelligence", Artificial Life III, Santa Fe Institute Studies in the Sciences of Complexity, Vol. 17, 1994.
10. Wolpert and K. Tumer, "An Introduction to Collective Intelligence", In Handbook of Agent Technology, J. M. Bradshaw, Editor, AAAI Press/MIT Press, 1999.
11. Wolpert, K. Wheeler, and K. Tumer, "General Principles of Learning-Based Multi-Agent Systems", In Proceedings of the Third Annual Conference on Autonomous Agents, May 1999.
12. Asperti and N. Busi, "Mobile Petri Nets", Technical Report UBLCS-96-10, Department of Computer Science, University of Bologna, Italy, 1996.
13. Sibertin-Blanc, "Cooperative Nets", In Application and Theory of Petri Nets, R. Valette, Editor, LNCS 815, pp. 471-490, Springer-Verlag, 1994.
14. Phil Buckle, Tom Moore, Steve Robertshaw, Alan Treadway, Sasu Tarkoma, and Stefan Poslad, "Scalability in Multi-agent Systems: The FIPA-OS Perspective", LNAI 2403, M. d' Inverno et al., Editors, pp. 110–130, 2002.
15. S. Sen and G. Weiss, "Learning in Multiagent Systems", in Multiagent Systems: A Modern Approach to Distributed Artificial Intelligence, G. Weiss, Editor, MIT Press, Cambridge, Mass., 1999.
16. R.G. Smith, "A Framework for Problem Solving in a Distributed Processing Environment", Stanford Memo STAN-CS-78-700, Department of Computer Science, Stanford University, 1978
17. J. L. Kolonder, "Case-based reasoning", Morgan Kaufmann, San Francisco, 1993.
18. Watson and F. Marir, "Case-based Reasoning: A review", In the Knowledge Engineering Review, Vol. 9, No. 4, pp. 327-354, 1994.
19. Umesh Deshpande, Arobinda Gupta, and Anupam Basu, "Performance Improvement of the Contract Net Protocol Using Instance Based Learning", IWDC 2003, LNCS 2918, S. R. Das, S. K. Das, Editors, pp. 290–299, Springer-Verlag Berlin Heidelberg, 2003.
20. U. Deshpande, A. Gupta, and A. Basu, "Adaptive Fault Tolerant Hospital Resource Scheduling", In Proceedings of the 10th International Conference on Cooperative Information Systems (CooPIS - 2002)
21. Zoltan Juhasz and Prasenjit Paul, "Scalability Analysis of the Contract Net Protocol", In Proceedings of the 2nd IEEE/ACM International Symposium on cluster Computing and the Grid, Berlin, Germany, May 21-24, 2002.
22. P. J. Turner and N. R. Jennings, "Improving the Scalability of Multi-Agent Systems", Proceedings of the 1st International Workshop on Infrastructure for Scalable Multi-Agent Systems, Barcelona, 2000.
23. Christian Gerber, "Self-adaptation and Scalability in Multi-agent Systems", PhD Thesis, Universität des Saarlandes, Dec. 1999.
24. H. Brooks and E. H. Durfee, "Congregation formation in information economies", In Proceedings of the AAAI-99 Workshop on AI in Electronic Commerce, pp. 62– 68, 1999.
25. H. Brooks, E. H. Durfee, and A. Armstrong, "An introduction to congregating in multiagent systems", In Proceedings of the Fourth International Conference on Multiagent Systems, pp. 79– 86, 2000.
26. Christopher H. Brooks and Edmund H. Durfee, "Congregation Formation in Multiagent Systems", In Autonomous Agents and Multi-Agent Systems, Vol. 7, pp. 145– 170, 2003.
27. M. Fenster, S. Kraus, and J. Rosenschein, "Coordination without Communication: An Experimental Validation of Focal Point Techniques", In Proceedings of the First International Conference on Multi-Agent Systems, pp. 102–116, San Francisco, California, 1995.

28. Edmund E. Durfee, "Scaling up Agent Coordination Strategies", In Computer, Vol. 34, No. 7, pp. 39-46, July 2001.
29. R. G. Smith, "the Contract Net Protocol: High-Level Communication and Control in a Distributed Problem Solver", In IEEE Transactions on Computers, Vol. 29, No 12, December 1980.
30. Jeffrey S. Rosenschein and Gilad Zlotkin, "Rules of Encounter: Designing Conventions for Automated Negotiation among Computers", MIT Press, 1994.
31. Y. Shoham, "Agent-oriented Programming", In Artificial Intelligence, Vol. 60, No. 1, pp. 51.92, 1993.
32. Piotr J. Gmytrasiewicz and Edmund H. Durfee, "Rational Coordination in Multi-Agent Environments", In Autonomous Agents and Multi-Agent Systems, Vol. 3, pp. 319-350, 2000.
33. Cora Beatriz Excelente-Toledo and Nicholas R. Jennings, "The Dynamic Selection of Coordination Mechanisms", In Journal of Autonomous agents and Multi-agent systems (to appear), 2004.
34. Rachel A. Bourne, Cora B. Excelente-Toledo and Nicholas R. Jennings, "Run-Time Selection of Coordination Mechanisms in Multi-Agent Systems", In Proceedings of the 14th European Conference on AI, pp. 348--352, Berlin, Germany, 2000.
35. K.S. Barber, D.C. Han, and T.H. Liu, "Coordinating Distributed Decision Making Using Reusable Interaction Specifications", PRIMA 2000, LNAI 1881, C. Zhang and V.-W. Soo, Editors, pp. 1-15, Springer-Verlag Berlin Heidelberg, 2000.
36. Rachel A. Bourne, Karen Shoop, and Nicholas R. Jennings, "Dynamic Evaluation of Coordination Mechanisms for Autonomous Agents", In Lecture Notes in Artificial Intelligence (LNAI) 2258, pp. 155-168, Springer-Verlag, 2001.
37. Rejane Frozza and Luis Otávio Alvares, "Criteria for the Analysis of Coordination in Multi-agent Applications", COORDINATION 2002, LNCS 2315, F. Arbab and C. Talcott, Editors, pp. 158-165, Springer-Verlag Berlin Heidelberg, 2002.
38. Tuomas W. Sandholm, "Distributed Rational Decision Making", In Multiagent Systems: A Modern Approach to Distributed Artificial Intelligence, Gerhard Weiss, Editor, The MIT Press, Cambridge, MA, USA, pp. 201—258, 1999.

Chapter 4 Coordination Models and Frameworks

Abstract The previous chapters have identified, highlighted, and addressed different issues and key aspects pertaining to coordination such as the need to understand scalability issues, as well as examples of the context in which coordination can occur, specifically, within the domain of distributed problem solving. With these issues and examples in mind, this chapter takes a higher level view and outlines the need for adequate models to provide support for studying coordination and building reliable organizations and systems. This chapter is thus devoted to presenting and describing relevant coordination models and frameworks designed to provide the foundation for understanding and managing the space of agent interactions.

4.1 Introduction

There has been a desire in the agent research community to develop and implement a more coherent, carefully crafted, and acutely relevant framework or model that serves as a sound basis for understanding existing principles and approaches and directing future research pertaining to the coordination function. Stemming from different disciplines, a large variety of models on how entities interact are indeed provided. These models can be used either to build middleware and languages or to express coordination strategies that lead to a coherent behavior of interacting entities [1]. Models of coordination are thus required to enable adequate technologies to be developed in order to support the design of applications that rely on the interaction of computational units or entities.

Commonalities amongst coordination models provide the ability to transfer coordination patterns across disciplines. In this respect, Tolksdorf [1] outlines the need to build models that "*have certain qualities such as being complete with respect to interaction forms and open to new patterns of interactions*". He considers that models of coordination have to be "*easy and safe to use to facilitate efficient software engineering*", must be "*scalable and efficient to implement*" so as "*to cope with the number of units to coordinate*", and be "*aware of the characteristics of future environments*". On the other hand, Tolksdorf recognizes the lack of consensus on the relations between coordination, communication and cooperation and outlines the need to work towards a standardized terminology which contains definitions and clarifications of basic notions including the term "coordination".

A. Bedrouni et al., *Distributed Intelligent Systems: A Coordination Perspective*,
DOI: 10.1007/978-0-387-77702-3_4, © Springer Science + Business Media, LLC 2009

Despite a growing amount of research in this area, Coates et al. have also similarly outlined the lack of a single widely accepted perception of coordination and its constituents [2]. Following a survey on research in coordination approaches and systems, these authors note the relative absence of efforts designed to satisfy *"the requirement to comprehensively understand the broader aspects of coordination"*. Within the same discipline, there is, according to Coates et al., *"a clear difference of opinion as to what constitutes coordination"*. This confusion results in "a rather liberal use and application" of the word *coordination,* and thus produces a diversity in definitions and understanding of the concept. From our point of view, we present below five of the most important coordination models and frameworks used in distributed intelligent systems.

4.2 Sikora & Shaw Framework

Sikora and Shaw present a general multi-agent framework for understanding and analyzing the different issues involved in coordinating and integrating a collection of stand alone units, each of which can be viewed as an agent [3]. This framework is presented to form *"the foundation for the development of a complete theory of coordination"*. The Sikora & Shaw framework is based on several dimensions, which includes the following:

1. Synthesis functions
2. Analytical model of a multi-agent information system & model of an agent
3. Taxonomy of interdependencies
4. Taxonomy of control structures / coordination mechanisms.

The authors first present the notion of a synthesis function, which relates the sub-goal of the agents or their performance measures to those of the overall performance of the system. This, they claim, is an important consideration in the design of complex multi-agent systems. Three synthesis functions are described by the authors: *competitive synthesis*, *additive synthesis* and *cooperative synthesis*.

Competitive synthesis is a competitive mechanism, in which the best solution from a single agent is chosen as the solution of the entire group of agents. This is similar to "survival of the fittest", and is similar to mechanisms found in the ecosystem as well as social systems. **Additive synthesis** is the mechanism whereby all of the agents contribute to the overall solution. As the authors describe, this is the most common type of mechanism where the goal is to subdivide a problem using a top-down approach, and assign the smaller problems to distributed agents which work on a part of the solution. **Cooperative synthesis** is described as a bottom-up approach, where the existing agents with different functional or operational perspectives must be integrated into a whole.

Next, the authors provide an analytical model of a multi-agent information system and a conceptual definition of an agent. The analytical model is characterized through:

1. A set of interaction variables that specify the interdependencies between the agents. The interactions among the agents equate to sending and receiving the values associated with the interaction variables.
2. The local states of the agents and environment. The local state of the agents also includes information about the interaction variables.
3. A notion of global structure that is defined as the set of all global states.
4. A set of joint activities that, when performed, transforms from global states to global states.

The components that comprise the functionality of the agent are then described. The components include knowledge or data, list of acquaintances, functional components, protocols and finally learning modules. The knowledge, or data component, contains information that the agent needs to perform its tasks. The list of acquaintances includes other agents that the agent in question knows directly. Furthermore, the agent may only communicate directly with its acquaintances and shares interdependencies and control structures with those acquaintances. The functional component contains numerical or computational procedures such as optimization routines or other heuristics. Lastly, the protocols specify the type of information exchanged and the response of those agents to the received information, while the learning module continually updates the agents' knowledge component based on interaction with other agents or through its functional components.

Next the authors describe the various taxonomies of interdependence, which include *temporal, resource* and *sub-goal interdependency*. These interdependencies, as the authors claim, require a different kind of coordination mechanism.

- *Temporal interdependency* is characterized by the temporal ordering of activities, for example, where a second activity cannot start until a first activity is completed. Alternatively, it may include synchronization whereby certain activities must be simultaneously performed.
- *Resource interdependency* is characterized by the fact that there is a competition for resources which are needed in order to accomplish a given set of tasks. Therefore, coordination is necessary in order to ensure proper resource allocation by the various agents.
- *Sub-goal interdependency* involves sub-goals that may be dependent across the various agents. In this case, the agents may need to share information regarding their partial goals.

Lastly, the authors describe the taxonomy of control structures and the supported coordination mechanisms. *Centralized control* mechanisms occur when there is a central coordinating agent and in the framework presented, this coordinating agent would have as a list of it's acquaintances all of the neighboring agents, while the neighboring agents would have as their acquaintances the coordinating agent. ***Decentralized control*** mechanisms would exist where there is no centralized coordinating agent, and all agents can interact among themselves.

After defining the various dimensions of the coordination framework, the authors provide an example of the utilization of the framework in the context of manufacturing of printed circuit boards. As the authors describe, the configuration consists of four assembly lines, and each line can hold at most two boards at a time. As the authors state, the scheduling problem is to find a weekly schedule that meets the daily demand, satisfies capacity constraints and minimizes the costs. The coordination problem is accomplished through a set of agents that make decisions on the lot size for each board, sequence the boards on the assembly lines and finally ensure capacity meets demand (Figure 4.1).

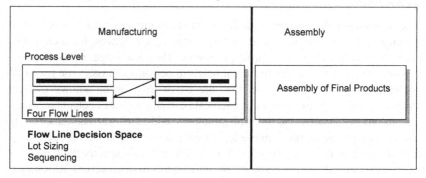

Figure 4.1: Multi-agent System Manufacturing Framework [3]

As stated by the authors, at the lowest level, the short interval scheduler that determines the production schedule for a flowline has to coordinate the functioning of the lot-sizing and sequencing modules. The need for coordination arises because the two modules have different and often conflicting objectives. For example, the lot-sizing module minimizes the holding and setup costs, whereas the sequencing module minimizes the total cycle time, or the *makespan*. These two objectives can be conflicting. For example, a decrease in the total cost of a schedule (i.e., setup and holding time) may increase the makespan. Hence it is necessary for the agents to coordinate by exchanging partial results. At the next level, there is a need for coordination among the short interval schedulers for each of the four flow-lines so the production of individual PCB's that comprise the same final product are synchronized. At the system level, there is a need for the different stages of manufacturing and assembly to coordinate their schedules in real-time so that any unexpected occurrences can be handled.

The authors describe the coordination problem in the context of the framework presented, and proceed to describe the temporal dependencies between the agents. For instance, the sequencing agent cannot initiate its activities until it receives a partial solution from the lot sizing agent. The capacity planning agent cannot start its process until the sequencing agent provides a partial solution. The authors also describe the interaction between the agents from the perspective of sub-goal interdependency. The authors describe this interdependency, for instance, between the lot sizing agent and sequencing agent as well as between sequencing agent and the capacity planning agents. In the former case, the lot sizing agent needs to know the exact sequence dependent setup time and available capacity, which can only be determined from the sequence provided by the sequencing agent. In the latter case, the sequencing agent uses a heuristic to give an initial sequence which is incrementally improved. In order to make such an incremental improvement, the sequencing agent needs to receive the evaluation of the sequence at every time step from the capacity planning agent. The authors proceed to describe the remaining coordination problem in the context of the framework. In other words, they describe the remaining analysis in terms of agent activities, functional components, list of acquaintances, and protocols used.

The general multi-agent framework, as presented by Sikora and Shaw enables the analysis of the different issues involved in coordinating and integrating a collection of stand alone units, each of which can be viewed as an agent [3]. This framework is presented to form "*the foundation for the development of a complete theory of coordination*". Sikora and Shaw suggest that future work would look at extending the proposed formalisms so as to:

1. Provide formal proofs of the best coordination schemes associated with different scenarios, and
2. Develop formal methods in order to derive coordination mechanisms suitable for any given scenario based on the interdependencies among agents.

In the context of applying the framework to an information system designed to manage the production of circuit boards, the proposed framework exhibited, according to the authors, several advantages, including the ability:

1. to provide uniformity of a general framework by treating heterogeneous components in a homogeneous fashion,
2. to recognize modularity by allowing different modules to be individually developed and implemented
3. to reconfigure the system easily
4. to represent distributed control by modeling agents as having local control with the capability to interact and coordinate their activities through message-passing.

4.3 Mintzberg Model

Mintzberg reveals what he calls "*a curious tendency to appear in five's*" [4, 5]. Interestingly, these findings do indeed suggest the possibility to logically isolate five basic parts of an organization, distinguish five basic mechanisms of coordination in the organization, and identify five fundamental types of decentralization. In exploring this possibility, Mintzberg proposes a theory on the structure of organization based on the postulate that any organization is composed of five parts. Thus, according to the Mintzberg model, the organization can – as shown in Figure 4.2: The Basic Parts of an Organization [4,5], be described in terms of the following basic elements:

1. *The operating core* – The operating core forms the basis of the organization where employees produce basic products and services, or directly support their production.
2. *The strategic apex* – The strategic apex refers to the top of the organization where top-ranking managers and their personnel staff are responsible for making strategic decisions.
3. *The middle line* – The middle line represents a chain of managers who *"sit in a direct line of formal authority"* between the staff of the strategic apex and the employees of the operating core. These managers are assigned the task of implementing decisions by *"supervising subordinates and reporting to the supervisors"*.
4. *The technostructure* – Out of the formal 'line' structure, the technostructure includes all members of the staff (e.g., accountants, work schedulers, long-range planners) responsible for "applying analytic techniques" to the design and maintenance of the structure and to allow the organization to achieve adaptability to its environment.
5. *The support staff* – The support staff includes people such as legal counsels, public relations, payroll, cafeteria employees, etc. This staff provides a number of indirect services to the rest of the organization.

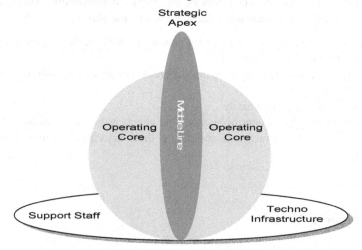

Figure 4.2: The Basic Parts of an Organization [4,5]

As pointed out, organizational structuring focuses on job specialization and a clear division of labor of a given organizational mission into a set of distinct tasks.

Then, it concentrates on appropriate coordination of the resulting tasks so as to allow the organization to accomplish its goals or mission in a unified way. In this respect, Mintzberg again identifies five basic ways or mechanisms through which the coordination of the tasks associated with the organization's mission can be affected. These mechanisms include:

1. *Direct supervision*: Direct supervision refers to coordination of tasks conducted through a supervisor who gives specific orders or instructions to his or her subordinates.
2. *Standardization of work processes:* Standardization of work processes indicates coordination of tasks that are achieved through standards – typically imposed by analysts of the technoinfrastructure in the form of work orders, rules and regulations, etc., that govern work in the organization.
3. *Standardization of outputs*: Standardization of outputs point to coordination of tasks conducted through standard performance measures and specifications regarding the output of the work – again this type of coordination mechanism is typically imposed by analysts of the technoinfrastructure.
4. *Standardization of skills*: Standardization of skills refers to coordination of work achieved as individuals internalize standard skills and knowledge – usually prior to starting a work.
5. *Mutual adjustment*: Mutual adjustment is a form of coordination of work conducted as participants communicate informally with each other.

Furthermore, Mintzberg identifies a list of nine mechanisms – design parameters – organizations can use to design their structures. The design parameters are defined as:

1. *Job specialization*: This parameter concerns the breadth of the tasks (i.e., horizontal job specialization) and the control over such tasks (vertical job specialization).
2. *Behavior Formalization*: This parameter concerns the formalization of work processes through rules, manuals, procedures, etc.
3. *Training and Indoctrination*: This parameter specifies the standardization of skills or knowledge through educational programs.
4. *Unit Grouping*: This parameter defines the clustering of positions into units.
5. *Unit Size*: This parameter, also called the span of control, defines the number of positions that comprise the units.
6. *Planning and Control Systems*: This design parameter may be of two kinds, *action planning* and *performance control*. Action planning focuses in an *a-priori* fashion regarding the output of specific decisions or actions; Performance control measures, in an *a-posteriori* fashion, the performance of all decisions or actions.
7. *Liaison Devices*: This design parameter defines how the use of specific positions such as liaisons or even larger groups might facilitate the interaction between other units.

8. *Vertical Decentralization*: This design parameter defines how well decision making authority might be delegated to a lower level chain of command.

9. *Horizontal Decentralization*: This parameter specifies the extent to which power might flow outside the normal chain of command.

Then, Mintzberg presents these parameters as levers organizations can turn to effect the division of labor and coordination. In addition, the author points to research efforts in organizational structuring designed to assess the effect of various so-called *contingency factors* on the design parameters. The contingency factors are described as: age / size, technical system, environment and power factors. According to Mintzberg, these research efforts are based on the *congruence* hypothesis, stating that effective structuring requires "*a close fit between contingency factor and design parameter*". While the *congruence* hypothesis relates the effectiveness of an organization to the fit between a given design parameter and a contingency factor, a second proposed hypothesis – called the *configuration* hypothesis – indicates that "*effective structuring requires an internal consistency among the design parameters*".

Mintzberg then presents five ideal types of organizational configurations described in terms of the above design parameters and contingency factors:

1. *Simple structure*: This structure is very simple, with little or no technoinfrastructure or support staff. Within this structure, the power tends to be very centralized and in the hands of a single individual – since a simple environment can be comprehended more easily by a single person. The author states that young organizations tend to be simple structures.

2. *Machine bureaucracy*: This structure tends to be very specialized; with tasks that are routine and standardized These types of structures tend to not rely on liaisons and are more centralized in their control. They also tend to have a fairly elaborate administrative structure, and are typically associated with environments that are stable and not very complex.

3. *Professional bureaucracy*: This structure contains entities called professionals that tend to work with some degree of autonomy in an environment that is complex, yet stable. It is stated that age and size are not factors in these types of organizations as the standard skills are the dominant factors.

4. *Divisionalized form*: This structure is defined as a market-based structure, with little interdependence between the various divisions. Each division has a certain degree of autonomy, and coordinates closely with a headquarters. It is suggested that performance control measures – those parameters that specify the performance of all decision or actions, as specified by the headquarters are used to coordinate the efforts of the various divisions.

5. *Adhocracy*: This structure is defined as one which is able to integrate experts from various disciplines, and can be divided into two types – *operating adhocracy* and *administrative adhocracy*. The operating adhocracy is driven by the demands of the clients, while the administrative adhocracy serves the organization itself. The environments in which these structures work well are both com-

plex and dynamic – and these structures are uniquely suited to provide the innovation which can be drawn from experts.

According to this theory, each of the above configurations depends on fundamentally different mechanisms of coordination. Thus, Mintzberg selects five configurations of coordination mechanism and the associated pre-eminent part in the organization, as shown in *Table 4.1*.

Table 4.1. The five structural configurations of organizations [4,5]

Name	Coordination mechanism	Key part
Simple structure	Direct supervision	Strategic apex
Machine Bureaucracy	Standardization of work processes	Technostructure
Professional bureaucracy	Standardization of skills	Operating core
Divisionalized form	Standardization of outputs	Middle line
Adhocracy	Mutual adjustment	Support staff

Tolksdorf notes that the Mintzberg model assumes "*a role for actors in an organization*" [1]. He argues that the choice of coordination mechanisms is determined by the choice of the organizational structure. Hence, mechanisms of coordination are not easily exchangeable. On the other hand, D. Harold Doty reports the Mintzberg typology and the underlying theory have little support, since they received little or no systematic empirical examination in large-scale comparative studies [6].

4.4 Tolksdorf Coordination Reference Model

Tolksdorf provides a brief review regarding various coordination models, such as the Mintzberg model (which we will not describe in this section, since it has already been covered earlier in the chapter), but also proceeds to describe other models such as Workflow Management Systems, formal models and uncoupled models.

The author describes workflow management systems as a mechanism to coordinate activities across human work. As such, the author provides a brief description regarding the activities that are taking place to standardize workflow systems, for example, through the Workflow Modeling Coalition (WMC). The WMC is a consortium of vendors who are defining a process definition language in order to enable basic specification of workflows.

As yet another example, the author describes formal models. These models are represented through mathematical techniques as well as language. An example of such a formal model, which is described by the author as a decentralized model of cooperation, is game theory. As the author elaborates, formal models are based on several key assumptions. The first is that they all assume that a utility and payoff function can be exactly defined and is static, and secondly, the agents behave rationally to maximize the payoff or utility function.

The author also briefly touches upon models that are uncoupled. He proceeds to discuss the language called "Linda", which enables agents to coordinate their activities by reading and writing a set of tuples from the tuplespace. The tuplespace is defined as a shared data space. The model is uncoupled, since it does not require the agents to know of one another in space or time; so in other words, the agents can remain anonymous to each other. The notion of a shared dataspace is very similar to blackboard architectures, which also enables access to a shared dataspace, called the blackboard, which may contain data, partial solutions, etc that have been provided by the various agents in the system. Such architectures may contain a mechanism to control the problem solving flow within the system.

Tolksdorf then proposes "a coordination reference model" [1] inspired by the 4-layer meta-model architecture for UML [7] (Figure 4.3). First, the author recalls the existence of situations associated with the real world where coordination is *"neither present nor necessary"*. Then, he further specifies that the model he proposes takes into consideration only the part of the world in which *"activities are managed in order to be coordinated"*.

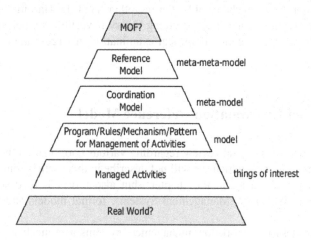

Figure 4.3. A structure for Tolksdorf coordination reference model[1] [1]

[1]   Meta Object Facility (MOF) is a standard of Object Management Group (OMG).

As described by Tolksdorf, the real world coordinated activities form the object-level in the proposed model-hierarchy. Considering a specific set of objects, the concrete management of activities can, as Tolksdorf explains, be described through a set of rules, specific mechanisms, programs or a selection of coordination patterns. According to the author, these objects are indeed models of specific managed activities or, in other terms, the blueprints for actual interactions.

As proposed by Tolksdorf, the coordination reference model is a meta-model to other coordination models such as the Mintzberg model described above. As a result, it contains terminologies and other concepts required to describe these coordination models. In this respect, Tolksdorf considers a set of concepts that he believes are necessary to incorporate into the reference model:

- *Interactors.* Interactors represent those entities related to other interactors.
- *Relations.* Relations are designed to associate in some way two or more interactors.
- *Non-interactors.* Non-interactors represent entities with no relations to interactors.
- *Operations.* Operations are performed by interactors on non-interactors.
- *Attributes.* Interactors, non-interactors or their corresponding current states can be described using attributes.
- *Meta-attributes.* Models built from the previous five concepts can be described through characteristics contained in the meta-attributes.

Finally, Tolksdorf claims that the reference model he proposes can be used to describe various coordination models, such as those he reviewed. As suggested, the reference model can thus be used to compare these coordination models through a set of meta-attributes:

- *Distinction*, or the degree to which interactors and non-interactors can be differentiated, as well as the management of their relations.
- *Orthogonality*, or how well the coordination model is in alignment with the computation model of the interactor.
- *Coupling between interactors*, or in other words, the degree of dependency between interactors. The author argues that the Mintzberg model is difficult to assess with regard to the degree of coupling.
- *Autonomy*, or the degree of independence of the interactors.
- *Management of relations*, for example, whether such management is handled externally or internally.
- *Awareness*, or how much the interactors need to be aware that relations need to be managed.
- *Interactor stability*, for example, whether there is a static set of interactors.
- *Relations stability*, or whether the relations are long term or short term. The author states that the Mintzberg model is characterized by stability, primarily due to the life-cycle of a given organization.
- *Reliability*, which in some measure denotes the reliability of the interactors.

- *Scalability*, with respect to the number of interactors and relations. The author argues that formal models of coordination are generally not scalable.
- *Usability for programming*, which describes whether the model is suited for prescriptive versus descriptive modeling to enable programming.
- *Qualitative* or *quantitative* measures on the management of relations.

The author concludes by stating that the models as described in his review appear to be well distinguishable along the primary dimensions of the meta-attributes as described above and that each of the models has a dominant meta-attribute characteristic.

4.5 Malone & Crowston theory of Coordination

Malone and Crowston advocate the notion of a "coordination theory" to refer to principles and ideas about how coordination can occur in diverse kinds of complex systems [8]. In this context, they estimate that many of the researchers whose efforts can contribute to, and benefit from, this new area are not yet aware of each other's work. The authors report having used the term "theory" with some hesitation since it connotes a degree of coherence that is not present in this field. They further describe the field as a collection of intriguing analogies, scattered results, and partial frameworks. In proposing an interdisciplinary study of coordination, they would like to both define a community of interest and suggest useful directions for future progress [9].

Malone and Crowston outline the need for *a coordination framework* required to "transport" concepts and results back and forth between the different kinds of systems. In their view, coordination involves organized actors engaged in sequences of interdependent activities to achieve desired goals. As a result, actors face coordination problems arising from dependencies that "constrain how tasks can be performed" [10]. Coordination is viewed as a response to problems induced by dependencies. The duality between coordination and dependencies implies the need to consider that there is nothing to coordinate in the absence of interdependence. Accordingly, coordination processes are, within the theory of coordination, viewed as ways of *"managing dependencies between activities"*.

Defined in a way that emphasizes its interdisciplinary nature, coordination can thus occur, as outlined above, in many kinds of systems: human, computational, biological, and others. To facilitate the transfer of concepts and results among these different discipline, Malone and Crowston propose as a second step to identify and study the basic processes involved in coordination. Since coordination is defined as managing dependencies between activities, it should be possible, according to them, to characterize different kinds of dependencies and identify the coordination processes that can be used to manage them. In this respect, the authors identify several common dependencies between activities and provide an analysis of alternative coordination processes to manage them.

The coordination theory concept suggests that a process consists of three types of elements: resources, activities, and dependencies. A resource is produced and/or consumed during a process. While an activity is indeed a partitioned action that produces and/or consumes resources, a dependency is a relation among activities mediated by producing or consuming resources. Arising from resources related to multiple activities, three basic types of dependencies are identified [11], as shown in Figure 4.4:

1. **Fit dependencies.** This type of dependency occurs when multiple activities collectively produce the same resource.
2. **Flow dependencies.** This type of dependency occurs all the time in almost all processes. It arises whenever one activity produces a resource that is used by another activity.
3. **Sharing dependencies.** This kind of dependency arises whenever multiple activities all use (or could use) the same resource.

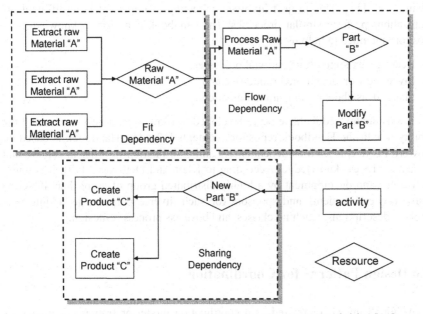

Figure 4.4: Three Basic Types of Dependencies among activities [11]

Later, Crowston develops a taxonomy of dependency types by considering possible combinations of activities using resources [12]. This taxonomy includes task-resource dependencies and three types of task-task dependencies: shared resources, producer-consumer and common output. For each type of dependency, alternative coordination mechanisms are described. To extend the above analysis within the theory of coordination, the authors categorize an exhaustive list of dependencies and their associated coordination processes.

According to Malone and Crowston, many specific processes that arise in particular kinds of systems can be seen as instances of more generic processes [9]. In this respect, dependencies that are not shown can be usefully analyzed as specializations or combinations of those that are more generic. It is thus believed that it is possible to identify and systematically analyze a wide variety of dependencies and their associated coordination processes. Designing a "handbook" of coordination processes could, in the view of Malone and Crowston, facilitate interdisciplinary transfer of knowledge about coordination. It could also provide a guide for analyzing the coordination needs in particular situations and generating alternative ways of fulfilling them. The author's further note that the power of analyzing processes in terms of dependencies and coordination mechanisms is greatly increased by access to a rich library of alternative coordination mechanisms for different kinds of dependencies.

Indeed, the Center for Coordination Science (CCS) at the Massachusetts Institute of Technology (MIT) conducted a project designed to develop a "Process Handbook" [11]. This project involved collecting examples of how different organizations perform similar processes. The handbook is a process knowledge repository intended to help users:

- Redesign existing organizational processes,
- Invent new organizational processes, and
- Share ideas about organizational practices.

In this context, tools have been developed to provide read-only access and the ability to edit the Handbook repository contents [13]. The Handbook is based on powerful concepts such as dependencies and coordination in order to capture and organize process knowledge. According to Klein and Dellarocas [13], it is under active use and development by a highly distributed group of more than 40 scientists, teachers, students and sponsors for such diverse purposes as adding new process descriptions, teaching classes, and business process re-design.

4.6 Design Patterns for Coordination

Although not characterized as a coordination model or framework, there has been some recent activity in the analysis of the coordination mechanisms within a multi-agent system that borrows from the notion of reusable design patterns, specifically from the field of object oriented technology. As Duego, et al., state *"patterns provide a means of documenting the building blocks in a format already accepted by the software engineering community"* [14]. The authors note that the minimal components that define a pattern include the following:

- *Name:* The name of the pattern should be clear, and specific in its meaning.
- *Context:* The context describes the circumstances under which the pattern could be used.
- *Problem:* The specific description of the problem that is to be solved.
- *Forces:* These are the items that influence when to apply the specific pattern in a given context.
- *Solution:* This is the solution to the problem, in the specific context and given the forces that are present.

The authors also state that other elements of a design pattern could be included, such as *related patterns, example code, aliases,* etc, but these might be optional. Furthermore, patterns themselves are not solutions to a given problem, but rather, they can be applied in order to arrive at a particular solution. The authors also makes two key statements, that if a pattern has the potential to be applied to a wide range of problem, then the more general it is, and that such general patterns can be used to form the foundation of a "pattern language". Such a pattern language might be formed by assembling related patterns or repositioning them with one another. As suggested by the authors, this so called "pattern language" could be utilized to build entire systems. The authors then proceed to define the global forces of coordination which impact when to choose a particular pattern. Several forces are described, namely:

- Time and space
- Mobility and Communication
- Standardization
- Temporal and Spatial Coupling
- Problem Partitioning
- Failures

Next, the authors describe several design patterns in relation to the context, problem, forces and solution. These include the *blackboard pattern, meeting pattern, market maker pattern, master-slave pattern* and *negotiating pattern.* We will briefly describe each of the patterns mentioned.

In the blackboard pattern (Figure 4.5), a set of specialist agents coordinate with each other through the sharing of data through a common blackboard. The specialist agents send signals to the blackboard when they want to add, remove or otherwise modify the data on the blackboard. The supervisor agent controls which agents may interact with the blackboard, as well as deciding on when the state of the blackboard has progressed sufficiently such that a solution has been reached. There is a certain degree of decoupling between the specialist agents in this pattern, as agents can post data or information on the blackboard and other agents can pick up that data at a later time – i.e., time transparency. Furthermore, this pattern is an example of passive coordination, since the architecture only supports the sharing of data, and does not specify how the individual specialist agents must use the data.

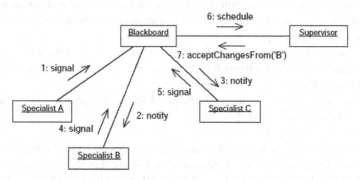

Figure 4.5: The Blackboard design pattern [14]

In the Meeting maker pattern, a place is created for the agents to meet. The meeting manager agent is responsible for notifying agents when a meeting is proposed, hence the interested agents must notify the manager who they are and where they can be located, as well as which meetings they are interested in so they can be notified when such meetings are instantiated. The meeting manager is also a local control point for the meeting, keeping a track of when agents enter or leave the meeting by registering or deregistering them. The meeting maker coordination pattern is depicted in Figure 4.6.

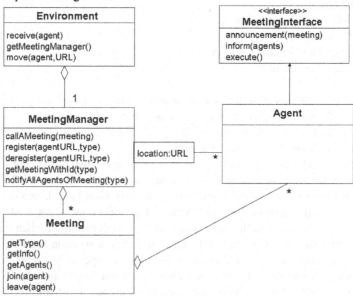

Figure 4.6: The Meeting Maker design pattern [14]

In the Market Maker Pattern (Figure 4.7), a buyer agent interacts with a broker agent, and the buyer agent is responsible for making requests for bids to the broker agent. The broker agent makes similar requests to seller agents, which provide bids back to the buyer agent via the broker. If a bid is accepted by the buyer agent, the message again goes back to the seller agent via the broker. As can be seen, the broker agent acts on behalf of the buyer and seller agent. When acting on behalf of the buyer agent, the broker agent passes the bid to the seller agent. When acting on behalf of the seller agent, the broker agent presents the list of bids to the buyer agent. The broker sets up a direct relationship between the buyer and seller once an agreement has been reached, which as stated by the authors, lasts until the goods have been delivered from the seller to the buyer.

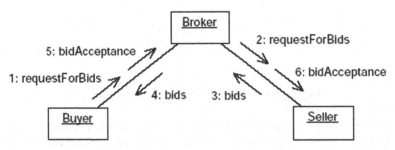

Figure 4.7: The Market Maker design pattern [14]

The Master-Slave Pattern consists of a master agent that delegates a set of tasks to slave agents for execution, which may be on different machines. The primary forces that drive the necessity to potentially use such a pattern are to improve the reliability, performance or accuracy with which the overall task can be performed. The master passes the tasks to the slaves, which compute their solutions and pass back the results to the master agent. The master agent is then responsible for passing the results to the client agents. The slaves may either continue to exist, or may terminate. As the author states, this model is an example of vertical coordination, where an agents carries out a subtask for another agent. The master-slave coordination pattern is depicted in Figure 4.8.

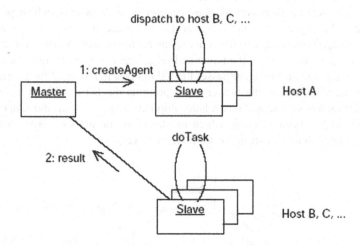

Figure 4.8: The Master-Slave design pattern [14]

The Negotiating Pattern is a model used to resolve conflicts between agents. In this model, an initiator agent indicates its intention to perform a given task to the other agents in the system. The other agents, in this context, act as critics and check whether the intended action by the initiator will conflict with any of their actions. If there are no conflicts the proposal is accepted. However, if conflicts are detected, then the critics may make counter-offers or reject the proposal. In the example of Figure 4.9, Agent *A* proposes its intention to perform action **A**, however Agent *B* detects that this action will conflict with its own action **D**. Therefore, Agent *B* counter proposes action **E**. After Agent *A* checks this action against its own action and finds no further conflicts, it accepts that Agent *B* will execute Action **E**, and therefore Agent *A* can execute Action **B**.

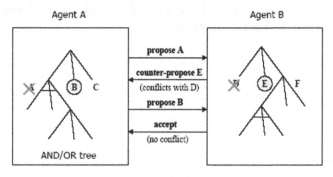

Figure 4.9: The Negotiating design pattern [14]

In a similar fashion, in [15], the authors examine architectural design patterns for agent coordination. They outline several design patterns, namely, *hierarchical, federated, peer-to-peer* and *agent-pair* patterns. The authors describe hierarchical patterns as those in which control is promulgated from the top down to the lower agents in the hierarchy, much like that in a supervisory role. The peer-to-peer pattern is described as one in which agents manage all aspects of coordination and resolve potential conflicts occurring in the system. The agent-pair pattern is described as a one-on-one interaction between the agents in the multi-agent system. The authors proceed to provide greater detail regarding the federated design pattern, which includes the *broker, embassy, mediator, monitor* and *wrapper*.

The broker pattern is described as a facilitator or matchmaker agent, which is responsible for matching client agents with service providers. In this model, the client agents are decoupled from the service provider, and the broker agent is aware of the other agents in the system, which has the potential to reduce the overhead associated with the number of messages that need to be sent in the agent network since the messages occur primarily with the broker agents. However, the broker agent can also become a bottleneck or result in a single point of failure. The authors indicate that it may be worthwhile to include several brokers in the system to overcome the single point of failure concern.

The embassy model, also known as an ambassador or surrogate, provides a bridge between many different agent domains which may be entirely independent in the agent language used for communication, The embassy agent may, in addition, provide access control mechanisms that enable some level of security to limit which agents can interact within the multi-agent system. The security model may be implemented through the use of digital certificates. The advantages of the embassy model, as stated by the authors, are in the decoupling between the two systems that are connected via the embassy agent.

The mediator design pattern is defined as "*a mechanism that encapsulates collective behavior, allowing control and coordination of the interactions of the group of agents*". This model incorporates a mediator agent, and a number of colleague agents. The mediator has knowledge of the colleague agents, while the colleagues have knowledge of the mediator agent. In this model, the colleagues interact with other colleagues through the mediator agent, which acts like a router in order to forward messages between colleague agents. As with the broker pattern, the mediator agent can become a single point of failure, but similarly to the broker pattern, this issue can be rectified through the use of multiple mediator agents.

The monitor design pattern is described as a publish-and-subscribe approach, in which a monitor agent subscribes to a particular subject which provides some information of particular interest to a subscriber agent. The limitation, as identified by the author, is that if an agent has multiple subscriptions, then the level of messaging can ripple through the agent network and place a great demand on the network.

The wrapper design pattern enables legacy applications to be "agentized" and integrated with a given multi-agent system. The authors state that the value of this pattern lies in the fact that if the legacy application cannot be easily rewritten in the agent paradigm, then this model permits the functionality of the legacy application to be more easily integrated in the agent system. The wrapper must translate or provide a mapping between the legacy application and agents.

In a similar fashion regarding design patterns, Tolksdorf [16] discusses coordination patterns for mobile information agents. He highlights the fact that mobility can exist in the context of *"passive but mobile information"*, *"active and mobile agents"*, and lastly *"mobile human users"*. He then describes the primary attributes that comprise a pattern, such as its *name, alias, intent, motivation, dependency, structure, collaborations, implementation, sample code, known uses* and *related patterns*. Based on this definition, he proceeds to describe three interaction patterns for mobile information systems, namely, *pull, push* and *index*.

The pull model is utilized when the source has more information than the client, and in order for the client to receive the necessary information, it sends a query to the source, executes the query, and receives the information as a result of the query execution. In the push pattern, the client moves an agent containing a query to the source, and this agent continuously monitors the source and provides any changes within the information back to the client. Lastly, in the index pattern the multiple sources are queried and indexed at a particular node, which may result in a much faster access by the agent/user. The author states that the intent is not to provide an exhaustive list of design patterns describing mobility of information systems in the context of coordination. Instead, he suggests that coordination is a much broader field of research, and design patterns need to be examined across other areas that support coordination such as auctions, etc. in order to begin categorizing such patterns.

References

1. Robert Tolksdorf, *"Models of Coordination"*, In Engineering Societies in the Agent' World, A. Omicini, R. Tolksdorf, and F. Zambonelli, Editors, ESAW 2000, LNAI 1972, Springer-Verlag, Berlin Heidelberg, 2000
2. Graham Coates, Robert Ian Whitfield, Alex H. B. Duffy and Bill Hills, *"Coordination Approaches and Systems – Part II: An Operational Perspective"* In Research in Engineering Design, No 12, pp. 73-79, 2000.
3. Riyaz Sikora and Michael J. Shaw, *"A Multi-Agent Framework for the Coordination and Integration of Information Systems"*, In Management Science, Vol. 11, Issue 11, Part 2 of 2, November 1998.
4. Henry Mintzberg, "The Structuring of Organizations: A Synthesis of the Research, Prentice Hall, Englewood Cliffs, N. J., 1979.
5. Henry Mintzberg, "Structure in 5'S: A Synthesis of the Research on Organization Design", In Management Science, Vol. 26, No. 3, March 1980.
6. Harold Doty, William H. Click, and George P. Huber, "Fit, Equifinality, and Organizational Effectiveness: A Test of Two Configurational Theories", In Academy of Management Journal, Vol. 36, No. 6, pp. 1196-1250, 1993

7. Cris Kobryn, "UML 2001: a Standardization Odyssey", In Communications of the ACM, Vol. 42, No. 10, pp. 29–37, October 1999.
8. B. A. Huberman, "*The Ecology of Computation*", In the Ecology of Computation, Elsevier Science Publishers, Amsterdam, Holland, 1988.
9. Thomas W. Malone and Kevin Crowston, "the Interdisciplinary Study of Coordination", In ACM Computing Surveys, Vol. 26, No 1, March 1994.
10. Kevin Crowston and Charles S. Osborn, "A coordination theory approach to process description and redesign", Report submitted to the Center for Coordination Science, Sloan School of Management, Massachusetts Institute of Technology – MIT, July 1998
11. Malone, T.W., K. Crowston, Lintae Lee, Brian Pentland, Chrysanthos Dellarocas, George Wyner, John Quimby, Charles S. Osborn, Abraham Bernstein, George Herman, Mark Klein, and Elissa O'Donnell, "Tools for Inventing Organizations: Toward a Handbook of Organizational Processes", In Management Science, Vol. 45, No 3, pp. 425-443, 1999.
12. Kevin Crowston, "A Taxonomy of Organizational Dependencies and Coordination Mechanisms", In Tools for Organizing Business Knowledge: the MIT Process Handbook, Malone, T. W., Crowston, K. and Herman, G. (Eds.), Cambridge, MA, MIT Press.
13. M. Klein and C. Dellarocas, "Towards a Systematic Repository of Knowledge about Managing Multi-Agent System Exceptions", Massachusetts Institute of Technology, Cambridge, MA, USA, ASES Working Paper ASES-WP-2000-01, February 2000.
14. Dwight Deugo, Michael Weiss, Elizabeth Kendall, "Reusable Patterns for Agent Coordination. Coordination of Internet Agents, Omicini, A.; Zambonelli, F.; Klusch, M.; Tolksdorf, R. (Eds.), pp. 347-368. Springer 2001.
15. Ra C. Hayden, Christina Carrick, Qiang Yang, "Architectural Design Patterns for Multiagent Coordination". In Proceedings of the 3rd International Conference on Autonomous Agents 1999.
16. Robert Tolksdorf, "Coordination Patterns of Mobile Information Agents. In Cooperative Information Agents II, Proceedings of the Second International Workshop in Cooperative Information Agents. Pp. 246-261. Springer-Verlag, 1998.

Chapter 5 Coordination Strategies and Techniques

Abstract This chapter is devoted to providing a broad overview of the various strategies and techniques designed and implemented to enable the coordination of autonomous entities within organizations, processes, and distributed multi-agent systems. In addition, examples are incorporated to illustrate the use of these strategies and techniques in various software implementations and prototypes. Finally, additional issues are discussed in order to help the reader further understand both the potential advantages and limitations of applying such strategies or techniques.

5.1 Introduction

This chapter will discuss various strategies and techniques that can be used for the coordination of entities within organizations, process and distributed multi-agent systems. Our goal will be to describe a broad range of strategies and techniques, in order to enable the reader to gain a better appreciation of the breadth of research being conducted in this field. For example, we will describe organizational structuring which leverages a-priori knowledge about the structure of organizations as an analogy for encoding coordination rules or knowledge, contracting which utilizes mechanisms for rewards in order to coordinate a set of distributed tasks or functions and multi-agent planning techniques. Furthermore, we will describe negotiation strategies such as game theory-based negotiation, plan-based negotiation and other negotiation approaches. We will also touch upon auctions as a way to reach agreements in multi-agent environments that leverage the notion of buying and selling goods through the process of bidding, and market-oriented models, that exploit the institution of markets as a mechanism to build computational economies in which multi-agent systems operate. Lastly, we will describe techniques such as coalition formation, argumentation and dialogue-systems. In some instances, we will provide examples from the literature that demonstrate how various software implementations and prototypes have been developed using these techniques. In many cases throughout the discussion, we will provide additional insight into the limitations that are imposed, or advantages that are gained, with each technique in order to enable the practitioner to better grasp the issues when considering the design of cooperating multi-agent systems.

A. Bedrouni et al., *Distributed Intelligent Systems: A Coordination Perspective*,
DOI: 10.1007/978-0-387-77702-3_5, © Springer Science + Business Media, LLC 2009

5.2 Organizational structuring

Organizational structuring is the simplest coordination scenario, which exploits *a priori* organizational structure. To support this claim, it is argued that the organization defines implicitly the agent's responsibilities, capabilities, connectivity and control flow. In defining the roles, communication paths and authority relationship, this type of coordination provides a framework for activity and interaction [1]. The organizational structuring technique is thus described as the predefined long-term relationships between agents [2].

Within this category, hierarchical organizations are generally identified as the dominant mode of coordination. This type of organization yields the classic master/slave or client/server coordination technique, which is used to enable a master agent to allocate tasks and resources among slave agents. Accordingly, this technique is implemented in two ways:

1. In the first, the slaves within a master/slave configuration have limited autonomy with respect to the master, while the latter exercise full autonomy with respect to the slaves. Thus, the master is devoted the task of planning and allocating sub-plans to the slaves. Ultimately bound to report their results to the master, the slaves may or may not communicate with each other.
2. In the second, a blackboard negotiation scheme exploiting the classic blackboard architecture is used to provide a "coordinating base". Agents replacing the blackboard's knowledge sources are used to post to and read from the general blackboard. A master agent is, on the other hand, devoted the role of scheduling other agents' reads/writes to/from the blackboard.

The blackboard architecture based approach has been implemented in various systems, such as the Werkman's DFI system [3] and the Sharp Multi-Agent Kernel (SMAK) system [4].

In addition, other organizational structures include both centralized and decentralized market structures [1]. The centralized market structure is identified as employing a master/slave coordination approach. On the other hand, the decentralized market structure suitably includes contracting techniques described in the next section.

Indeed, these strategies are useful in a multi-agent system configuration based on master/slave relationships. It is generally argued that the approach implies much control over the slaves' actions and, consequently, over the problem-solving process. However, such control can, at its highest level, compromise the numerous advantages offered by DAI: speed, reliability, concurrency, robustness, graceful degradation, minimal bottleneck, etc. A blackboard-based scheme engaging a great number of agents may result in a severe bottleneck, even in a multi-partitioned blackboards-based configuration.

As a result, most blackboard-based systems tend to incorporate homogeneous and rather small-grained agents [1], as the Distributed Vehicle Monitoring Testbed

(DVMT) prototype [5]. The centralized control required in the master/slave technique does not comply with the basic assumptions of DAI [1,2]. It presumes that at least one agent has a global view of the entire agency. Such an assumption is unrealistic in many domains.

5.3 Contracting

Deployed in a multi-agent environment, an agent may be faced with certain tasks that cannot be accomplished locally or can be performed more efficiently through appropriate assistance of other agents. In this respect, a self-interested agent may be able to take advantage of the presence of other agents and hire the services of appropriate entities to ensure that the assigned tasks are effectively accomplished [6]. Commonly known as contracting, the approach consists in allowing a self-interested agent to take the necessary steps − say through promises of rewards − in order to convince other self-interested agents to assist it in performing its tasks.

The contracting-oriented approach raises the question of how one agent can convince other self-interested agents that do not share a global task to provide it with assistance in carrying out some tasks. Another issue lies in the need to explore how the manager-agent can convince the contractor-agent to perform a given task with a desired level of effort without the need for close observation. The contractor-agent is able to choose different levels of effort when carrying an assigned task.

5.3.1 Different Types of Contracting

The issue of incentive contracting has indeed been the subject of numerous studies over the last three decades [6-12]. Conducted in both economics and game theory, research focused on different contracts for different applications. Different types of contracts have thus been examined between:

- A firm and an employer or employers [13-16].
- A government and taxpayers [17].
- A landlord and a tenant [7].
- An insurance company and a policy holder [18-21].
- A buyer and seller [22-23].
- A government and firms [24].
- Stockholders and managers [7].
- A professional and a client [25].

Two parties usually exist in situations reflected through such types of contracts [6]:

- *The agent,* or the first party, is required to choose *"an action or a level of effort from a number of possibilities."*
- *The principal,* or the second party, has the additional function of prescribing payoff rules.

Prior to the agent choosing an action, the principal determines a rule, i.e. a contract, designed to specify *"the fee to be paid to the other party as a function of the principal's observations"*. Though similar, the applications mentioned above reveal differences in several aspects, such as the number of agents, the amount of information available to the parties involved, and the observations peculiar to the principal. Several concepts and techniques are applied to the principal-agent paradigm in the relevant economics and game theory literature [6].

Indeed, the Contract Net protocol is a well-known framework for achieving automated contracting. A contract initiated through the Contract Net protocol represents an explicit agreement between, on the one hand, an agent that generates a task (the manager) and, on the other hand, an agent willing to execute the task (the contractor). While the manager has the responsibility to both monitor the execution of a given task and process the results, the contractor has the duty of actually executing the task.

Thus, the Contract Net protocol provides a scheme that enables the manager to issue an announcement of the existence of a task. In response, available agents are consequently required to evaluate the task announcements made by managers. Acting as potential contractors, these agents then submit bids or proposals on tasks for which they are well suited to undertake. Initially developed for and implemented in distributed problem solving environments, where benevolent agents are organized to achieve common goals, the protocol does not require the need to stimulate and motivate an agent to bid for tasks and deploy all its capabilities in favor of the execution of the contracted tasks.

Smith and Davis originally developed the Contract Net protocol and addressed problems related to the distribution of tasks and sub-tasks and synthesis of the overall solution [26-28]. The protocol has been implemented within numerous applications relevant to various domains [29- 32]. Initially, the Contract Net protocol was applied to a simulated distributed acoustic sensor network to provide a framework of a negotiation process involving mutual selection by both managers and contractors. In this application, the agents are totally cooperative, and the selection of a contractor is based on suitability, such as adjacency, processing capability, and agent's current load.

Absent in the original Contract Net protocol, a formalized decision making process regarding tasks announcement, bidding, and awarding [33] was proposed to allow agents to locally calculate their marginal costs for performing desired tasks. In this respect, self-interested agents with different local criteria can thus interact to distribute tasks within a more effective system. The proposed pricing mechanism offers a new generalized version of the Contract Net protocol that can effectively handle both competitive and cooperative agents. In addition, a backtracking method, known as *leveled commitment contract*, has been developed and proposed to allow each party involved in a contract to unilaterally de-commit by paying a predetermined penalty [34, 35]. This method has demonstrated the ability to improve expected social welfare even if agents de-commit strategically in Nash equilibrium.

On the other hand, techniques have been proposed to enable agents to efficiently make incentive contracts in various situations of automated agent environments [36]. As a result, different situations and contexts have been explored:

- Certainty versus uncertainty.
- Full information versus partial information.
- Symmetric information versus asymmetric information.
- Bilateral situation versus a situation where more than two automated agents are involved in an environment.

Economics-based mechanisms and techniques that can be used for contracting in automated agents environments are fitted for each of the situations and contexts mentioned above. Given the constraints of the other entities, the agent that designs the contract is, in all the cases, provided with appropriate mechanisms and techniques to maximize its personal expected utilities.

5.3.2 Contract Net Protocol

The *Contract Net Protocol* [26-27] is a classic coordination technique for decentralized allocation of tasks and resources among agents. In this approach, the description of activities is specified in terms of roles. Agents can be assigned two functions:

1. *A manager* to assume the role of dividing a problem into sub-problems and searching for contractors to tackle them. The manager is also assigned the task of monitoring the overall solution of the global problem.
2. *A contractor* to accomplish a sub-task. The contractors may however recursively assume the role of managers to further decompose sub-tasks assigned to them and search for sub-contractors to undertake them.

In this respect, agents endowed with managerial responsibilities locate contractors via the following bidding process:

1. A manager issues a task announcement,
2. Contractors evaluate the announced task with respect to their abilities and commitments,

3. Contractors send bids to the manager to announce their willingness and ability to perform a given task,
4. The manager then evaluates received bids, select the most appropriate contractor to which it awards a contract,
5. The manager finally waits for results emanating from the contractor.

The Contract Net Protocol is a completely distributed scheme, where a node can simultaneously assume the role of manager and contractor. This approach has been implemented and generalized in various applications, such as the discrete manufacturing environment that partitions tasks [31] or the multistage negotiation paradigm involved in monitoring and control of complex communication systems [37].

The Contract Net Protocol is a high-level coordination strategy, which provides the ability to distribute tasks and self-organize a group of agents [38]. The conditions in which this protocol can be best used are:

• A well-defined hierarchical nature of the application task,
• A coarse-grained decomposition of the problem,
• A minimal coupling among sub-tasks.

The Contract Net Protocol has been acknowledged as a reliable mechanism for distributed control and failure recovery. It provides various advantages, such as:

• Better agreements through self-bidding in dynamic task allocation,
• Dynamic introduction and removal of agents,
• Natural load-balancing, as busy agents need not bid.

On the other hand, the basic drawback associated with the Control Net Protocol lies in its inability to anticipate the existence of agents with contradictory demands. Hence, the approach can neither detect nor resolve possible conflicts, whereas coordination is required to detect and resolve conflicts. Agents in the Contract Net are rather *"passive, benevolent, and non-antagonistic"*. Having agents with such attributes is unrealistic in many real-world problems. This limitation has been tackled essentially by introducing an iterative mechanism to enable agents with conflicting goals to reach a consensus [37]. It is generally argued that the Contract Net approach is rather communication-intensive. The costs associated with this property may outweigh its advantages in real-world applications.

5.4 Multi-Agent Planning

Classified under a unique category, multi-agent planning is described as a coordination approach designed to avoid inconsistent and conflicting actions and interactions. This approach is implemented to allow agents to build a multi-agent plan containing details of all future actions and interactions. Agents can thus achieve their goals and interleave execution with more planning and re-planning. Two types of multi-agent planning are identified, namely:

1. Centralized multi-agent planning.
2. Distributed problem solving.

The centralized multi-agent planning based approach is usually characterized by the need to incorporate a coordinating agent. On receipt of all partial or local plans from individual agents, the coordinating agent analyzes these plans to identify potential inconsistencies and conflicting interactions, such as those associated with limited resources. Then, the coordinating agent attempts to modify the partial plans in order to eliminate conflicting interactions before they are combined into a multi-agent plan.

In the 1980's, research conducted separately focused on the implementation of the centralized multi-agent planning approach [38-40]. In this context, a method was introduced to synthesize multi-agent plans from single-agent plans. The idea consists in inserting communication acts into single-agent plans to enable agents to synchronize activities and avoid harmful interactions. It is acknowledged that the approach does not guarantee solutions where problems involve complex interactions between single-agent plans. However, the method has a wide applicability in many real-world domains, such as automated factories and cooperative robot assembly tasks.

Later, a more general model of action has been proposed to provide the ability to synthesize or verify multi-agent plans and concurrent programs [38-39]. On the other hand, various problem solvers based on a *task centralization* approach have been developed and simulated in the air-traffic control domain [40]. This scheme imposes on agents associated with aircrafts involved in any conflict the need to select and decide which one of them can appropriately assume the role of the coordinating agent. The latter is required to only modify his flight plan to resolve the conflict. In adopting passive information-gathering roles, the remaining agents will thus perform no planning or actions, but merely send their intentions or plans to the selected coordinating agent.

The MATPEN model has been proposed for coordinating autonomous and distributed agents based on centralized planning [1,41]. A ship collision avoidance system has thus been developed and implemented using MATPEN. In this approach, two agents sharing a conflict form a conflict group and initiate a negotiation process through an expectation-based negotiation protocol. "Expectations" are thus exchanged in order to decide which agent should assume what role in the negotiation process. As a result, agents generate a multi-agent plan required to resolve the conflict. The idea behind the distributed multi-agent planning lies in the need to provide each agent with a model of other agents' plans [42]. In a system based on this approach, agents communicate until all conflicts are resolved. In this context, each agent takes responsibility for building its individual plan and a model of other agents' plans.

Indeed, research efforts have been dedicated to performing this style of distributed processing. The *Functionally Accurate and Cooperative* (FA/C) protocol has been proposed and later used to develop the Distributed Vehicle Monitoring Testbed for testing coordination strategies [43-44]. The FA/C is described as an approach where loosely coupled agents form high-level, but possibly incomplete, plans, results and hypothesis [1]. The objective behind this approach is to bring agents sharing the same environment to exchange and refine incomplete input data and possibly incomplete, incorrect and inconsistent tentative results received from other nodes until all agents reach a convergence on some global complete plan. Another application of distributed multi-agent planning, i.e. the Partial Global Planning (PGP) approach, has been proposed to allow agents to execute their local plans with each other [1,45]. In turn, these plans are continuously modified based on partial global plans built by exchanging local plans. Agents within this framework are always searching for potential improvements to group coordination.

Centralized or distributed multi-agent planning imposes on agents to share and process substantial amounts of information. Thus, it is commonly argued that such an approach is likely to require more computing and communication resources than other approaches. The centralized multi-agent planning approach and the master/slave coordination technique described above share many common limitations. On the other hand, the distributed multi-agent planning oriented coordination is much more complex than the centralized multi-agent planning based coordination. Finally, the scope of applicability of various existing multi-agent planning techniques, such as PGP, may be better in some domains than in others, since coordination resulting from these techniques is a gradual process [1,46].

5.5 Negotiation

A significant part of the research conducted world-wide in the area of coordination has been dedicated to negotiation, since negotiation mechanisms are involved in most coordination schemes [1]. Negotiation represents the most significant part of distributed artificial intelligence research in the area of coordination [47]. An abundant literature is devoted to coordination through negotiation mechanisms. Negotiation is thus the subject of considerable interest in multi-agent systems, as it is in economics, political science, and social studies. In multi-agent domains, negotiation is used to resolve conflicting situations arising, for example, over the usage of joint resources or task assignments, problematic issues concerning document allocation in multi-server environments, or conflicts between a buyer and a seller in electronic commerce.

Kraus dedicated a comprehensive survey to negotiation, where various techniques on reaching agreements in multi-agent environments are described [6]. While focusing on negotiation between self-interested agents, the survey describes game theory and economics based techniques, and discusses logical based mechanisms for argumentations. It also presents several mechanisms designed for cooperative agents attempting to resolve conflicts arising from conflicting beliefs about different aspects of their environment.

On the other hand, Wooldridge devoted a chapter to aspects related to the issue of cooperation and conflict resolution in a society of self-interested agents via negotiation and argumentation [48]. The author examines, in more details, the question pertaining to the design of mechanisms or protocols that govern negotiation scenarios. He provides a comprehensive description of desirable properties that should characterize negotiation protocols to govern multi-agent interactions. Finally, he presents auctions, negotiation protocols and strategies and discusses argumentation.

Indeed, the choice of a negotiation technique or mechanism depends on what properties the designer wants the overall system to have. As agents are self-interested, the evaluation of the results of multi-agent techniques becomes a difficult task. Each agent engaged in a negotiation process is concerned only about its own benefits and losses. Hence, the success of any negotiation outcome is not easy to assess, as the appropriate question regarding the identification of the successful agent remains to be answered. Both Kraus and Wooldridge describe various criteria or properties for evaluating negotiation protocols and mechanisms. These criteria include: *negotiation time, guaranteed success, maximizing social welfare, efficiency and Pareto efficiency, individual rationality, stability, simplicity, distribution* and *money transfer*.

Negotiation can be succinctly defined as "*the communication process of a group of agents in order to reach a mutually accepted agreement on some matter*" [49]. To negotiate effectively, agents must reason about beliefs, desires and intentions of other agents [50]. Such an approach to negotiation led to the development of various techniques designed to represent and maintain belief models, reason about other agents' beliefs, and influence intentions and beliefs of other agents.

Negotiation based approaches are implemented to solve complex problems related to distributed planning and distributed search [6]. These approaches are used in environments where agents are either cooperative or self-interested. Conry et al. are attributed the development of the multi-stage negotiation approach suggested to solve distributed constraint satisfaction problems in the absence of a central planner [37]. Furthermore, Moehlman et al. [51] used negotiation as a tool for distributed planning. Applied to the Phoenix fireman array, this approach offers each agent, subjected to certain constraints, the opportunity to find a feasible solution using a negotiation process. Finally, Lander and Lesser [52] developed a method relevant to multi-stage negotiation and used it as a means of cooperation, while searching and solving conflicts among agents.

Rosenschein and Zlotkin [53] identified three distinct domains where negotiation is applicable:

- Task-oriented Domain: It characterizes a situation where the problem is to *"find ways in which agents can negotiate to come to an agreement and allocate their task in a way that is beneficial to every entity"*.
- State-oriented Domain: It features a particular situation where the problem is *"to find actions which change the state of the world and serve the agents' goals"*.
- Worth-oriented Domain: It is similar to the state-oriented domain. However, in the worth-oriented domain, the decision is *"taken according to the maximum utility the agents gain from the states"*.

Among other efforts directed towards developing approaches relevant to negotiation in multi-agent environments, Sycara has proposed a model of negotiation that combines case-based reasoning and optimization of multi-attribute utilities [54, 55]. This approach offers an environment where agents attempt to *"influence the goals and intentions of their opponents"*. Another attempt attributed to Zeng and Sycara lies in the development of a negotiation approach suitable for a marketing environment endowed with a learning process [56]. In this approach, the buyer and the seller can update their beliefs about the opponent's reservation price using the Bayesian rule. On the other hand, Kraus and Lehmann proposed and implemented an automated Diplomacy player that negotiates and plays well in actual games against human players [57]. Sierra et al. devised a model of negotiation to provide a framework for autonomous agents to reach agreements for the provision of services [58]. This model *"defines a range of strategies and tactics distilled from intuition about good behavioral practice in human negotiation that agents can employ to generate offers and evaluate proposals"*. Sandholm and Lesser discuss issues, such as levels of commitment that arise in automated negotiation among self-interested agents, whose rationality is bounded by computational complexity [59].

Issues pertaining to negotiation are also tackled in areas other than distributed artificial intelligence, such as social studies [6]. Indeed, there are two main approaches to the development of theories pertaining to negotiation in the social studies. ,

The first approach, known as the formal theory of bargaining, represents a formal game-theoretic approach [60-61]. It provides both *"clear analyses of various situations and accurate results relative to the strategy a negotiator is bound to choose"*. Limited to situations that satisfy very restricted assumptions, this approach assumes, in particular, that agents are acting rationally, have large computation capabilities, and follow strict negotiation protocols.

The second approach is referred to as the negotiation guides approach. It includes informal theories to identify possible general beneficial strategies for a negotiator. Methods based on this negotiation approach are designed to advise a negotiator on how to behave in order to reach beneficial results [62-67].

The first approach is less difficult to apply, since it incorporates formal theories or strategies that can be used. Within the application of this approach, Kraus tackled the issue of strategic negotiation [84]. In this context, various situations have been considered, where a set of agents need to reach an agreement on a given issue.

Based on a comprehensive literature, Nwana et al. classify negotiation techniques into three broad categories [1]:

1. Game theory-based negotiation.
2. Plan-based negotiation.
3. Human-inspired and miscellaneous AI-based negotiation approaches.

5.5.1 Game Theory Based Negotiation

Indeed, game theory-based negotiation has become a growing area of research [1]. The origin of such work can be traced to the doctoral thesis of Rosenschein [68]. The content of this thesis and results of earlier research conducted by Rosenschein have been later synthesized, refined, and compiled [53].

The resulting collection highlights several strategies and protocols for negotiation. A game theory negotiation based approach is proposed to achieve coordination among a set of rational and autonomous agents with no a priori and explicit mechanism. The approach does not presume "*the benevolent agent assumption*".

The key elements pertaining to this approach are the concepts of utility functions, space of deals, strategies, and negotiation protocols. Utility is defined as "*the difference between the worth of achieving a goal and the price paid in achieving it*". On the other hand, a deal is presented as "*an action that can be taken, which has an attached utility*". Finally, a negotiation protocol is viewed as a concept designed to "*define the rules which govern negotiation, including how and when it ends*".

In an actual negotiation process, utility values for each outcome related to a given interaction are built for each agent into a pay-off matrix [1]. This matrix represents a common knowledge to (typically) both parties involved in the negotiation. As a result, the negotiation process implies an interactive process of offers and counter-offers in which each agent chooses a deal which maximizes its expected utility value. The approach implicitly assumes that each agent involved in a negotiation is an expected utility maximizer. An agent engaged in this process is, as noted by Nwana et al., devoted the task of evaluating, at each step of the negotiation, the offer emanating from another party [1].

Zlotkin and Rosenschein have extended the work described above to cover agents that are not truthful and can be deceptive [69]. In this respect, simple demonstrators were used to show that an agent may strike better negotiation deals if it withholds certain information or deliberately misinforms other agents. On the other hand, negotiation is viewed as a two-stage process: the actual negotiation and the execution of the resulting plans. Using game theory-based techniques with appropriate modifications, Kraus & Wilkenfield proposed a strategic model that takes time into consideration during a negotiation process [71]. Time is incorporated into the model in order to influence the outcome of negotiations and avoid delays in reaching agreements.

Nwana et al. claim that game theory-based negotiation fails to address some crucial problems in reference to a report on project NOMADS-001 conducted at British Telecom Labs in the U.K. [1,72]. Indeed, game theory-based negotiation presumes that agents are fully rational entities that act to maximize utility using pre-defined strategies. Unlike the real world, agents are also presumed to have full knowledge of other agents' preferences through the payoff matrix. For truly non-benevolent and loosely-coupled agencies, this assumption is unrealistic, as an entity which has partial or incomplete knowledge of its own domain cannot determine other agent's preferences. Another problem related to this approach lies in the fact that a payoff matrix resulting from a negotiation involving too many agents and outcomes could well become very large and intractable.

When deciding on their deal, agents using the game theory-based negotiation approach only consider the current state and ignore past interactions and future implications [1]. In addition, agents are considered to have identical internal models and capabilities. Much of the research conducted in the area of game theory-based negotiation presumes that negotiation involves two agents, though later work addressed *n-agent* negotiation [73]. Considering that these assumptions are untenable in real-world problems, doubt and uncertainty are raised about the effectiveness of the game theory-based negotiation in dealing with real-life industrial agent-based applications [1].

5.5.2 Plan-Based Negotiation

Plan-based negotiation is an important area of research that attracted many experts. Adler et al. have investigated negotiated agreements and discussed methods pertaining to conflict detection and resolution in the area of telephone network traffic control [74]. The authors of this investigation strongly maintain that negotiation and planning are very tightly intertwined. According to them, agents need information from others to function effectively and efficiently and instill these entities with planning knowledge.

On the other hand, Kreifelt and von Martial view negotiation as a two-stage process: agents plan their activities separately and then coordinate the resulting plans [75]. The authors proposed a negotiation strategy for autonomous agents based on this approach. The devised strategy consists in devoting a separate agent solely for activities related to the coordination of the remaining agents. In this context, a negotiation protocol is also presented in terms of agents' states, message types, and conversation rules between agents.

In an attempt to highlight the limitations associated with this protocol, Bussman & Muller [49] pointed out that the approach proposed by Kreifelt and von Martial prescribes rather than really presents a negotiation model. This approach leaves to the agents how to really achieve consensus. Finally, Nwana et al. [1] consider that the protocol itself also needs some further clarification, stating that, in general, plan-based negotiation suffers from limitations related to centralized or distributed multi-agent planning.

5.5.3 Human inspired AI-Based Negotiation

Almost every form of human interaction requires some degree of explicit or implicit negotiation [3]. With this in mind, many researchers in the area of negotiation draw from human negotiation strategies, often leading to the usage of miscellaneous AI techniques, including logic, case-based reasoning, constraint-directed search, etc. However, various negotiation approaches are strictly AI-based and are not similar to human interaction based negotiation approaches.

Sycara has proposed a general negotiation model to handle multi-agent, multiple-issues, single and repeated type negotiations [76]. Considering negotiation as an interactive activity, the author has exploited both case-based reasoning and multi-attribute utility theory. As far as the case-based approach is concerned, Sycara argues that human negotiators draw from past experience to guide present and future negotiations. In the absence of past cases, the author resorts to preference analysis based on multi-attribute theory, where issues involved in negotiation are represented by utility curves. These curves are combined in additive and multiplicative fashions so as to select a proposal that maximizes the utility.

Sycara has developed PERSUADER, a framework based on the integration of case-based reasoning and multi-attribute utility theory [55]. This system operates in labor management dispute to provide negotiation support in conflict resolution with the aid of two practicing negotiators. It creates and handles cooperative interactions, where agents can modify beliefs, behaviors and intentions of other entities through persuasion. The use of case-based reasoning was at the time quite novel to the negotiation problem.

Another approach to negotiation proposed by Sathi and Fox amounts to a *constraint directed search* of a problem space using negotiation parameters [77]. The proposed strategy views negotiation as a two-phase process including a communication phase and a bargaining phase. The communication-oriented phase enables the transfer of information to all participating agents. The bargaining phase offers a framework, where deals are made within a group or between individuals. Agents using this technique negotiate through a relaxation of various conflicts and constraints until final agreement is reached. While the solution may be modified, negotiation preferences are modeled as constraints. Based on observations and experience in human negotiation, negotiation operators, including operators which simulate relaxation, reconfiguration and composition, are used to generate new constraints [78].

Using this approach, a system designed to *"perform marginally better than experts"* has been built to handle resource allocation. However, the approach is described as an iterative method that presents a major problem, as agents can easily get caught in an infinite loop of exchanging offers. This limitation results from the fact that the process of selecting relaxations is conducted with no criteria provided.

Werkman proposed the Designer Fabricator Interpreter (DFI), a knowledge-based model of an incremental form of negotiation [3]. This model is largely inspired from various human models of negotiation. The proposed scheme uses a shared knowledge representation called *shareable agent perspectives.* It provides agents with the ability to perform negotiation in a manner similar to cooperating or competing experts sharing a common background of domain knowledge [1]. This scheme is also designed to basically exploit a blackboard with partitions for requested proposals, rejected proposals, and accepted proposals and a partition for communications and shared knowledge. In addition, it provides agents with rich detail and knowledge of other entities perspectives, thus giving them invaluable information to make better proposals in the future. Werkman considers the negotiation process as a three-phase cycle [1,3]:

- Phase I – A proposing agent announces a proposal that is received and evaluated by a receiving agent.
- Phase II – The initial proposal is then simply accepted. In case the receiving agent is not satisfied with the initial proposal, a counter proposal is thus generated.
- Phase III – The counter proposal is finally submitted for review by other agents.

Two agents may engage in an incessant process of reviewing the negotiation dialogue to generate alternative proposals, using the mutual information network at their disposal. In this context, it is expected that an arbitrator agent handles and breaks a deadlock in negotiations via relaxation techniques or an intelligent proposal generator. In case this procedure fails, the arbitrator may set time limits or use other techniques. Considering the use of arbitration as a relatively novel approach, Werkman's proposal is described as both interesting and definitely worth examining in more detail [1].

However, the bottleneck problem associated with this approach lies in the use of the centralized blackboard, where reading and posting to the blackboard seem to generate chaos in the absence of an explicit scheduler. The approach proposed by Werkman provides agents with the ability to communicate via the blackboard through a speech-act based language. Implemented in the DFI system, this approach has a good understanding of the negotiation process.

Indeed, the research by Conry et al. has focused on developing negotiation strategies designed to tackle *distributed constraint satisfaction* problems, where local constraints give rise to a complex set of global and inter-dependent constraints [37]. These efforts were specifically directed towards investigating problems, where agents in a network have a goal and each node or agent has limited resources. Research conducted by Conry et al. involved developing algorithms for multi-agent planning, while considering the inevitable conflicts. It examined whether specific generic tasks may be linked with specific negotiation strategies.

On the other hand, Bussmann and Muller focused on developing a negotiation framework for cooperating agents [49]. This effort aimed at addressing limitations associated with various existing negotiation approaches and models. Largely inspired by Gulliver's eight phases of the negotiation process [79], Bussmann and Muller gradually developed a general and simple cyclic negotiation model as a way to address the thorny issue of conflict resolution. The general adopted strategy consists in starting the negotiation process with one, some or every agent making a proposal. In response, activities are engaged so that agents evaluate and check out the resulting proposals against their own preferences. Then, agents can present a criticism of these proposals through a list of violated preferences. The evaluation procedure offers agents the opportunity to update their knowledge regarding the preferences of other entities. This procedure is followed by a resumption of the negotiation cycle, where new proposals are introduced in the light of newly gleaned information. Such an interesting negotiation model was designed to handle conflicts between agents in a concurrent resolution cycle.

Finally, other efforts directed towards the development of negotiation protocols include Kuwabara and Lesser's extended protocol for multistage negotiation [80] and Durfee and Montgomery's hierarchical protocol for coordinating multi-agent behavior [81].

In conclusion, Nwana et al. synthesize key lessons learned and put forward conclusions drawn from conducting this review. In this respect, they question the scope, applicability, and usability of one-off coordination strategies. They further notice the lack of enough studies designed to validate many proposed strategies. In this context, Nwana et al. highlight the absence of information regarding when, where, how, and why various negotiation and coordination strategies or a combination of them are used in various applications. On the other hand, Nwana et al. state that the contract net and master/slave models, including variations of them, are simple and the most used strategies. According to them, the contract net approach, like various other techniques, presumes truly benevolent, trustful, non-conflicting, and helpful agents. They add that most coordination or negotiation strategies do not involve any complex meta-reasoning required of most domains. Finally, Nwana et al. refer to the lack of fundamental analysis of the process of coordination, but point to the work of Jennings [82] as a first step in this direction.

5.5.4 Strategic Negotiation

Based on Rubinstein's model of alternating offers [83], the strategic-negotiation model proposed by Kraus consists of a protocol designed to govern interactions between agents, utility functions associated with these entities, and negotiation strategies that each agent is required to adopt [84]. In this strategic model, a set of N self-interested autonomous agents effectively seek, or need to reach, a negotiated agreement on a given issue. As noted, the agents are assumed to be able to take actions in the negotiation at certain definite and pre-determined times that are known to them in advance.

In this respect, Kraus provides sufficient details pertaining to the strategic negotiation protocol. She explains that if the current negotiation has not terminated, the agent required to make an offer at the prescribed time will suggest a possible agreement with respect to the specific negotiation issue. Once the offer is put forward, each of the other entities may indeed accept it, reject it, or opt out of the negotiation. In case it is accepted by all of the agents, the available offer is implemented and the negotiation process between the agents is thus stopped. On the other hand, if at least one of the agents chooses to opt out, the negotiation engaged between these entities would stop to result in a conflicting outcome. Finally, the negotiation process would proceed as engaged if at least one agent has rejected the offer, while no other entity has chosen to opt out. In this context, the next expected agent would make a counteroffer, the rest of the other agents would thus respond, and the negotiation process would then continue. In the course of the negotiation process, it is assumed that an agent responding to a given offer is not informed of the responses from the other entities.

To demonstrate the notions outlined in the description of the strategic-negotiation protocol, i.e. *the simultaneous response protocol*, Kraus considers the problem pertaining to data allocation in large databases. It is an example of a system that includes several information servers scattered across different geographical areas. Each server (i.e., agent) is designed to store and provide information to clients from the same geographical area but also from other locations.

Kraus further explains that the interests of each agent change dynamically over time. While the set of clients may also change over time, new data is periodically received and thus located at a given server. In this distributed system, each server is both independent and driven by its own commercial interests. Given these attributes, the servers would thus prefer to cooperate in order to provide more information to their clients. However, conflicts among the interests of various servers may arise, since each server has its own preferences regarding data allocations.

According to Kraus, a specific example of a distributed information system lies in the Data and Information System component of the Earth Observing System[1]

---

[1]   Consult EOSDIS home page at http://www-v0ims.gsfc.nasa.gov/v0ims/index.html

(EOSDIS) attributed to NASA. She describes it as a distributed system supporting data archival and distribution at multiple and independent data centers, called DAACs (Distributed Active Archive Center). Based on a static data allocation policy, a DAAC receives new data, checks its relevance to one of the available topics, and then uses various criteria, such as storage cost, to determine whether or not to accept and store the data in its database. As explained, in case the data presented to it encompasses the topics of multiples DAACs or clearly fall under the jurisdiction of another DAAC, the DAAC would communicate with other DAACs and a discussion would be engaged among the relevant DAAC managers.

Kraus further states that the distributed system used by NASA does not however take into consideration the location of the information clients. According to her, this approach may thus cause delays and higher transmission costs, as data items could be stored far from their potential users. She explains that the method used can also lead to a rejection of data items that either do not fall within the criteria of any DAAC or respond to the criteria of a DAAC which is unable to support the new product because of limited financial resources.

In the example provided by Kraus, the agents negotiate to reach an agreement that specifies the location of all the relevant data items. In accordance with the strategic-negotiation protocol, it is explained that the first server opens the negotiation process and offers an allocation. Following this offer, the other agents either accept it or opt out of the negotiation. In this context, the negotiation process comes to an end and the proposal is implemented whenever the offer is accepted by all the agents. However, it is explained that a predefined conflict allocation is implemented, as described in [85], when at least one of the agents opts out of the negotiation. Finally, if at least one of the agents has rejected the offer and no other has chosen to opt out, the negotiation proceeds to the next time period, then another agent proposes an allocation, the other entities respond, and the process continues in accordance with the established protocol.

Finally, Kraus describes the strategic-negotiation as a model where there are no rules to bind the agents to any specific strategy. She adds that no assumptions are made about the offers put forward during the negotiation. In this context, Kraus notes that the agents are not bound to any previous offers that have been made. She adds that an agent expected to suggest a new offer following the rejection of an offer can decide either to renew the same offer or propose a new one. She further explains that the protocol is designed to only provide a framework for the negotiation process and specify the termination condition, with no limit on the number of periods.

Arranging agents randomly in a specific order before the negotiation begins represents, according to Kraus, a fair and reasonable method pertaining to the decision on the order in which these entities will make offers. In this respect, the author notes that a distributed algorithm for randomly ordering the agents can be based on the methods presented in [86]. She reveals that the agents' time preferences and the preferences between agreements and opting out are, on the other hand, the driving force of the model that influence the outcome of the negotiation.

Kraus finally points out that agents will not reach an agreement which is not at least as good as an outcome based on opting out from the negotiation process.

Negotiation strategies

Kraus attempts to clarify the question pertaining to negotiation strategies. According to her, a negotiation strategy peculiar to an agent aims at specifying the rules and procedures that govern the actions of this entity at each sequence of offers. This strategy is thus deployed to specify for the right entity, i.e. the agent whose turn is to make an offer, which offer to make next. Kraus explains in more detail that a negotiation strategy is indeed designed to indicate to a particular agent which offer to make at a particular time in case the sequence of offers made previously have been rejected by at least one of the agents, while none of them has opted out. She adds that the strategy similarly specifies to an agent, whose turn it is to respond to an offer, whether to accept it, reject it, or opt out of the negotiation process. Referring to the work of Osborne and Rubinstein [87], Kraus briefly notes that a strategy profile represents a collection of strategies, one for each agent.

Sub-game perfect equilibria

Kraus further tackles the problem of how a rational agent can choose a suitable negotiation strategy. In this respect, the author puts forward notions and concepts for choosing a strategy or analyzing a negotiation process. Described as useful, the first notion considered is commonly known as the Nash Equilibrium [88, 89].

Given a set of agents $\{A_1, ..., A_N\}$, a strategy profile $F = \{f_1, ..., f_N\}$ is a Nash equilibrium of a model of alternating offers, if, as defined, "*each agent A_i does not have a different strategy yielding an outcome that it prefers to that generated when it chooses f_i, given that every other agent A_j chooses f_j*". Briefly, no agent can profitably deviate, given the actions of the other agents. In an attempt to comprehensively clarify the above definition through more fundamental and necessary details, Kraus explains that having all agents use the strategies designed and specified for them in the strategy profile of the Nash Equilibrium induces a state where all of them lose the motivation to deviate and implement another strategy. However, the use of the Nash equilibrium in a model of alternating-offers leads, as she points out, to absurd Nash equilibria. Referring to the research by Tirole [90], Kraus thus states that an agent may use a threat that would not be carried out if it were put in the position to do so, since the threat move would give this entity lower payoff than it would get by not taking the threatened action. According to her, the reason behind this lies in the fact that

Nash Equilibrium strategies may be in equilibrium only at the beginning of the negotiation process, but may be unstable in intermediate stages.

In addition, Kraus further presents another stronger concept for negotiation analysis known as the **sub-game perfect equilibrium** [87]. In her attempt to define this concept, she states that "*a strategy profile is a sub-game perfect equilibrium of a model of alternating offers if the strategy profile induced in every sub-game is a Nash equilibrium of that sub-game*". In other terms, Kraus attempts to better clarify the above definition, explaining briefly that at any step of the negotiation process, no matter what the history is, all agents lack the motivation to deviate and use a different strategy that is not defined in the strategy profile. According to her, the sequential equilibrium [91], which takes the beliefs of the agents into consideration, can be used in incomplete information situations where there is no proper sub-game.

Next, Kraus illustrates the application of the strategic-negotiation model to the data allocation problem described in the earlier example. While a full description of this application is presented in [92], the author reports that using this model provides the servers with simple and stable negotiation strategies that result in efficient agreements without delays. Then, she clearly reaffirms that the methods implemented yield better results than the static allocation policy currently used in the EOSDIS distributed data and information system.

In addition, Kraus reports that the application of the strategic negotiation model to the data allocation problem has particularly shown that various agreements can be reached when the servers possessing complete information negotiate to reach an agreement. According to her, the implementation of this model has also proved that "*for any possible allocation of the data items that is not worse for any of the agents than opting out, there is a set of stable strategies (one for each server) that leads to this outcome*". Furthermore, Kraus explains that a strategy for each of the servers can be designed such that the strategy profile will be in equilibrium. Thus, if the servers use this strategy profile, the negotiations will, according to her, end at the first time period of the negotiation with an agreement on a specific allocation which all the servers prefer than opting out of the negotiation.

As pointed out, the details of the allocations that are not worse for any of the agents over opting out depend on the specific settings of the environment in a given negotiation session. While there is no way to identify these allocations in advance, there are usually, as noted, several intractable allocations that are not worse for any of the agents than opting out. Kraus explains that once these allocations are identified, the servers should agree upon one of them as the basis for the negotiation. In this respect, the author notes that each of the servers may indeed prefer a different allocation as the latter may yield a higher utility. According to her, a mechanism is developed and implemented to enable the servers to choose one of these profiles of stable strategies. Described as successful, this mechanism is designed such that each server proposes an allocation and the entity that is selected is the one which maximizes a social welfare criterion, such as the sum of the utilities associated with the servers. In this context, Kraus finally reports that several heuristic search algorithms were proposed and implemented to allow the servers to find such allocations.

In situations where the servers have incomplete information about each other, a preliminary step was, according to Kraus, added to the strategic negotiation to allow the servers to report, preferably more truthfully, some of their private information. According to her, once the preliminary step is completed through the use of the revelation mechanism, the negotiation continues according to the procedure related to the complete information case. The author states that the introduction of the preliminary step to tackle the lack of incomplete information leads to better results for all of the servers than the static allocation policy currently used in EOSDIS.

Kraus explains that the overall process pertaining to this case, i.e. incomplete information, consists first in allowing each server to broadcast its private information. Without providing details on the nature of the punishment, the author notes that a server transmitting false information, i.e. a liar, is punished by the group when detected. Next, all the servers individually search for and then, as noted, simultaneously propose an allocation. It is then reported that the allocation which maximizes the pre-defined social-welfare criteria is thus selected. Based on this allocation, the servers next construct the equilibrium strategies and, as the author further explains, start the negotiation using the alternating offers protocol. Following this process the first agent proposes the selected allocation as part of the first step of negotiations, and then the rest of the entities accept it.

On the other hand, Kraus presents simulation results that demonstrate the effect of different parameters of the environment on the negotiation results. In this respect, she notes that better agreements can be reached when, for example, the servers are more willing to store data locally. She argues that in such situations, where it is easier to reach a beneficial compromise, there are fewer constraints on finding agreements which are better for all the servers than opting out. She finally adds that the servers are indeed more willing to store data locally when the storage and delivery costs of documents stored locally to other servers is low.

Summarizing the above discussion, Kraus states that the strategic negotiation model provides a unified solution to a wide range of problems. This model is, according to her, appropriate for dynamic real-world domains. She reports that the strategic-negotiation model was, in addition to the above application, used to tackle resource allocation and task distribution problems and other problems related to pollution allocation [84]. In this respect, Kraus explains that the strategic-negotiation model implemented in these domains provides the negotiators with ways to reach mutually beneficial agreements without delay. She finally reports that the strategic-negotiation model was also applied to domains characterized by human high-pressure crisis negotiations [93, 94].

5.6 Auctions for Resolving Conflicts

In [6, 84], Kraus briefly tackles the question of using auctions, another game-theory based technique, as a way of reaching agreements in multi-agent environments. While recalling the example relating to the information server environment described above, Kraus emphasizes that most of the conflicts occurring in such domains where agreements concerning the distribution of a set of items should be reached can be resolved efficiently by providing agents with a monetary system. Referring to Ronen's work on algorithms for rational agents [95], she explains that agents in this system are modeled as buyers and sellers to provide the ability to resolve occurring conflicts using money transfer.

Wooldridge devotes a lengthy discussion to address rules, terms and conditions pertaining to using auctions for resolving conflicts in agent-based environments. Both Kraus and Wooldridge put forward the emergence of the Internet to highlight how auctions have been transformed from a comparatively rare practice to an area of increased interest with a large, international audience. In this respect, they quote the example of eBay to explain how large virtual businesses and auction houses have recently sprung up around the idea of online auctions. According to Wooldridge, the current popularity of online auctions lies in the fact that auctions are extremely simple interaction scenarios. Easy to automate, auctions have thus become, as further noted, a good first choice to implement as a way for agents to reach agreements. While considered as a rich collection of problems for the research community despite their simplicity, auctions represent, as Wooldridge notes, a powerful tool that automated agents can indeed use for allocating goods, tasks, and resources.

As described by Wooldridge, an auction takes place between an agent known as the *auctioneer* and a collection of agents known as the *bidders*. The author notes that the auction offers the auctioneer the opportunity to allocate the good to one of the bidders. In his terms, Wooldridge adds that in most settings – and certainly most traditional auction settings – the auctioneer desires to maximize the price at which the good is allocated, while bidders desire to minimize the price paid. In this respect, he further explains that the auctioneer attempts to achieve his desire through the design of an appropriate auction mechanism – the rules of encounters – while the bidders attempt to achieve their desires by using a strategy that will conform to the rules of encounter, but that will also deliver an optimal result.

Kraus identifies two patterns of interactions in auctions. According to her, the most common are the one-to-many [96, 97, 33] and many-to-many [98] auction protocols. She explains that the first pattern of interaction is the one-to-many auction protocols designed to enable one agent to initiate an auction so that a number of other agents can bid in the auction. The second pattern represents the many-to-many protocols where several agents initiate an auction and several other agents can bid in the auction. Kraus then points out that given the pattern of interaction, the first issue is to determine the type of protocol to use in the auction [99]. Similarly, she explains that given the protocol, the agents then need to opt for their bidding strategy.

For Wooldridge, several factors can affect the protocol and the strategy that agents can use. He further states that the most important factor is related to whether the good for auction has a *private* or a *public/common* value. In this respect, he adds that a good for auction has a *common value* if it is worth exactly the same to all bidders in the auction. However, a good for auction is said to have a *private value* if each agent values it differently. Another type of valuation as identified by Wooldridge is *correlated value*. He defines this as a setting at which an agent's valuation of the good depends partly on private factors, and partly on other agent's valuation of it. In an attempt to provide a clearer understanding of this type of valuation, Wooldridge gives the example of an agent that was bidding for a painting it liked, but wanted to keep open the option of later selling the painting. He further explains that, in this case, the amount it would be willing to pay would depend partly on how much it liked it, but also partly on how much it believed other agents might be willing to pay for it if it were put up for auction later. Furthermore, Wooldridge considers and identifies three dimensions along which auction protocols may indeed vary:

- The first dimension is identified as *Winner determination*. It is about who gets the good that the bidders are bidding for. It is observed that the answer to this question is obvious since in familiar auctions, the agent that bids the most is commonly allocated the good. As stated, such protocols are commonly known as *first-price* auctions. However, it is pointed out that another possibility could be that the good is allocated to the agent that bids the highest, but pays only the amount of the second highest bid. This type of protocol is known as *second-price* auctions.

- The second dimension that characterizes an auction protocol lies in the answer to whether or not the bids made by the agents are known to each other. In this respect, it is stated that an *open-cry* auction imposes common knowledge bids. In other terms, an *open-cry* auction is defined as an auction where every agent can see what every other agent is bidding. It is also specified that if the agents are not able to determine the bids made by other agent, the auction is said to be a *sealed-bid* auction.

- The third dimension relates to the mechanism through which bidding proceeds. In this respect, it is pointed out that auctions defined as *one shot* auctions represents the simplest event characterized by a single round of bidding followed by the allocation of the good to the winner. It is also mentioned that a second possibility consists in starting with a low price – often at a *reservation price* – and then successive bids will be conducted for increasingly large amounts. As stated, such protocols are known as *ascending* auctions. The alternative possibility finally referred to – *descending* auctions – imposes upon the auctioneer that he starts off with a high value, and to decrease the price in successive rounds.

Indeed, both Kraus and Wooldridge attempt to examine and classify various types of auctions according to the set of dimensions extensively described above. While Kraus provides a brief discussion, Wooldridge proposes a classification together with an extensive and informative description of the most familiar auctions. Covered in both studies, the most important ones are discussed below.

5.6.1 Types of Auctions

English Auctions

Made famous by the houses of Sothebys, English auctions are, according to Wooldridge, the most commonly known type of auction. Kraus describes the English auction as an ascending auction in which *"the price is successively raised until only one bidder remains, and that bidder wins the item at the final price"*. She reports that in one variant of the English auction *"the auctioneer calls higher prices successively until only one willing bidder remains, and the number of active bidders is publicly known at all times"*. According to her, the bidders in other variants of the English auction call out prices themselves, or have the bids submitted electronically and the best current bid is posted.

Wooldridge describes the English auctions as *first-price, open cry, ascending* auctions where:

- The auctioneer starts off by suggesting a *reservation price* for the good which may be 0. However, the good is allocated to the auctioneer if none of the agents is willing to bid more than the reservation price.
- Otherwise, the auction process continues and agents are invited to submit their bids that must be more that the current highest bid.
- If no other agent is willing to raise the bid, the good is then allocated to the agent that has made the current highest bid. The price paid for the good is the amount of that bid.

Wooldridge then brings up the question of what strategy an agent should use to bid in English auctions. According to him, the dominant strategy for an agent is to successively bid a small amount more than the current highest bid until the bid price reaches its current valuation, and then to withdraw.

While considering English auctions as a simple bidding process, Wooldridge attributes some interesting properties to this type of auction. He highlights an interesting feature of English auctions arising from the uncertainty about the true value of the good being auctioned. In this respect, he gives the example of a sale where he imagines an auctioneer who has limited geological information to provide about some land he is selling to agents desiring to exploit the mineral resources. As Wooldridge further points out, none of the agents knows exactly the value of the land being auctioned in an environment where scarce information is deployed. The author then assumes that the agents, each using the dominant strategy mentioned above, engage in an English auction to obtain the land. In this context, he raises the question about the attitude and feelings the winner should have at the end of the auction. In other terms, Wooldridge wonders whether the winner should feel happy that it has obtained the land for less than or equal to its private valuation or worried that no other agent valued the land so highly. As he finally points out, the latter situation, known as the *winner's curse*, occurs most frequently in English auctions.

Dutch Auctions

Dutch auctions are examples of *open-cry descending* auctions. Both Kraus and Wooldridge describe this type of auction as an event where:

- The auctioneer begins by offering the good at an artificially high value.
- He then continuously lowers the offer price of the good by some value, until an agent makes a bid for the good which is equal to the current offer price.
- The good is finally allocated to the agent that made the offer.
- According to Wooldridge, there is no dominant strategy for Dutch auctions in general.

First Priced, Sealed Bid Auctions

Considered as the simplest of all the auction types, first-price sealed-bid auctions are, according to Wooldridge, examples of *one-shot* auctions. It is described by both Kraus and Wooldridge as a single round event in which bidders submit a bid for the good to the auctioneer. Then, without subsequent rounds, the good is, as explained, awarded to the agent that made the highest bid. It is finally stated that the winner pays the price of the highest bid. In this respect, Wooldridge highlights the absence of any opportunity for the participating agents to offer larger amounts for the good. He then raises the question on how an agent should act in first-price sealed-bid auctions. To answer this question Wooldridge considers an event where every agent bids its true valuation. Since there is only a single round, the author notes that the good is allocated to the agent that bid the highest amount. Considering the second highest bid, he then observes that the winner still has been awarded the good while it could have offered an amount that is just a tiny fraction more than the second highest price. As a result, most of the difference between the highest and the second highest price is, in effect, as Wooldridge points out, money wasted as far as the winner is concerned. As a result, the author finally highlights the need for a participating agent to bid less than its true valuation, depending on what the other agents bid. Described as a sealed-bid auction, the second-price auction represents, according to Kraus, the event where the buyer making the highest bid claims the object, but pays only an amount equal to the second highest bid.

Vickery Auctions

Wooldridge considers the Vickery auction [100] as "*the most unusual and perhaps the most counterintuitive*" of all the auction protocols described in [48]. On the other hand, Kraus reports that this type of auction is widely used in distributed artificial intelligence [101, 68, 102, 103, 104] and in research on electronic commerce [103, 104] for the case of one-to-many auctions. She further claims that, under various assumptions, the Vickery auction-based protocol is incentive compatible. As she further explains, each participating bidder has incentives to bid truthfully. Indeed, the Vickery auction falls, according to Wooldridge, within the category of the *second-price sealed-bid* auctions. In an attempt to give a more comprehensive description, he explains that the Vickery auction, which is based on a single negotiation round, is designed to provide each bidder with the opportunity to submit a single bid in the absence of appropriate information about the bids made by other agents. He further points out that the good is finally awarded to the agent that made the highest bid. In this respect, he notes that the amount the winner pays for that good represents the price of the second highest bid.

Kraus states that, under various assumptions, the Vickery auction-based protocol is incentive compatible. In other words, each participating bidder has incentives to bid truthfully. In response to the question of why one would even consider using Vickery auctions, Wooldridge similarly argues that these types of auctions "*make truth telling a dominant strategy*". In an attempt to explain why a bidder's dominant strategy in a private value Vickery auction is to bid his true valuation, he supposes that an agent bids more than its true valuation. In this case, Wooldridge observes that the agent may indeed be awarded the good, but it runs the risk of paying more than the amount of its private valuation. In such circumstances, the agent will, as stated, make a loss, since it paid more than it believed the good was worth. On the other hand, Wooldridge imagines that the same agent bid less than its true valuation. In this case, he notes that the bidder stands less chance of winning than if it had bid its true valuation. He further explains that even if the agent wins, the amount it pays will not have been affected by the fact that it bid less than its true valuation. The reason lies in the fact that the agent will, as noted, pay the price of the second highest bid. In conclusion, Wooldridge states that the best conduct for an agent engaged in a Vickery auction is to bid truthfully, no more and no less than its private valuation.

Referring to a research work on distributed rational decision making in multi-agent systems [105], Wooldridge notes that Vickery auctions have received a lot of attention in the literature. According to him, this wide interest within the research community on Vickery auctions lies in the fact that "truth telling" is indeed imposed as a dominant strategy. He further reports that this type of auction has not, however, been widely adopted in auctions among humans. The reason mentioned as perhaps the most important is that humans frequently find the Vickery mechanism hard to understand, since, according to him, it seems so counterintuitive at first sight.

Furthermore, Wooldridge highlights the fact that Vickery auctions can lead to antisocial behavior. In this respect, he describes a situation where an agent wants to acquire a good through a Vickery auction. While its private valuation is $90, he knows that another agent desires the same good and values it at $100. He explains that in case truth telling is the dominant strategy, the first agent can do no better than bid $90, while the second agent will eventually bids $100. In this context, the latter will be awarded the good, but will pay only $90. However, Wooldridge further argues that the first agent may not be too happy about the whole procedure and may thus decide to punish its successful opponent. The author then suggests that the agent can bid $99 instead of $90. As a result, the second agent will still be awarded the good, but it will pay $9 more than it would do if the first agent had been truthful.

According to Kraus, situations are likely to occur where the value of some items to a bidder depend upon which items are won. As explained, such situations may indeed result in the need for bidders to submit bids for combinations of items. Often referred to as *combinatorial auctions*, such auctions highlight the need to determine, as Kraus points out, the revenue of maximizing the set of non-conflicting bids. In this respect, the author mentions various approaches where researchers attempt to develop polynomial algorithms, either to respond to specific cases [83] or to provide sub-optimal solutions [106, 107, 108]. Also mentioned is another interesting research work pertaining to combinatorial auctions [109] where the author considers two aspects related to this market mechanism, namely the bidding language and the allocation algorithm.

Although not classified as one of the major four auction types, the *double auction* is another type of auction finally referred to as the most known auction protocol for many-to-many auctions. In double auction, buyers submitting bids and sellers submitting minimal prices are, according to Kraus, treated symmetrically [110]. In addition, the author mentions the existence of several algorithms that are implemented to match buyers and sellers and determine the transaction price. Referring to the work of Wurman et al. on flexible double auctions for electronic commerce [111], Kraus finally underlines the need for the double auction-based protocol to be *incentive compatible*, *individual rational* and *Pareto optimal*.

5.6.2 Issues Related to the Types of Auctions

We discuss below some of the more important issues related to auctions that can influence the coordination mechanisms. We briefly discuss the issues related to expected revenue, lies and collusion, and counter-speculation.

Expected revenue

It is observed that in all likelihood the overriding consideration of an auctioneer will be to maximize his revenue. In other words, the auctioneer is much more likely to prefer an auction protocol that will get him the highest possible price for the good. In addition, the question of whether or not agents are truthful may well not be of interest to the auctioneer. It is pointed out that some protocols – Vickery's mechanism in particular – may seem not to address these considerations. With reference to the work performed by Sandholm [105], it is stated that the answer to the question of which protocol the auctioneer should choose depends partly on the attitude to risk of both auctioneers and bidders. The attitude to risk of these actors is summed up as follows:

- *Risk-neutral bidders* – In the four main types of auctions discussed above, the expected revenue to the auctioneer is probably identical in case the attitude of bidders is risk-neutral. Using all of these types of auction, the auctioneer can, in other words, expect on average to get the same revenue for the good.
- *Risk-averse bidders* – These bidders would prefer to get the good even when they have to pay slightly more than their private valuation. In this context, higher expected revenue for the auctioneer can result from Dutch and first-price sealed-bid protocols, since a risk-averse agent using these protocols can 'insure' itself by bidding slightly more for the good than would normally do a risk-neutral bidder.
- *Risk-averse auctioneers* – In this case, an auctioneer can do better using Vickery or English auctions.

Finally, Wooldridge recommends guidelines for understanding which protocol the auctioneer should choose. Given risk-neutral bidders, the author notes, for example, that the first result relating to the revenue equivalence of auctions depends critically on the fact that bidders really do have private valuations. He further adds that it becomes critical to ensure that the properties of the auction scenario – and the bidders – are correctly understood when choosing an appropriate protocol.

Lies and collusion

Another interesting issue brought forward and discussed concerns the extent to which the auction-based protocols presented above are susceptible to anti-social behavior likely to come from both bidders and auctioneer. Indeed, an auctioneer would ideally prefer a protocol that is immune to collusion by bidders. In other words, the protocol can be designed to make it in the best interest of bidders not to engage in collusion with other bidders. Similarly, a potential bidder is also likely to prefer a protocol that imposes honesty as the dominant strategy on the part of the auctioneer.

The four main auction types are believed to be vulnerable to collusion. In this respect, it is claimed that all agents involved in any of these types of auction can form a 'grand coalition' so as to agree beforehand to put forward artificially low bids for the good on offer. As noted, the bidders can thus obtain the true value of the acquired good and split the profits. Then, it is argued that the most obvious approach to preventing collusion is to modify the protocol to prevent bidders from identifying each other. As stated, such an approach is of course unpopular with bidders engaged in open-cry auctions, since the concerned bidders prefer to be sure the information about the bids placed by other agents is accurate.

As further noted, the auctioneer engaged in a Vickery auction can overestimate the price of the second highest bid so as to force the winner to pay more than the true bid. To overcome this problem, bids can in some way– through a digital signature - be signed to offer the winner the opportunity to independently check the value of the second highest bid. Another possibility is to appoint a trusted third party to handle bids. However, open-cry and first-price sealed-bid auctions are reported to be lies-resistant protocols that are not susceptible to allow the auctioneer to make false statements. While open-cry auctions provide all agents with the ability to see bids formulated by others, the winner in a first-price sealed-bid auction is, on the other hand, allowed to examine the offers made by the other agents. In other cases, the auctioneer may place bogus bids to artificially inflate the current bidding price. Commonly known as shills, these bids represent a potential problem only in English auctions.

Counter-speculation

Counter-speculation is widely recognized as an issue worth tackling. It is characterized by *"the process of a bidder engaging in an activity in order to obtain information either about the true value of the good on offer, or about the valuations of other bidders"*. Indeed, every agent would be tempted to engage in such activity if it were free and accurate. However, in most types of auction, counter-speculation may result in time and monetary costs. Investing in this activity would be wasteful and counterproductive, since the time cost is an important factor in auctions – e.g. English or Dutch auction - that depend heavily on the time at which a bid is made. On the other hand, engaging in counter-speculation can be advantageous and worthwhile only in the case where the bidder can, as a result, expect to be no worse off than if it behaved otherwise. Hence, it appears that prior to engaging into counter-speculation, a clear trade-off analysis has to be made between the potential gains and the associated costs.

5.7 Market-oriented programming

Kraus provides a brief overview of market-oriented programming largely based on the research and experience of Wellman [112, 113, 114]. This methodology is presented as a programming paradigm and a new approach to distributed computation based on market price mechanisms. In exploiting the institution of markets and the models associated to them, the approach is implemented to build, as Kraus states, *"computational economies to address and solve particular problems of distributed resource allocation"*. Based on Wellman's view, the author discusses that the idea of market-oriented programming is inspired *"in part by economists' metaphors of market systems 'computing' the activities of the agents involved, and also by AI researchers' view of modules in a DAI system as autonomous agents"*. Referring to the agents involved in such market systems, Kraus explains that the modules interact in a very restricted manner by offering to buy and sell quantities of commodities at fixed unit prices. Indeed, as the system reaches equilibrium, the computational market has, as noted, computed the allocation of resources throughout, and dictates the activities and consumptions of the various modules.

While it is applicable in systems characterized by incomplete information, the market-oriented programming approach does not necessarily, as Kraus points out, require money transfer. The author adds that the method is however applicable only in the presence of several units of each kind of goods and in the case the number of agents is large. It is argued that otherwise it is not rational for the agents to ignore the effect of their behavior on the prices when they actually have an influence. Referring to the work of Wellman [114], Kraus reports that reaching equilibrium may be time consuming and that the system based on the market-oriented programming approach may not even converge. Finally, the author notes that the approach also requires the implementation of mechanisms – possibly distributed mechanisms – to manage auctions.

5.8 Coalition Formation in Coordination

Kraus outlines the usefulness of the formation of coalitions for executing tasks in both Multi-agent Systems (MAS) and Distributed Problem Solving (DPS) environments. Referring to the literature pertaining to this method, the author presents the act of creating coalitions as an important way for agents to cooperate. DPS is, according to Kraus, usually characterized by the absence of the need to motivate the individual agent to join a coalition. In this context, agents involved in a distributed problem-solving environment can be built to try to maximize the overall performance of the system. It is thus required to only consider the problem pertaining to the nature of the coalitions that should be formed to maximize the overall expected utility of these entities. Note that the problem of finding the coalition structure that maximizes the overall utility of the system is NP-complete.

It is reported that a self-interested agent in a multi-agent environment will join a coalition only if it could derive a clear advantage from the coalition formation than it could gain otherwise. In this context, the problem associated with the division of the coalition's joint utility represents indeed another very important issue. As Kraus suggests, this issue can be tackled using game theory techniques for coalition formation. Indeed, numerous research papers and reports devoted to game theory [115, 116, 117, 118] provide a description of which coalitions will form in NP-person games under different settings and how the players will distribute the benefits resulting from the inter-players cooperation. As noted, the profit sharing process is conducted through the application of several stability-based notions such as the *core, Shapley value* and the *kernel* [119]. In this respect, Kraus argues that each of the stability notions just mentioned "*is motivated by a different method of measuring the relative strengths of the participating agents*". She further explains that the game-theory solutions to the coalition formation problem "*do not take into consideration the constraints of a multi-agent environment – such as communication costs and limited computation time – and do not present algorithms for coalition formation*".

Shehory and Kraus [120] present a multi-agent approach to the coalition formation problem. As stated, the main contribution of this work lies in the provision of algorithms dedicated to self-interested agents. The approach is indeed designed to handle both the coalition structure and the division of the utility problems. It rests on an *anytime* algorithm developed to enable the formation of coalitions that satisfy a certain stability based on the kernel stability criteria mentioned above. As reported, simulations were indeed conducted in order to examine the properties of the proposed algorithm. According to Shehory and Kraus, the results which were applied to the formation of coalitions among information agents [121] show that the model increases the benefits of the agents within a reasonable time period and more coalition formations provide more benefits to the agents.

In a study pertaining to the key topic of coalition formation in multi-agent environments, Sandholm et al. focus on establishing a worst case bound on the quality of the coalition structure while only searching a small fraction of the coalition structures [122]. This work shows that a threshold – a minimum number of structures – is, as Kraus points out, necessary to search in order to establish a bound. As a result, an *anytime* algorithm is devised and implemented to establish a tight bound within this minimal amount of search. In case additional time is available, the algorithm is allowed to search further and progressively establish a lower bound.

As reported by Kraus, another interesting research relative to coalition formation has been described by Sandholm and Lesser [123]. Sandholm and Lesser analyze coalitions among self-interested agents that need to solve combinatorial optimization problems to operate efficiently. Then, they adopt a model of bounded rationality where computational resources are costly. In this study, the authors concentrate, as Kraus points out, on the problem of computing the value of a coalition. In the adopted model, the computed value depends on the computation time available to the agents. Kraus also mentions a research study conducted by Zlotkin and Rosenschein in the area of coalition formation [124]. In this study, the authors consider the general case of n-agent coalition formation and present a simple mechanism that uses cryptographic techniques for sub-additive task-oriented domains. Considering only the grand coalition structure where all the agents belong to the same coalition, the authors provide, as Kraus reports, a linear algorithm that guarantees each agent an expected utility that is equal to its Shapley value. On the other hand, Ketchpel has also devoted a study to the analysis of a more difficult problem where agents have different estimates of the value that a coalition will obtain [125]. As noted, the author proposes and describes a utility distribution mechanism designed to perform in situations where there is uncertainty in the utility that a coalition obtains. The "two agent auction" mechanism suggested for complementing an existing coalition formation algorithm to solve the problem presents certain properties:

- First, the agent valuing the collaboration more highly is always selected manager.
- Second, the agreement price is a deterministic function of the agent's initial offers and estimates of the value of collaboration.

Finally, another research work mentioned by Kraus refers to the use of coalition formation to manage task execution in DPS environments – multi-agent environments requiring cooperation among agents – [126]. While tackling only the coalition structure problem, the study presents efficient distributed algorithms with low ratio bounds and with low computational complexities for task allocation among computational agents in a non super-additive environment. The proposed approach is suitable for coalition formation where each agent must be a member of only one coalition, and overlapping coalitions.

5.9 Argumentation in Coordination

Centered on the trading of proposals, the approaches to reaching agreement discussed so far - game-theoretic and heuristic approaches - have a number of advantages. Perhaps, the most important advantage associated with these approaches lies in the ability to prove some desirable properties of the negotiation protocols [48]. However, various disadvantages associated with these types of negotiation approaches have been identified [127, 48]. According to Jennings et al. [127], the proposals made in the course of a negotiation process generally denote a single point in the space of negotiation agreements, as shown in Figure 5.1 where **X** and **O** represent single points in space. In addition, the authors note that the only feedback that can be made to a proposal through game theory and heuristic approaches is a counter-proposal – which itself is another point in the space – or an acceptance or withdrawal. In this respect, Wooldridge observes that positions in a negotiation process cannot be justified using game-theoretic approaches [48]. He argues that humans engaged in a negotiation process tend to justify their negotiation stances. In this context, the author gives the example of a person who attempts to sell his car to somebody else. He explains that the seller may justify the price of the car with respect to a set of features – say a particularly powerful engine. He adds that the buyer may, in response, justify his proposal for a lower price by pointing out that he needs the car for short inner-city journeys, making the use of a powerful engine less meaningful.

Wooldridge outlines another limitation associated with game-theoretic techniques [48]. He argues that using this technique may make it very hard to understand how an agreement has been reached. According to him, this issue is particularly important in case a person wants to delegate specific tasks such as buying and selling to particular agents. In this respect, Wooldridge provides an example of someone who delegates the task of buying a car to his agent. He explains that once the agent purchases the car, the person concerned would, reasonably enough, be eager to know how the agreement was reached. He would thus ask for clarification on the details of this agreement. Without such clarification, the person who delegated the task of buying the car to the agent may however find the agreement rather hard to accept. In this context, Wooldridge finally outlines the need for people to be able, in such scenarios, to trust and relate to the decisions made by other agents acting on their behalf.

Another limitation associated with game-theoretic and heuristic approaches lies in the difficulty of changing the set of issues under negotiation in the course of a negotiation process [127]. As pointed out, changing the issues under negotiation corresponds to changing the negotiation space of Figure 5.1 by adding new dimensions.

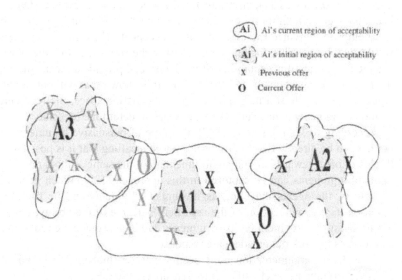

Figure 5.1: The space of negotiation agreements [127]

Wooldridge notes that game theory tends to assume that a utility function associated with an agent is fixed and immutable [48]. He points out that an objective, external, omniscient observer can indeed consider an agent's utility function as fixed during negotiation. However, he further adds that from a subjective and personal point of view, preferences certainly do change during the negotiation process. Based on the previous car-buying example, Wooldridge argues that a person setting out to buy a car may initially desire a car with an electric sun roof. He then adds that this person might however well change his preferences in case he learns that electric sun roofs are unreliable and tend to leak.

Argumentation-based negotiation has thus emerged as an alternative approach designed to overcome the limitations discussed above [48,50,127,128]. The basic idea behind this approach is to allow *"additional information to be exchanged over and above proposals* [127]. As Wooldridge points out, argumentation in a multi-agent context can be crudely assimilated to *"a process by which one agent attempts to convince another of the truth or falsity of some state of affairs"* [48]. As also noted, this process involves agents using arguments for and against propositions, together with justifications regarding the acceptability of these arguments.

Indeed, the information that can be exchanged beyond proposals conveys, in a number of different forms, arguments that explain explicitly the opinion of the agent making the argument. As Jennings et al. explain, an agent can, in addition to rejecting a proposal, offer an explanation on why the proposal is unacceptable

[127]. Such an explanation results in the identification of "*an entire area of the negotiation space*" as inappropriate for the other agent to explore. On the other hand, an agent can similarly provide an argument along with a given proposal in an attempt to convince the other agent to accept it. Through such arguments, it would thus be possible for one agent to alter the preferences of the other agent, change the region of acceptability of the latter, and provide a means of modifying the negotiation space itself. In other words, it is shown that without the ability to argue for the worth of a new object in the negotiation space, the receiving agent would not, in general, have any basis on which to determine its value.

According to Jennings et al. [127], this type of persuasive argumentation does not have to be directly tied to proposals. While recalling that it is possible to make threats or offer rewards in human argumentation, the same authors note that these kinds of arguments can be captured in this approach [129]. When generating the arguments, the agents may not, as in human argumentation, be truthful. Thus, based on its own perception of the argument's degree of credibility, the recipient has to assess the argument on its own merits and then provide the required modification so as to work out an adequate response.

Considering argumentation as it occurs between humans, Gilbert [130] suggests that arguments be classified into four different modes:

1. **Logical mode** – The logical mode is the kind of argument that is generally employed in "*courts of law and scientific papers*". Wooldridge suggests that this mode is perhaps the paradigm example of argumentation [48]. While it resembles mathematical proof, it tends to be deductive in nature.
2. **Emotional mode** – The emotional mode of argumentation is indeed recognized through arguments that appeal to feelings, attitudes, and the like.
3. **Visceral mode** – The visceral mode of argumentation allows a participant to make arguments stemming from the physical or social human aspect. For instance, this mode occurs when a participant bangs his fist down firmly on a table as a way to emphasize the strength of his feeling.
4. **Kisceral mode** – The kisceral mode – in Japanese the term "ki" means "energy" – covers the intuitive, mystical, religious, and non-sensory arenas.

Wooldridge reports that people might not be inclined to accept some modes of argumentation [48]. In this respect, he provides the example of courts of law in most western societies where the emotional and kisceral modes of argumentation are not permitted. He further notes that lawyers, of course, still attempt to use such arguments, but one of the roles of a judge is to declare them unacceptable. In contrast, other societies explicitly allow people to refer to religious beliefs in legal settings. While arguments based on emotions are ruled out in a court of law, people are, as noted, inclined to permit such arguments with children or spouse.

5.9.1 Logic-based argumentation

Indeed, Wooldridge suggests that the logical mode of argumentation be regarded as the *"purest"* or *"most rational"* kind of argument [48]. Wooldridge introduces a system of argumentation inspired from research work attributed to Fox et al. [131] and Kraus et al. [132]. This system functions through the construction of a series of logical steps or arguments against or in support of propositions of interest. Already used by Parsons and Jennings [133] as a basis for negotiation, the system represents, as stated, a promising option for building a framework for dialectic argumentation through which agents can negotiate.

In an extensive review of logical approaches to argumentation [6], Kraus reports that several researchers have developed frameworks for negotiation through argumentation. As noted, these frameworks allow agents to exchange proposals and counter-proposals backed by arguments that summarize the reasons for accepting the proposal. In addition, the author further states that this type of argumentation is persuasive since the exchanges are able to alter the mental state of the participant – the agent involved. Indeed, most of the frameworks referred to above are based on logical models representing the mental states – such as beliefs, desires, intentions, and goals – of the agents participating in the negotiation-based exchanges. A logic-based model of argumentation has been used in argumentation-based negotiation systems [128,133]. The approach is designed to allow, for example, a given agent to negotiate with a peer over which agent will carry out a particular task. As Wooldridge points out [6], the idea is to bring an agent to argue with the other agent intending to perform the task in an attempt to convince it of the acceptability that it should carry out the task.

In an attempt to provide an adequate treatment of the collaborative behavior exhibited in dialogues, a formal model is developed to deal with collaboration [134]. As stated, this model is used as a specification for agent design to constrain certain planning and negotiation processes. On the other hand, the formal model can also be used either by the agents or as a way to check the agents' behavior.

In a complex and dynamic multi-agent setting, the coherence of collective actions from agents is often harmed in the presence of conflicting beliefs about different aspects of the environment, resource availability, and individual or collective capabilities and performance. In this context, team members are thus forced to communicate and negotiate to restore team coherence. Indeed, numerous research projects on teamwork have made progress in enabling agents to coordinate and communicate in a flexible manner without addressing the problem of inter-agent negotiation to resolve conflicts. However, Zhun Qiu et al. focus on the problem of negotiation in teamwork to resolve such conflicts [135]. As noted, the basis of such negotiation lies in inter-agent argumentation where agents assert their beliefs to others with supporting arguments. According to the authors, this work introduces a key novelty which consists in using agents' argumentation that exploits previous research on general, explicit teamwork models. Through such models, it is possible, as Zhun Qiu et al. argue, to categorize the conflicts that arise into different classes, and more importantly provide a generalized and reusable argumentation facility based on teamwork constraints. This approach to resolving agents' conflicting beliefs is effectively implemented within the Collaborative Negotiation System based on Argumentation (CONSA).

Indeed, as self-motivated agents in a multi-agent environment are inclined to pursue their own goals, cooperation is organized and achieved through communication and negotiation. Often, negotiation involves argumentation in the form of an exchange of *"messages or a dialogue"*. Kraus et al. have developed a formal logic that forms a basis for the development of a formal "axiomatization" system for argumentation [129]. In addition, the authors present a logic model of the mental states of the agents based on a representation of their beliefs, desires, intentions, and goals. Using categories identified in human multi-agent negotiation, the authors demonstrate how the logic can be used both to specify argument formulation and evaluation and describe different types of agents. In this context, Kraus et al. present argumentation as an *"iterative process emerging from exchanges among agents to persuade each other and bring about a change in intentions"*. As pointed out, argumentation is seen as a mechanism that can be implemented to achieve cooperation and agreement.

In addition, Kraus et al. further introduce a general Automated Negotiation Agent based on the logical model mentioned above [129]. The Automated Negotiation Agent is implemented to act and negotiate in a simulated multi-agent environment. As stated, several Automated Negotiation Agents can thus be defined and created. The resulting simulation system infrastructure allows a user to analyze and explore different methods for negotiating and arguing within a noncooperative environment that lacks a centralized coordination mechanism. An example of agents that are able to plan, act, and resolve conflicts via negotiation in a "Blocks World" environment is used to illustrate the development of negotiating agents in the framework of the Automated Negotiation Agent.

As proposed by Kraus et al. [129], the formal model consists of *"a set of agents, not necessarily cooperative, with the ability to exchange messages"*. Concepts such as beliefs, goals, desires, intentions, and local preferences are indeed incorporated in the formal models so as to characterize the mental states of these agents. Having a set of desires, each agent develops and implements activities motivated by the will to fulfill these desires. Thus, at a given time, a participating agent selects a consistent and suitable subset of desires that serve as its peculiar set of current goals. Preferring to fulfill goals of higher importance, the agent *"ascribes different degrees of importance to different goals"*. This exercise results in a set of properly prioritized goals that motivate and actively direct the agent's planning process.

According to Kraus, the planning process may generate several intentions [6]. Referring to actions that are within the direct control of the agent, some intentions are classified as the *"intent-to-do"* category. On the other hand, classified in the *"intent-that"* category [134, 135, 136, 137], these other intentions represent propositions that are not directly within the agent's realm of control. In order to fulfill or satisfy such propositions, the agent must, in this case, rely on other agents. However, in the presence of "intent-that" actions in a plan, there is often room for argumentation, as Kraus reports [6].

Argumentation is thus the process through which one agent – the *persuader* – attempts to modify the intention structure of another agent – the *persuadee* – so as to convince it to include the actions it wants it to achieve. In the course of a negotiation process, the persuader and the persuadee are attributed or assigned a dynamic rather than a static role. Thus, each participating agent may, once it receives a message from another agent, update its own intentions and goals. Furthermore, the agent dispatching an unsuccessful argumentation is then required "*to revise its arguments, its plans*", *and/or seek other sources of satisfying the portion of its plan in question*" [6].

A belief set peculiar to an agent includes beliefs concerning the mental states of other agents and beliefs related to the world. Associated with each agent, the mental model of other agents is thus used to determine the actions a particular agent undertakes. As Kraus reports [6], an agent may indeed be mistaken in both kinds of beliefs. As a result, it may update its beliefs following the reception of messages from other agents and through the observation of the world.

Kraus argues that arguments offer the opportunity either to add an intention to the belief set of a persuadee, change the latter's preferences, or retract an intention [6]. Without being exhaustive, she then attempts to present a list of several argument types. However, presenting an authoritative classification proved to be difficult to achieve, since arguments are both liable to interpretation and effective within a particular context and domain [138]. Given this consideration, Kraus proposes a list of arguments loosely classified into six categories. The argument types presented are commonly thought to have persuasive force in human negotiations [78,139,140]. The author suggests that argumentations which proved to be successful in human negotiation may also be successful in automated inter-agent negotiation. In this respect, Kraus further expresses the willingness regarding the need to provide agents with the ability to negotiate with humans. As noted, these agents are therefore required to at least understand human argumentation. Finally, the arguments classified in distinct categories are presented as follows [6]:

- Arguments containing threats designed to lead a persuadee to adopt or abandon a goal.
- Arguments accompanied by a promise of a future reward intended to entice or incite a persuadee.
- Arguments in the form of an appeal to past reward.
- Arguments appealing to precedents as counterexamples to convey to the persuadee a contradiction between what she/he says and past actions.
- Arguments referring to "*prevailing practice*" as an appeal designed to convey to a persuadee that the proposed action will further his/her goals as it has helped others to successfully achieve their goals in the past.

- Arguments appealing to self-interest in order to convince a persuadee that taking the proposed action is susceptible of enabling the achievement of a high-importance goal.

Indeed, the most common arguments used in human negotiation contain threats and promises as a strategy of persuasion [141]. On the other hand, it is reported that the appeal to prevailing practice represents the most common argument used in the legal system. In this respect, presenting example instances – in other terms, prevailing practice cases – appears to be much more persuasive than presenting statistical summaries [142, 143, 144, 145]. Assuming that a person will be willing to keep his/her promises as a way to maximize the internal consistency of his/her cognition, the cognitive dissonance theory supports arguments based on an *"appeal to past promise"* [140]. In repeated interactions, arguments appealing to past promise are indeed important since agents prefer to preserve their established credibility. Finally, bounded rational agents with limited inferential resources are likely or prefer to use the types of arguments in the form of *"an appeal to self-interest"* and in the form of *"a counter example"* [129].

5.9.2 Dialogues and Dialogue Systems

Wooldridge points out that many authors are interested in studying agents *"that argue with themselves, either to resolve inconsistencies or else to determine which set of assumptions to adopt"* [48]. While recalling that an agent engages in a dialogue in order to convince another agent of some state of affairs, he reports that, in contrast, his interest lies in the study of agents that are involved in a dialogue with other agents.

Table 5.1. : *Walton and Krabbe's classification of dialogues [48,146,147].*

Type	Initial Situation	Main goal	Participants aim
Persuasion	Conflict of opinion	Resolve the issue	Persuade the other
Negotiation	Conflict of interest	Make a deal	Get the best for oneself
Inquiry	General ignorance	Growth of knowledge	Find a 'proof'
Deliberation	Need for action	Reach a decision	Influence outcome
Information seeking	Personal ignorance	Spread knowledge	Gain/pass on personal knowledge
Eristics	Conflict/antagonism	Reaching an accommodation	Strike the other party
Mixed	Various	Various	Various

Wooldridge defines the notion of dialogue and investigates the concept of winning an argument [48]. Similarly, Parsons et. al. present a well-grounded framework for describing the reasoning process of negotiating agents that is based upon the use of argumentation both at the level of an agent's internal reasoning and at the level of negotiation between agents [128]. In addition, they further provide a concrete example of how a dialogue – a series of arguments – can be used to solve negotiation problems.

As mentioned in various studies pertaining to argumentation-based dialogue [48, 128, 148, 149, 146, 150], Walton and Krabbe identify a set of dialogues classified into different categories [147]. Considered as an important contribution, the proposed typology is based exclusively on dialogue encounters between human interlocutors [150]. Although it is not exhaustive, this classification is, according to Chris Reed [150], both formal and robust to withstand applications to multi-agent system domains.

Indeed, Walton and Krabbe introduce a classification that distinguishes seven types of dialogue summarized in Table 5.1. As noted, 'eristics' represents a category of dialogue that *"serves primarily as a substitute for physical fighting"* [150]. As such, it is thus unlikely that it plays a significant role in current research pertaining to agent systems. However, Wooldridge explains that an 'eristic' dialogue may result from the need to air in public a conflict between agents [48]. According to him, the objective of such a dialogue may be to reach an accommodation, but need not be. The remaining types of dialogue are characterized through:

1. the initial situation – in particular, the absence of conflicts,
2. the private objectives of the participating agents, and
3. the joint intents or purposes to which all participating agents "*implicitly sub-scribe*".

Initiated from a position of recognized conflict – both agents are mutually aware of the situation, a **persuasion dialogue** is conducted through a sequence of argumentation where "*the elements at stake*" are primarily a particular set of beliefs. In this context, each agent adhering to a system of beliefs is motivated by the objective of offering compelling arguments in support of its thesis. Entering a persuasion dialogue implies the need to implicitly agree to the joint aim of resolving a particular conflict. Hence, a successful persuasion dialogue requires that each participating agent had beforehand prepared itself to alter its beliefs with respect to its thesis. In this respect, an agent participating in a persuasion dialogue can therefore "*assume that the other agent is at least prepared to alter its beliefs*".

In contrast, a **negotiation dialogue** is an argumentation process that "*involves a utility*". From another point of view, this type of dialogue arises from a situation characterized by a real, potential or perceived "*conflict of interest*". It may thus involve, for instance, an attempt to reach agreement either over scarce resources or on a division of labor between agents. Sharing the common and strong overarching aim of reaching a deal, selfish agents adopt goals aimed at maximizing "*their own share of any resource*". The goal of reaching a deal is not highly important in many multi-agent scenarios, as any agent may be able to negotiate and strike a better deal with a third party [150]. However, there are multi-agent scenarios where agents are faced with extremely limited options. In this case, sharing a common desire to reach a deal can be considered an important factor affecting the progress and outcome of the negotiation process. In addition to the contextual differences, another important difference between negotiation and persuasion refers to the procedure or way of doing things. As points out by Reed, coherence between beliefs is not required and the relevant beliefs of the participating agents may very well remain at odds after negotiation [150].

In an **inquiry dialogue**, participating agents engage in a process of argumentation pertaining to a matter of common interest, where the object of the inquiry is "a belief". Resulting from a perceived lack of knowledge, the inquiry dialogue thus provides evident differences with the negotiation and persuasion dialogues, in that the argumentation process is not based on any conflict. Rather than challenging any still existing knowledge, the participants would instead try to establish "truth or falsity". In this respect, Wooldridge provides the best-known example of an inquiry: a public inquest into some event such as a train crash [48]. He notices that the aim of an inquiry is simply to determine facts, as it takes place when a group of people have some mutual interest in determining something.

A *deliberation dialogue* represents the process through which a group of participants attempt to form and decide upon a course of action. This type of dialogue expresses shared similarities with negotiation: the joint goal is to reach an agreement and the individual goal associated with each participating agent is to influence this agreement to suit its benefit [150]. While the deliberation dialogue results from the need for action, negotiation arises from a situation of conflict. Rather than displaying the proposal-counterproposal associated with a negotiation process, the deliberation dialogue is thus usually oriented around means-ends discussion.

Closely related to an inquiry, an *information-seeking dialogue* occurs as a result of an agent taking the individual necessary step *"to find out something for itself"*. Reed argues that the information-seeking dialogue is initiated to deal with a recognized asymmetry between one agent having more information than another *"in regard to some particular data"* [150]. He then outlines the agreement between the joint aim and the individual goals of the agents.

Finally, a *mixed dialogue* occurs through the combination of different types of dialogues discussed above. In this respect, Wooldridge recalls that committee meetings involve negotiation, deliberation, inquiry, and frequently, eristic dialogue [48].

Reed presents an initial work designed at introducing rich models developed in informal logic into multi-agent settings [150]. This work provides a formal characterization of inter-agent communication which clearly distinguishes persuasion from negotiation. It further introduces the notion of a dialogue frame that is used to explore the dialogue typology and the concept of functional embedding. A dialogue frame is described as a tuple consisting of four elements: dialogue type, dialogue topic, the interlocutors or agents engaged in the dialogue and finally the series of utterances between interlocutors. As noted, the dialogical frame in the context of a negotiation dialogue is initiated through a *propose-accept* sequence of utterances, and terminates with an utterance which indicates either an acceptance or concession to the topic on the part of the one of the agents. The notion of *argument supports* is also described, which is a technique to enrich the standard model of communication by providing supporting information which can lead to a more efficient dialogue. Functional embedding is the nesting of dialogue types. The scenario provided by the author that illustrates functional embedding is of two agents engaged in a persuasion dialogue in which one of the agents is perceived as having more knowledge than the other agent. The dialogue may shift to an information seeking dialogue until both parties have the appropriate information, at which time the dialogue may shift back to persuasion dialogue. The author argues that differentiating between different dialogue types is important in complex multi-agent societies. For example, understanding the relationship between dialogue types and agent goals enables, as suggested by the author, a formal definition of the terms that comprise an encounter. Such a formal dialogue can lead to a common framework in which the dialogue can be assessed / characterized. The author also states that the approach offers several benefits, such as better computational efficiency as well as greater expressive power. As noted, the approach demonstrates that *"the typology designed on the basis of empirical research into natural argumentation can be successfully formalized and applied in a multi-agent domain"*.

Furthermore, in an attempt to advance knowledge in the area pertaining to the use of argumentation techniques as a basis for negotiation dialogues, Amgoud et al. present a model for inter-agent dialogues based on argumentation [146]. It is a general model incorporating a precisely defined protocol for the exchange of arguments. As explained, this model extends the general approach suggested by Reed as a way to capture a range of dialogue types [150]. In contrast, Parsons et al. concentrate more on the interaction between beliefs and intentions in a specific negotiation/deliberation form of dialogue [128]. Introduced by Amgoud et al. [146], the general model provides an underlying argumentation system and the illocutions necessary to carry out the kinds of dialogues discussed in [150]. As suggested, this approach can thus be regarded as an attempt to bridge the gap between the low level detail of handling beliefs and intentions described in [86] and the general approach discussed in [150].

Parsons et al. explore three types of argumentation-based dialogues between agents – *information seeking*, *inquiry*, and *persuasion*, define a precise protocol for each type of dialogue, and examine various important properties of the resulting protocols [148]. While also considering some aspects of the complexity associated with these dialogues, the authors show in particular that each protocol leads to dialogues that are guaranteed to terminate. In a follow-on work [149], Parsons et al. extend this analysis of formal inter-agent dialogues to provide a first detailed characterization of the outcome of such dialogues. Then, they investigate the extent to which outcomes are dependent *"on tactical play"* by the participating agents. The results of this investigation show that tactics can have an important effect on the outcome. In this respect, Parsons et al. identify how to rule out the effect of tactics. According to them, excluding the effect of tactics is desirable from the perspective of mechanism design.

References

1. H. S. Nwana and L. C. Lee and N. R. Jennings, "Coordination in Software Agent Systems", In the British Telecom Technical Journal, Vol. 14, No 4, pp. 79-88, 1996.
2. E. H. Durfee, V. R. Lesser and D. D. Corkill, "Coherent Cooperation among Communicating Problem Solvers", IEEE Transactions on Computers, 36 (11), pp. 1275—1291, 1987.
3. K. Werkman, *"Knowledge-based model of negotiation using shareable perspectives"*, In the Proceedings of the 10th International Workshop on DAI, Texas, 1990.
4. P. Kearney, A. Sehmi, and R. Smith, *"Emergent behavior in a multi-agent economics simulation"*, In the Proceedings of the 11th European Conference on Artificial Intelligence, A. G. Cohn, Editor, London, John Wiley, 1994.
5. V. Lesser and D. Corkill, "the Distributed Vehicle Monitoring Testbed: a Tool for Investigating Distributed Problem-Solving Networks", In Artificial Intelligence Magazine, Vol. 4, No 3, pp 15—33, 1983.
6. Sarit Kraus, "Automated Negotiation and Decision Making in Multiagent Environments", Lecture Notes in Artificial Intelligence 2086, pp. 150-172, 2001

7. K. J. Arrow, "the Economics of Agency", In Principals and Agents: the Structure of Business, J. Pratt and R. Zeckhauser, Editors, pp. 37–51, Harvard Business School Press, Cambridge, MA, 1985.
8. S. Grossman and O. Hart, "an analysis of the principal-agent problem", In *Econometrica*, Vol. 51, No. 1, pp. 7–45, 1983.
9. J. Hirshleifer and J. Riley, "The Analytics of Uncertainty and Information", Cambridge University Press, Cambridge, 1992.
10. J. Laffont and J. Tirole, "a Theory of Incentives in Procurement and `Regulation", the MIT Press, Cambridge, Massachusetts, 1993.
11. Rasmusen, "Games and Information", Basil Blackwell Ltd., Cambridge, MA, 1989.
12. S. Ross, "the Economic Theory of Agency: the Principal's Problem", In the American Economic Review, Vol. 63, No. 2, pp. 134–139, 1973.
13. S. Baiman and J. Demski, "Economically Optimal Performance Evaluation and Control Systems", In Journal of Accounting Research, Vol. 18, pp. 184–220, 1980.
14. Banerjee and A. Beggs, "Efficiency in Hierarchies: Implementing the First-best Solution by Sequential Actions", In the Rand Journal of Economics, Vol. 20, No. 4, pp. 637–645, 1989.
15. Nalebuff and J. Stiglitz, "Information, Competition, and Markets", In American Economic Review, Vol. 73, No. 2, pp. 278–283, 1983.
16. Macho-Stadler and J. P´erez-Castrillo, "Moral hazard and cooperation", In Economics Letters, Vol. 35, pp. 17–20, 1991.
17. Caillaud, R. Guesnerie, P. Rey, and J. Tirole, "Government Intervention in Production and Incentives Theory: a Review of Recent Contributions", In the Rand Journal of Economics, Vol. 19, No. 1, pp. 1–26, 1988.
18. M. Harris and A. Raviv, "Some Results on Incentive Contracts with Applications to Education and Employment, Health Insurance, and Law Enforcement", In the American Economic Review, Vol. 68, No. 1, pp. 20–30, 1978.
19. M. Landsberger and I. Meilijson, "Monopoly Insurance under Adverse Selection when Agents Differ in Risk Aversion", In Journal of Economic Theory, Vol. 63, pp. 392–407, 1994.
20. Rubinstein and M. Yaari, "Repeated Insurance Contracts and Moral Hazard", In Journal of Economic Theory, Vol. 30, pp. 74–97, 1983.
21. M. Spence and R. Zeckhauser, "Insurance, Information and Individual Action", In the American Economic Review, Vol. 61, No. 1, pp. 380–391, 1971.
22. S. Matthews, "Selling to Risk Averse Buyers with Unobservable Tastes", In Journal of Economy Theory, Vol. 30, pp. 370–400, 1983.
23. R. Myerson, "Mechanism Design by an Informed Principal", In *Econometrica*, Vol. 51, pp. 1767—1798, 1983.
24. R. P. McAfee and J. McMillan, "Bidding for Contracts: a Principal-agent Analysis", In the Rand Journal of Economics, Vol. 17, No. 3, pp. 326–338, 1986.
25. S. Shavell, "Risk Sharing and Incentives in the Principal and Agent Relationship", In Bell Journal of Economics, Vol. 10, pp. 55–79, 1979.
26. R. Davis and R. G. Smith, "*Negotiation as a Metaphor for Distributed Problem Solving*", In Artificial Intelligence, No 20, pp. 63-109, 1983. – Reprinted in Communications in Multiagent Systems, LNAI 2650, M.-P. Huget, Editor, pp. 51-97, 2003.
27. R. G. Smith, "the Contract Net Protocol: High-Level Communication and Control in a Distributed Problem Solver", In IEEE Transactions on Computers, Vol. 29, No 12, December 1980.
28. R. Smith and R. Davis, "Framework for Cooperation in Distributed Problem Solvers", IEEE Transactions on Systems, Man and Cybernetic, Vol. C-29, No. 12, pp. 61–70, 1981.
29. T. W. Malone, R. E. Fikes, K. R. Grant, and M. T. Howard, "Enterprise: a Market-like Task Schedule for Distributed Computing Environments", In The Ecology of Computation, B. A. Huberman, Editor, pp. 177–205, North Holland, 1988.

30. T. Ohko, K. Hiraki, and Y. Anzai, "Reducing Communication Load on Contract Net by Case-based Reasoning: Extension with Directed Contract and Forgetting", In Proceedings of the First International Conference on Multi–Agent Systems, Cambridge, MA, MIT Press, 1995

31. H. Van Dyke Parunak, "Manufacturing Experience with the Contract Net", In Distributed Artificial Intelligence, M. N. Huhns, Editor, pp. 285-310, 1987.

32. Sandip Sen and Edmund Durfee, "a Contracting Model for Flexible Distributed Scheduling", In Annals of Operations Research, Vol. 65, pp. 195–222, 1996.

33. T. Sandholm, "An Implementation of the Contract Net Protocol based on Marginal Cost Calculations", In Proceedings of AAAI-93, pp. 256–262, Washington D.C., July 1993.

34. T. Sandholm, S. Sikka, and S. Norden, "Algorithms for Optimizing Leveled Commitment Contracts", In Proceedings of IJCAI99, pp. 535–540, Stockholm, Sweden, 1999.

35. T. Sandholm and Y. Zhou, "Surplus Equivalence of Leveled Commitment Contracts", In Proceedings of ICMAS-2000, pp. 247–254, IEEE Computer Society, Boston, MA, 2000.

36. S. Kraus, "an Overview of Incentive Contracting", In Artificial Intelligence Journal, Vol. 83, No 2, pp. 297–346, 1996.

37. Suzan E. Conry, Robert A. Meyer and Victor R. Lesser, "Multistage Negotiation in Distributed Planning", In Readings in Distributed Artificial Intelligence, Alan H. Bond and Les Gasser, Editors, Morgan Kaufmann Publishers, Inc., San Mateo, California, 1988.

38. M. P. Georgeff, "Communication and Interaction in Multi-agent Planning", In Readings in Distributed Artificial Intelligence, Alan H. Bond and Les Gasser, Editors, Morgan Kaufmann Publishers, Inc., San Mateo, California, 1988.

39. M. P. Georgeff, "A Theory of Action for Multi-agent Planning", In Readings in Distributed Artificial Intelligence, Alan H. Bond and Les Gasser, Editors, Morgan Kaufmann Publishers, Inc., San Mateo, California, 1988.

40. S. Cammarata, D. McArthur, R. Steeb, "Strategies of Cooperation in Distributed Problem Solving", In Readings in Distributed Artificial Intelligence, Alan H. Bond and Les Gasser, Editors, Morgan Kaufmann Publishers, Inc., San Mateo, California, 1988.

41. Y. Jin and T. Koyama, "Multi-agent Planning Through Expectation-based Negotiation" In Proceedings of the 10th International Workshop on Distributed Artificial Intelligence, M. N. Huhns, Editor, Texas University, 1990.

42. D. D. Corkill, "Hierarchical Planning in a Distributed Environment", In Proceedings of the 6th International Joint Conference on Artificial Intelligence, pp. 168-179, August 1979.

43. Victor R. Lesser and Daniel D. Corkill, "Functionally Accurate, Cooperative Distributed Systems", In IEEE Transactions on Systems, Man, and Cybernetics, Vol. 11, No 1, pp. 81-96, January 1981.

44. Victor R. Lesser and Daniel D. Corkill, "the Distributed Vehicle Monitoring Testbed: A Tool for Investigating Distributed Problem-Solving Networks", In AI Magazine, Vol. 4, No 3, pp 15-33, 1983.

45. Edmund H. Durfee and Victor R. Lesser, "Using Partial Global Plans to Coordinate Distributed Problem Solvers", In Proceedings of the 1987 International Joint Conference on Artificial Intelligence, pp. 875-883, 1987.

46. M.N. Huhns and M. P. Singh, "CKBS-94 Tutorial: Distributed Artificial Intelligence for Information Systems", Dake Centre, University of Keele, 1994.

47. M. Schumacher, "Multi-agent Systems", In Objective Coordination in Multi-agent Systems Engineering: Design and Implementation, M. Schumacher, Editor, Lecture Notes in Artificial Intelligence, Vol. 2039, Springer Verlag, Heidelberg, Germany, April 2001.

48. M. Wooldridge, "Reaching Agreements", In an Introduction to Multi-agent Systems, John Wiley & Sons, Ltd, 2002.

49. S. Bussmann and J. Muller, "A Negotiation Framework for Cooperating Agents", In Proceedings CKBS-SIG, S. M. Deen, Editor, Dake Centre, University of Keele, pp. 1-17, 1992.

50. Katia P. Sycara, "Multi-agent Compromise via Negotiation", In Distributed Artificial Intelligence 2, Les Gasser and M. Huhns, Editors, Morgan Kaufmann Publishers, Inc., San Mateo, California, 1989.
51. T. Moehlman, V. Lesser, and B. Buteau, "Decentralized negotiation: An approach to the distributed planning problem", In Group Decision and Negotiation, Vol. 2, No 2, pp. 161–191, January 1992.
52. Susan E. Lander and Victor R. Lesser, "Customizing Distributed Search among Agents with Heterogeneous Knowledge", In Proceedings of the. First International conference on Information Knowledge Management, pp. 335–344, Baltimore, 1992.
53. Jeffrey S. Rosenschein and Gilad Zlotkin, "Rules of Encounter: Designing Conventions for Automated Negotiation among Computers", MIT Press, 1994.
54. K. P. Sycara, "Resolving Adversarial Conflicts: An Approach to Integrating Case-Based and Analytic Methods", PhD thesis, School of Information and Computer Science, Georgia Institute of Technology, 1987.
55. K. P. Sycara, "Persuasive argumentation in negotiation", In Theory and Decision, Vol. 28, pp. 203–242, 1990.
56. Dajun Zeng and Katia Sycara, "Bayesian learning in negotiation", In International Journal of Human-Computer Studies, Vol. 48, pp. 125–141, 1998
57. S. Kraus and D. Lehmann, "Designing and building a negotiating automated agent", In Computational Intelligence, Vol. 11, No 1, pp.132–171, 1995
58. C. Sierra, P. Faratin, and N. Jennings, "A Service-oriented Negotiation Model between Autonomous Agents", In Proceedings of the 8th European Workshop on Modeling Autonomous Agents in a Multi-Agent World (MAAMAW-97), pp. 17–35, Ronneby, Sweden, 1997.
59. T. W. Sandholm and V. R. Lesser, "Issues in Automated Negotiation and Electronic Commerce: Extending the contract net framework, In First International Conference on Multiagent Systems (ICMAS-95), pp. 328–335, San Francisco, 1995.
60. M. J. Osborne and A. Rubinstein, "Bargaining and Markets", Academic Press Inc., San Diego, California, 1990.
61. E. Roth, "Axiomatic Models of Bargaining", Lecture Notes in Economics and Mathematical Systems No. 170, Springer-Verlag, Berlin, 1979.
62. D. Druckman, "Negotiations", Sage Publications, London, 1977.
63. R. Fisher and W. Ury, "Getting to Yes: Negotiating Agreement Without Giving In", Houghton Mifflin, Boston, 1981.
64. Lavinia Hall, editor, "Negotiation: Strategies for Mutual Gain", Sage Publications, Newbury Park, CA, 1993.
65. R. Johnson, "Negotiation basics", Sage Publications, Newbury Park, 1993.
66. L Karrass, "The Negotiating Game: How to Get What You Want", Thomas Crowell Company, NY, 1970.
67. H. Raiffa "The Art and Science of Negotiation", Harvard University Press, Cambridge, MA, 1982.
68. Jeffrey S. Rosenschein, "Rational Interaction: Cooperation among Intelligent Agents", PhD Thesis, Stanford University, 1985.
69. Gilad Zlotkin and Jeffrey S. Rosenschein, "Blocks, Lies, and Postal Freight: the Nature of Deception in Behavior", In Proceedings of the 10th International Workshop on DAI, 1990.
70. Rosenschein, J.S. and Zlotkin, G., "Rules of Encounter: Designing Conventions for Automated Negotiation among Computers", MIT Press, 1994,
71. Kraus, S. and Wilkenfield, J., "the Function of Time in Cooperative Negotiations: Preliminary Report", Department of Computer Science, University of Maryland, 1991.
72. M. Busuioc and C. Winter, "Negotiation and Intelligent Agents", Project NOMADS-001, BT Labs, Martlesham Heath, U.K., 1995.
73. G. Zlotkin, G. and J. S. Rosenschein, J.S., "One, Two, Many: Coalitions in Multi-Agent Systems", In Proceedings Of the 5th European Workshop on Modeling Autonomous Agents in Multi-Agent World, August, 1993.

74. M. R. Adler, A. B. Davis, R. Weihmayer, and R. W. Forest, "Conflict-resolution strategies for non-hierarchical distributed agents", In Distributed Artificial Intelligence II, L. Gasser and M. N. Huhns, Editors, Morgan Kaufmann, 1989.

75. T. Kreifelt and von F. Martial, "A Negotiation Framework for Autonomous Agents", In Decentralized Artificial Intelligence, Y. Demazeau and J. P. Muller, Editors, Vol. 2, Elsevier Science, 1991.

76. K. Sycara, "Multi-agent Compromise via Negotiation", In Distributed Artificial Intelligence II, L. Gasser and M. Huhns, Editors, Morgan Kaufmann, 1989.

77. Sathi and M. S. Fox, "Constraint-directed Negotiation of Resource Allocations", In Distributed Artificial Intelligence II, L. Gasser and M. Huhns, Editors, Morgan Kaufmann, 1989.

78. D. G. Pruitt, "Negotiation Behavior", Academic Press, New York, N.Y., 1981.

79. P. H. Gulliver, "Disputes and Negotiations - a Cross-cultural Perspective", Academic Press, 1979.

80. K. Kuwabara and V. R. Lesser, "Extended Protocol for Multistage Negotiation", In Proceedings of the 9th Workshop on Distributed Artificial Intelligence, 1989.

81. E. H. Durfee and T. A. Montgomery, "a Hierarchical Protocol for Coordinating Multi-agent Behavior", In Proceedings of the 8th National Conference on Artificial Intelligence, Boston, MA, pp. 86-93, 1990.

82. N. R. Jennings, "Coordination Techniques for Distributed Artificial Intelligence", In Foundations of Distributed Artificial Intelligence, G. M. P. O'Hare and N. R. Jennings, Editors, John Wiley & Sons, Inc., New York, p. 187-210, 1996.

83. Rubinstein, "Perfect equilibrium in a bargaining model", In Econometrica, Vol. 50, No 1, pp. 97–109, 1982.

84. Sarit Kraus, "Strategic Negotiation in Multiagent Environments", the MIT Press, Cambridge Massachusetts, 2001.

85. R. Schwartz and S. Kraus, "Negotiation on data allocation in multi-agent environments", In Proceeding of AAAI-97, pp. 29–35, Providence, Rhode Island, 1997.

86. M. Ben-Or and N. Linial, "Collective Coin Flipping, Robust Voting Games and Minima of Banzhaf Values", In Proceedings of the 26th IEEE Symposium on the Foundations of Computer Science, pp. 408–416, Portland, 1985.

87. M. J. Osborne and A. Rubinstein, "A Course in Game Theory", MIT Press, Cambridge, Massachusetts, 1994.

88. R. D. Luce and H. Raiffa, "Games and Decisions", John Wiley and Sons, New York, 1957

89. J. F. Nash, "Two-person Cooperative Games", Econometrica, Vol. 21, pp. 128–140, 1953.

90. Jean Tirole, "the Theory of Industrial Organization", the MIT Press, Cambridge, MA, 1988.

91. Kreps and R. Wilson, "Sequential equilibria", In Econometrica, vol. 50, pp. 863–894, 1982.

92. Rina Azoulay-Schwartz and Arit Kraus, "Negotiation on Data Allocation in Multi-agent Environments", In Autonomous Agents and Multi-agent Systems, Vol. 5, No 2, pp. 123-172, 2002.

93. S. Kraus and J. Wilkenfeld, "A Strategic Negotiations Model with Applications to an International Crisis", In IEEE Transaction on Systems Man and Cybernetics, Vol. 23, No 1, pp. 313—323, 1993.

94. J. Wilkenfeld, S. Kraus, K. Holley, and M. Harris, "Genie: A decision support System for Crisis Negotiations", In Decision Support Systems, Vol. 14, pp. 369–391, 1995.

95. Amir Ronen, "Algorithms for rational agents", In Conference on Current Trends in Theory and Practice of Informatics, pp. 56–70, 2000.

96. M. R. Andersson and T. W. Sandholm, "Contract Types for Optimal Task Allocation: II Experimental Results", In AAAI 1998 Spring Symposium: Satisficing Models, Stanford University, California, 1998.

97. Gimenez-Funes, L. Godo, and J. A. Rodriguez-Aguilar, "Designing Bidding Strategies for Trading Agents in Electronic Commerce, In ICMAS98, pp. 136–143, Paris, 1998.

98. R. Wurman, W. E. Walsh, and M. P. Wellman, "Flexible Double Auctions for Electronic Commerce: Theory and Implementation", In Decision Support Systems, Vol. 24, pp. 17–27, 1998.
99. P. Klemperer, "Auction Theory: a Guide to Literature", In Journal of Economic Surveys, Vol. 13, No 3, 1999.
100. William Vickrey, "Counterspeculation, auctions, and competitive sealed tenders", In Journal of Finance, Vol. 16, pp. 8-37, March 1961.
101. Huberman and S. H. Clearwater, "A multi-agent system for controlling building environments" In Proceedings of ICMAS-95, pp. 171–176, San Francisco, 1995.
102. R. Schwartz and S. Kraus, "Bidding mechanisms for data allocation in multiagent environments", In Intelligent Agents IV: Agent Theories, Architectures, and Languages, Munindar P. Singh, Anand S. Rao, and M.J. Wooldridge, Editors, pp. 61–75, Springer-Verlag, 1998.
103. M. B. Tsvetovatyy and M. Gini, "Toward a virtual marketplace: Architectures and strategies", In the first International Conference on the Practical Application of Intelligent Agents and Multi Agents Technology, pp. 597–614, London, 1996.
104. M. Tsvetovatyy, M. Gini, B. Mobasher, and Z. Wieckowski, "Magma: An agent-based virtual market for electronic commerce", In Applied Artificial Intelligence, special issue on Intelligent Agents, Vol. 6, pp. 501–523, 1997.
105. Tuomas W. Sandholm, "Distributed Rational Decision Making", In Multiagent Systems: A Modern Approach to Distributed Artificial Intelligence, Gerhard Weiss, Editor, The MIT Press, Cambridge, MA, USA, pp. 201—258, 1999.
106. Y. Fujishima, K. Leyton-Brown, and Y. Shoham, "Taming the Computational Complexity of combinatorial Auctions: Optimal and Approximate Approaches", In Dean Thomas, editor, Proceedings of the 16th International Joint Conference on Artificial Intelligence (IJCAI-99-Vol1), pages 548–553, S.F., July 31–August 6 1999, Morgan Kaufmann Publishers.
107. L. Hunsberger and B. Grosz, "a Combinatorial Auction for Collaborative Planning", In ICMAS-2000, Boston, USA, 2000.
108. Daniel Lehmann, Liadan Ita O'Callaghan, and Yoav Shoham, "Truth Revelation in Rapid, Approximately Efficient Combinatorial Auctions", In Proceedings of the ACM Conference on Electronic Commerce (EC'99), pages 96–102, N.Y., November 3–5 1999. ACM Press.
109. Noam Nisan, "Bidding and Allocation in Combinatorial Auctions", In ACM Conference on Electronic Commerce", pp. 1–12, 2000.
110. R. Wilson, "Incentive Efficiency of Double Auctions", Econometrica, Vol. 53, No 5, pp. 1101–1116, 1985.
111. P. R. Wurman, W. E. Walsh, and M. P. Wellman, "Flexible Double Auctions for Electronic Commerce: Theory and Implementation", Decision Support Systems, Vol. 24, pp. 17–27, 1998.
112. Gerber, C. Russ, and G. Vierke, "On the Suitability of Market-based Mechanisms for Telematics Applications", In Proceedings of Agents99, pp. 408–409, 1999.
113. M. Wellman, "A Market-oriented Programming Environment and its Application to Distributed Multicommodity Flow Problems", Journal of Artificial Intelligence Research, Vol. 1, pp. 1–23, 1993.
114. M. P. Wellman and P. R. Wurman, "Market-aware agents for a multi-agent world", In Robotics and Autonomous Systems, Vol. 24, pp. 115–125, 1998.
115. Rapoport, "N-Person Game Theory", University of Michigan, Michigan, 1970.
116. K. I. Shimomura, "the Bargaining Set and Coalition Formation", Technical Report 95-11, Brown University, Department of Economics, 1995.
117. R. Vohra, "Coalitional Non-cooperative Approaches to Cooperation", Technical Report 95-6, Brown University, Department of Economics, 1995.
118. L. Zhou, "a New Bargaining Set of an N-person Game and Endogenous Coalition Formation", Games and Economic Behavior, Vol. 6, pp. 512–526, 1994.
119. J. P. Kahan and A. Rapoport, "Theories of coalition formation" Lawrence Erlbaum Associates, Hillsdale, New Jersey, 1984.

120. O. Shehory and S. Kraus, "Feasible Formation of Stable Coalitions among Autonomous Agents in Non-super-additive Environments", In Computational Intelligence, Vol. 15, No 3, pp. 218–251, 1999.

121. M. Klusch and O. Shehory, "a Polynomial Kernel-oriented Coalition Formation Algorithm for Rational Information Agents", In Proceeding of ICMAS-96, pp. 157–164, Kyoto, Japan, 1996.

122. T. Sandholm, K. Larson, M. R. Andersson, O. Shehory, and F. Tohm, "Coalition Structure Generation with Worst Case Guarantees", In Artificial Intelligence Journal, Vol. 111, pp. 209–238, 1999.

123. T. W. Sandholm and V. R. Lesser, "Coalition Formation among bounded rational agents", In Proceeding of IJCAI-95, pp. 662–669, Montreal, 1995.

124. G. Zlotkin and J. S. Rosenschein, "Coalition, Cryptography, and Stability: Mechanisms for Coalition Formation in Task Oriented Domains", In Proceeding of AAAI94, pp. 432–437, Seattle, Washington, 1994.

125. S. P. Ketchpel, "Forming Coalitions in the Face of Uncertain Rewards", In Proceedings of AAAI94, pp. 414–419, Seattle, Washington, 1994.

126. O. Shehory and S. Kraus, "Methods for task allocation via agent coalition formation", In Artificial Intelligence, Vol. 15, No 3, pp. 218–251, 1998.

127. N. R. Jennings, P. Faratin, A. R. Lomuscio, S. Parsons, C. Sierra, and M. Wooldridge, "Automated Negotiation: Prospects, Methods, and Challenges", In International Journal of Group Decision and Negotiation, Vol. 10, No. 2, pp. 199-215, 2001.

128. S. Parsons, C. A. Sierra, and N. R. Jennings, "Agent that Reason and Negotiate by Arguing", Journal of Logic and Computation, Vol. 8, No. 3, pp. 261-292, 1998.

129. S. Kraus, K. Sycara, and A. Evenchik, "Reaching Agreements through Argumentation: a Logical Model and Implementation", In Artificial Intelligence, Vol. 104, pp. 1–69, 1998.

130. M. Gilbert, "Multi-modal Argumentation", Philosophy of the Social Sciences, Vol. 24, No. 2, pp. 159-177, 1994.

131. J. Fox, P. Krause, and S. Ambler, "Arguments, Contradictions, and Practical Reasoning", In Proceedings of the 10th European Conference on Artificial Intelligence (ICAI-92), Vienna, Austria, pp. 623-627, 1992.

132. Paul Krause, Simon Ambler, Morten Elvang-Gøransson, and John Fox, "a Logic of Argmentation for Reasoning under Uncertainty", In Computational Intelligence, Vol. 11, pp. 113-131, 1995.

133. S. Parsons and N. R. Jennings, "Negotiation through Argumentation – a Preliminary Report", In Proceedings of the 2nd International Conference on Multi-agent Systems (ACMAS-96), Kyoto, Japan, pp. 267-274, 1996.

134. J. Grosz and S. Kraus, "Collaborative Plans for Complex Group Activities", In Artificial Intelligence Journal, Vol. 86, No. 2, pp. 269–357, 1996.

135. Z. Qiu and M. Tambe, "Flexible Negotiations in Teamwork: Extended Abstract", In Proceedings of the AAAI Fall Symposium on Distributed Continual Planning, 1998

136. J. Grosz and S. Kraus, "the Evolution of Sharedplans", In Foundations and Theories of Rational Agency, A. Rao and M. Wooldridge, Editors, pp. 227–262, Kluwer Academic Publishers, 1999.

137. Vermazen, "Objects of Intention", Philosophical Studies, Vol. 71, pp. 223–265, 1993.

138. S. Toulmin, R. Rieke, and A. Janik, "An Introduction to Reasoning", Macmillan Publishing Co., Inc., 1979.

139. M. Karlins and H. I. Abelson, "Persuasion: How Opinions and Attitudes are Changed", Springer Publishing Company, Inc., second edition, 1970.

140. Daniel J. O'Keefe, "Persuasion: Theory and Research", SAGE Publications, 1990.

141. J. Boster and P. Mongeau, "Fear-arousing Persuasive Messages", In Communication yearbook 8, R. N. Bostrom, Editor, SAGE Publications, 1984.

142. R. Hamill, T. D. Wilson, and R. E. Nisbett, "Insensitivity to sample bias: Generalizing from atypical cases", In Journal of Personality and Social Psychology, Vol. 39, pp. 579–589, 1980.

143. R. R. Jr. Koballa, "Persuading Teachers to Reexamine the Innovative Elementary Science Programs of yesterday: The effect of Anecdotal versus Data-summary Communications", In Journal of Research in Science Teaching, Vol. 23, pp. 437–449, 1986.
144. R. E. Nisbett, E. Borgida, R. Crandall, and H. Reed, "Popular Induction: Information is not Necessarily Informative", In Cognition and social behavior, Lawrence Erlbaum, J. S. Carroll and J. W. Payne, Editors, 1976.
145. S. E. Taylor and S. C. Thompsons, "Staking the Elusive Vividness Effect", In Psychological Review, Vol. 89, pp. 155–181, 1982.
146. Leila Amgoud, Nicolas Maudet, and Simon Parsons, "Modelling dialogues using argumentation", In Proceedings of the Fourth International Conference on Multi-Agent Systems, E. Durfee, Editor, pp. 31-38, Boston, MA, USA, 2000. IEEE Press.
147. N. Walton and E. C. W. Krabbe, "Commitment in Dialogue: Basic Concepts of Interpersonal Reasoning", State University of New York Press, Albany, NY, 1995.
148. S. Parsons, M. Wooldridge, and L. Amgoud, "an Analysis of Formal Inter-agent Dialogues", In 1st International Conference on Autonomous agents and Multi-agent Systems, ACM Press, 2002.
149. S. Parsons, M. Wooldridge, and L. Amgoud, "on the Outcome of Formal Inter-agent Dialogues", Proceedings of the Second International Joint Conference on Autonomous Agents and Multi-agent Systems (AAMAS 2003), Melbourne, Victoria, Australia, ACM 2003, July 14-18, 2003.
150. Chris Reed, "Dialogue Frames in Agent Communication" In Proceedings of the Third International Conference on Multi-agent Systems, Y. Demazeau, Editor, pp. 246-253, IEEE Press, 1998.

Chapter 6 Learning and Coordination

Abstract Adaptive learning techniques can automate the large-scale coordination of multi-agent systems and enhance their robustness in dynamic environments. Several learning approaches have been developed to address the different aspects of coordination, from learning coordination rules to the integrated learning of trust and reputation in order to facilitate coordination in open systems. Although convergence in multi-agent learning is still an open research question, several applications have emerged using some of the learning techniques presented.

6.1 Introduction

An agent in a multi-agent system (MAS) has to decide (1) what task to do next, (2) whether to accept a task from another agent, (3) whether to ask another agent to achieve a task on its behalf, and (4) what information to share with other agents in order to achieve its goals [1]. In cooperative, distributed MAS, the agents share the same global goal and the problem there is to coordinate on local goals which can eventually lead to the satisfaction of global goals. Open systems, where agents come and go, are non-cooperative because agents do not necessarily share the same global goals but can occasionally cooperate on local goals. It is convenient to model large dynamic multi-modal problems through an open MAS paradigm to reduce the problem complexity and to use indirect methods, such as negotiations and incentives, to induce coordination so that most goals can be achieved.

Learning is a process, described by the tuple *{T, P, E}* where *T* is a task, *P* is the performance metric, and *E* the experience, whereby a machine is said to learn to improve its performance *P* at task *T* given experience *E* [2]. Defining the performance metric is essential in measuring the amount of learning accomplished. In MAS, the performance of a task depends on the coordination quality which can be evaluated in two ways: (1) as a managerial cost (for example, communication costs) or (2) as an emergent property. When considered as a managerial control cost, some meta-level reasoning has to take place to balance the benefit of an action and its cost [3]. For example, asking another agent to achieve a task might require some delays for negotiations. The absence of interference (including role conflicts and collisions) reflects coordination and the time taken to resolve or prevent interference represents the coordination cost. Instead of explicit coordination mechanisms to reduce the coordination cost, coordination can emerge from local interactions of autonomous behavior. For example, simple adaptation mechanisms of reactive behavior can induce self-organization [4, 5]. Consequently, a coordination quality metric describing the efficiency of a multi-agent algorithm must at least combine three aspects: performance, resources, and failures (Figure 6.1) [6].

A. Bedrouni et al., *Distributed Intelligent Systems: A Coordination Perspective,*
DOI: 10.1007/978-0-387-77702-3_6, © Springer Science + Business Media, LLC 2009

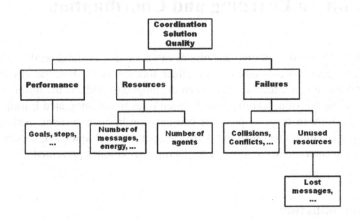

Figure 6.1: Taxonomy for coordination metric

There are three basic approaches to machine learning: (1) supervised learning where the correct output is provided by a teacher during a training phase; (2) unsupervised learning where there is no knowledge of the correct output but where it is possible to distinguish equivalence classes in the input itself to guide the learning process; and (3) reward-based or reinforcement learning where only a feedback is provided by the environment on the utility of the performance. Using this feedback as a guide, a learner can incrementally modify its performance. Table 6.1 summarizes some current machine learning strategies relevant to multi-agent learning (MAL). Learning coordination strategies is important in MAS to scale up to large state spaces using inductive techniques and for robust and flexible coordination behavior in dynamic systems. Learning by individual agents can, however, make a system more dynamic, but at the same time, may be problematic and prevent the system from reaching an equilibrium state. Convergence in MAL and its relevance in complex domains [7, 8] remains an open area of research that has stimulated countless workshops.

Table 6.1: Machine Learning Strategies

Machine Learning Strategy	Description
Case-based Learning	Instance-based method that adapts solutions to previous similar instances.
Decision-tree learning	Supervised method for instance classification that discovers the hierarchies of relevant features describing the search space.
Bayesian Learning	Incremental learning method that

	learns pattern approximations through the update of posterior distributions using Bayes' theorem.
Transfer Learning	Knowledge learned in one task can be reused to speed up learning in a different task.
Sequential Learning	Leverages from temporal contiguity in the data to formulate inferences.
Online Learning	Learns from one example at a time from multiple "experts." The goal is to learn to weight an expert's advice to minimize mistakes.
Active Learning	Learns by selecting the relevant training examples to maximize information gain.
Relational Learning	Learns inductively from relational features linking examples together.
Layered Learning	Learns at different degrees of abstraction.
Reinforcement Learning	Learns action utilities by trial and error from environmental feedback alone.
Evolutionary Learning	Population-based and policy-based reinforcement learning based on the biological metaphor of survival of the fittest.
Temporal Difference Learning	Reinforcement learning of a Markov decision process from two temporally successive estimates.
Collective learning	Distributed and emergent intelligence based on the metaphor of social insects.

In MAL, it helps to distinguish between learning coordination behavior, team learning of joint solutions, and the integrated learning of indirect coordination mechanisms. The merits of the different approaches depend on the problem context. In learning coordination behavior, the behavior of the other agents is ignored (or assumed stationary) in favor of maximizing performance alone. In team learning, anticipating the behavior of other agents is key to improving performance. In integrated learning, societal interaction issues between agents are considered.

6.2 Learning Coordination Behavior

Coordination can be learned as a behavior itself. For example, learning conventions and learning when to communicate can improve the outcome due to less interference and conflicts. Learning coordination behavior can occur offline in a centralized manner or concurrently online by each agent.

6.2.1 Coordination Rules

One of the inherent limitations of multi-agent systems is the restricted knowledge and view of its agents of the global situation which can be compensated by information sharing. Monitoring traces from the context-specific situations of the agents can be collected offline, consolidated into a global picture, and divided into positive and negative problem-solving instances depending on the global outcome of the application of a task (or action). A supervised learning method, such as decision-tree learning, can then be used to determine the information necessary to execute a task. For example, in a disaster management scenario, the urgency of a refueling task for a firetruck depends on the knowledge of the intensity of nearby fires, the number of other rescuers in the area, the wind direction, the level of fuel, etc. Learning the relevant variables in the application of each task that drive the overall outcome can produce coordination rules that will determine the context-specific situation to establish in order to instantiate a task. The determination of this context will drive the need for information sharing in a multi-agent system.

Coordination rules can be learned using feedback from other agents and the environment in a collective way assuming homogeneity and cooperation. In a reinforcement learning approach, the action selection problem is modeled as a Markov decision process (MDP) represented by the tuple $\{S,A,P,r\}$ where S represents the set of states, A represents the set of actions, P is the probability of going from state s_i to state s_j performing action a_i, and r is the reward obtained in state s_j. The goal is to learn a policy specifying the action to take in each state. In temporal difference learning methods such as Q-learning, the expected reward at the next step, modulated by a decay factor, constitutes the credit assignment used to update the utility of performing action a_i in state s_i. In classifier systems where rules are evolved with a genetic algorithm [9], it is the final outcome that is propagated back (with a decay factor) as the credit assignment to each state-action rule in the sequence of actions leading to it. Those two learning methods have been shown to be theoretically equivalent [10]. To avoid convergence problems due to the non-stationary environment of MAL, cooperative agents can bid on possible actions according to their action estimates [11] given their local context. The joint action set with the highest bid is executed and the sum of its bids propagated back to the actions of the previous joint action set to refine their estimates. Finding the maximum overall bid for an action set can be determined through distributed algorithms such as Adopt [12]. After a training phase, a policy can be learned by each agent that can be followed without additional communication overhead.

6.2.2 Conventions

In social systems, external mechanisms induce coordinated behaviors. For example, certain holidays coordinate the behavior of producers and consumers in the market without need for explicit communication. Similarly, agents can agree on certain conventions, based on common knowledge, to minimize conflicts and maximize gains without the added expense of communication. To learn conventions, agents must be homogeneous and cooperative, that is, the set of possible joint actions and transition functions must be commonly known and the agents must desire a global payoff (social maximum in game-theoretical terms) instead of an individual payoff. Conventions can be learned through incremental methods such as Bayesian learning where the probability of a best response leading to a coordinated joint action gets reinforced through the exploration of randomized strategies [13] in repeated play. In this approach, what is learned are the beliefs about the actions of the other agent(s) from which to construct a best response. In addition, as noted in [13], agents must recognize when to stop learning for conventions to emerge where actions are selected without deliberation and random fluctuations.

6.3 Team Learning

It is possible to achieve coordination by learning a team model instead of learning individual reactive behaviors in two ways. First, less interference will result by learning a team composition of behaviors and discovering the internal hierarchical structure of the task. In this approach coordination occurs by "growing" the behaviors together. Second, when a task decomposition is given, the problem becomes to learn to coordinate within that hierarchical abstract space.

6.3.1 Composition of Behaviors

Evolutionary algorithms offer offline and centralized solutions to the problem of learning team models. Complementary agent behaviors can be learned through co-evolution for cooperative tasks. In cooperative co-evolution [14], populations of specialized agents are evolved separately. The "best" of each population is then drafted to perform a cooperative task in an elitist fashion. The success of this task will readjust the fitness value of the agents in their respective population. This approach learns the needed component behaviors of a task by evolving single solutions modulated by coordinated solutions.

In swarm intelligence [15], experience shapes behavior by lowering response thresholds to stimuli from the environment. In turn, behavior also shapes experience by affecting the demands of the environment. A response threshold T is an adaptive reaction likelihood to perform an action (or task) as a function of the stimulus intensity s and tendency θ of an agent to perform the task. Several response threshold functions are possible. For example,

$$T_\theta(s) = \frac{s^n}{s^n + \theta^n}$$

where n is a constant parameter determining the steepness of the threshold. The stimulus intensity is then adjusted according to the relative proportion of active agents N_{act} in a population of N agents and learning rate α as follows:

$$s(t+1) = s(t) + \alpha \frac{N_{act}}{N}$$

In other words, the more an agent performs a task, perhaps due to local stimulus conditions, the more specialized it will become in this task in contrast to other tasks by adjusting its response threshold. This gives rise to a dynamic division of labor of heterogeneous "specialists" within a team of stochastically homogeneous agents. [1]

6.3.2 Role Conflicts

Case-based learning of situations where team members didn't perform according to expectation can improve the performance of single agent learners [16]. Here, an existing coordination strategy is adapted to prevent future conflicts by storing exceptions to the strategy. Heuristics or optimization techniques are not enough sometimes to disambiguate certain situations. For example, in the predator-prey domain where predators concurrently and independently decide which location to select (north, south, east, or west) in order to encircle the prey, a situation might require moving away from the prey to avoid collisions with other predators but a greedy strategy prevents predators from considering alternatives and yielding their place. Figure 6.2 illustrates the type of conflict that can arise in the predator-

---

[1] Homogeneous agents that have different parameter values initially determined stochastically according to a specific distribution.

prey domain [17] using constraint optimization agents [6] and Manhattan distance. Here, the predator immediately west of the prey is unable to move east of the prey without colliding with other predators to the north and south. A better alternative of equal cost would be for one of the predator located north or south of the prey to yield its place and to move east. To consider this alternative as an exception to the standard constraint optimization strategy, progression to the goal by the team needs to be monitored. In case of failure, a new case will be learned and a solution proposed for negotiation among the members of the team.

Figure 6.2: Conflict in the predator-prey domain

6.3.3 Hierarchical Approaches

Teamwork occurs at different abstract levels requiring different learning approaches to seamlessly work together. In the RoboCup soccer domain [18], the individual, multi-agent and team abstract hierarchical levels motivate a layered learning approach [19]. What and how to learn at each layer needs to be specified a priori by the programming of the task. The behavior learned at one layer constrains the behavior learned at the upper layer. At the individual level, a skill not requiring the participation of other team members is learned. For example, in robotic soccer, intercepting the ball and dribbling are individual behaviors. At the multi-agent level, skills requiring the participation of other team members are learned (e.g., how to pass the ball to another player). Those multi-agent skills assume that individual complementary skills, such as ball interception, are learned. Learning at this layer feeds into the upper team layer learning where strategic behaviors are learned through policy evaluation methods such as reinforcement learning. For example, the decision of whether to pass the ball or to make a goal takes into consideration results from the mid-level layer on the evaluation of possible passes. A layered learning approach addresses the issue of non-stationarity in MAL by learning individual behaviors separately from multi-agent and team level behaviors. This approach requires a careful design of the *a priori* task decomposition.

Hierarchical reinforcement learning is a temporal difference learning method that offers a unified incremental learning approach for team learning at different levels of abstraction [20]. In the theory of semi-Markov decision processes (SMDPs), rewards for high-level abstract actions of strategic behavior, such as those found at the upper levels of a task decomposition, are a function of the mean reward accrued by their underlying primitive temporal actions weighted by the probability of reaching their goal in t time steps [21]. Given a task decomposition, the MAXQ hierarchical reinforcement learning algorithm [20] combines the utility value returned by a subtask with the predictive utility value of the task. This algorithm seamlessly and incrementally composes tasks at different levels of abstraction.

6.4 Integrated Learning Techniques

Instead of directly learning coordination strategies, learning mechanisms for adjustable autonomy, incentives, negotiation, trust and reputation can help facilitate coordination among heterogeneous agents.

6.4.1 Trust

Learning who to interact with is essential in open multi-agent systems. Trust can overcome the uncertainty associated with the outcome of an encounter and sway the decision of an agent to cooperate. Trust is a socio-cognitive belief that can be learned from experience but also acquired indirectly from the experience of other agents through recommendations. There are many aspects to trust and in the context of enhanced coordination, trust as a belief entails (1) that an agent will do as proclaimed (competence), (2) that an agent will do as predicted (commitment with no deception) and (3) that an agent will reciprocate. Reciprocation is a necessary component of trust to achieve a common social payoff through cooperation while non-reciprocating behavior provides short-term higher payoffs. Experiments have shown the emergence of trust and reciprocating behaviors from interacting evolving agents in Prisoner's dilemma tournaments [22].

In addition to evolving trust implicitly through the evolution of coordination strategies such as tit-for-tat [22], trust can be learned socially as a trust function [23] for interacting with "trustworthy" agents. This trustworthiness attribute can be expressed through different values or labels l in applying the trust function. A trust function for a certain label l can be updated directly as a function of the interaction payoff P and learning rate $\alpha \in (0,1)$ as follows:

$$trust(l)[t] = (1 - \alpha)trust(l)[t-1] + \alpha P \frac{N_l}{N}$$

where N_l is the number of agents with label l and N is the total number of agents. In conjunction, agents learn when to use different behaviors corresponding to a specific label to gain the trust of other agents and maximize the global social payoff. Labels do not have any intrinsic meaning but become signals for selective learning. For example, outer appearance and non-verbal messages often constitute labels around which trust is formed. Trust is learned and groups are formed through interaction and the exchange of labels. As noted in [23], because agents can learn to use labels deceptively, there is no convergent solution in this approach.

6.4.2 Adjustable Autonomy

Learning when to transfer control of certain decisions, or adjustable autonomy, is a key issue in teams of heterogeneous agents that may include humans. Transfer of control can leverage from the unique expertise of the different agents but can incur coordination costs in delaying decisions. Similarly, mixed-initiative interaction provides a flexible way to harness the cognitive capabilities of the human-in-the-loop. The key control of transfer decisions involve knowing *when* to task for help, *when* to ask for more information, and *when* to inform the user of a decision. Learning mechanisms include the reinforcement learning of Markov decision processes maximizing the utility of control transfer decisions based on the overall coordination performance as well as expectations and preferences [24]. For example, a scheduling agent could autonomously decide to cancel a meeting if it thinks that somebody will be late rather than incurring coordination costs in waiting for a confirmation while people sit idle. However, if the meeting is important, it is not expected or desired that it be canceled. Because reinforcement learning takes into account delayed rewards, it can avoid taking the wrong action minimizing short-term costs.

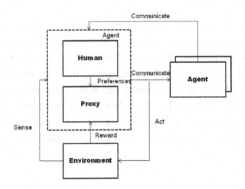

Figure 6.3: Coordination proxy system architecture with interactions from the
environment and with other agents

Coordination proxy agents are personal agents that take on the coordination
role on behalf of a human user (Figure 6.3) [25]. While coordination proxies
might prescribe optimal actions, switching tasks involves preferences such as loy-
alty, boredom and persistence thresholds. A learning approach for training coordination proxies in making decisions include the reinforcement learning of hierarchical abstract actions. Hierarchical abstract actions are high-level decisions, for
example a planning decision, that are implemented by several primitive actions
but are temporally abstract or "offline." Based on the theory of SMDPs, hierarchical abstract machines (HAMs) [26] addresses the issue of constraining a non-
deterministic finite state machine of primitive actions by specifying valid transitions through high-level decisions or choice points. Machine states superimpose to
environmental states to identify behavioral states and choice points. In the reinforcement learning of user preferences [27], coordination proxies learn whether to
interrupt their users by reducing the ambiguity of a goal selection at a choice
point. The intermediate reward r_c is obtained by similarity to a user decision at a
choice point while the discounted reward $\gamma_c r$ is obtained from the temporal MDP
upon reaching the goal selected. Figure 6.4 illustrates the application of HAMs for
coordination proxies in the prey/predator domain [27].

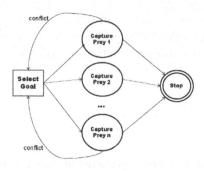

Figure 6.4: Prey/Predator HAM

6.5 Applications of Machine Learning Techniques for Coordination

Adaptive learning techniques have emerged in several application domains characterized by dynamic and uncertain environments.

6.5.1 Adaptive Routing

Routing algorithms for communication networks rely on information provided at each node by a routing table for transmitting packets to their destination. A routing table typically specifies the next node to select along with its cost in terms of transmission delay. Routing tables should be consistent among all nodes to avoid loops and should be dynamically updated as new nodes are brought up and old nodes fail or are congested. In distributed routing, local routing table information is shared among neighboring nodes until all nodes contain information on how to send packets to every other node.

In AntNet [28], a swarm intelligence approach based on the artificial ant colony paradigm [10] is used to update the routing tables in a distributed fashion. In this approach, mobile agents are dispatched from each network node to a random destination node in the network. Those agents traverse the network with a shortest path algorithm and added exploration so that alternative routes can be evaluated. In addition, they record the cost of each link and update the routing tables of the nodes traversed by returning to the source node along the same path. Those updates on the return trip are accumulated and aggregated much like the stigmergy process found in ant colonies whereby signals are embedded in the environment. With the help of those mobile agents, the network nodes collectively learn to maximize throughput. What is learned specifically are the probabilities to reach a destination node going through an intermediary node as a function of the associated trip time. In addition, probabilistic routing avoids congestion by using all probable good paths.

6.5.2 Robotics

As the deployment of robots is predicted to increase, the control of teams of robots has become a key issue. Self-organization through effective and robust coordination mechanisms to prevent collisions and interference between tasks reduces the amount of control necessary.

Adaptive coordination methods (without communication) in response to the environment were found to perform better than static methods [29]. Characteristics of the environment include group size, scenario type, uncertainty, etc. Machine learning techniques can be used for automatically tuning the parameters of heuristic coordination algorithms [30] or to automatically learn when to switch between heuristics. For example, one such coordination heuristic in robotics would be to move away from a teammate for a certain period of time. The size of the group was found to be a good indicator of the optimal amount of time required [29] for such a strategy. Evolutionary algorithms can search and optimize the parameter space of coordination algorithms by simulating their effect on relevant environmental conditions.

The ALLIANCE architecture [4] is a behavioral-based system for heterogeneous mobile robots applying multi-robot learning to control parameters. In this architecture, robots decide which task to perform based not only on the goals of the mission and environmental conditions, but also on their motivations for performing the task. Two such motivations are modeled: (1) impatience, whereby a robot takes up a task (possibly from another robot) and (2) acquiescence, whereby a robot gives up a task (possibly to another robot). The rate of impatience and acquiescence for a task characterizes different dynamic task allocation and reallocation strategies. Here, a scale factor by which to update those rates is learned by evaluating performance time first in a training phase and then in an adaptive phase. In the training phase, robots are experimenting with different behaviors and are maximally patient and minimally acquiescent. In an adaptive learning phase leading to lifelong learning, the rates of impatience and acquiescence guide the task allocation of robots and are continuously updated. The robots collectively learn to adjust to each other in the performance of tasks in a dynamic environment.

6.5.3 Intelligence, Surveillance, and Reconnaissance

The use of unmanned aerial vehicles (UAVs) to support intelligence, surveillance, and reconnaissance (ISR) has become a key enabler of network-centric operations to maintain situation awareness [31]. One key issue in teams of UAVs is the coordination of path planning to maximize surveillance.

Several metrics affect the optimization of coordinated paths such as track continuity, area coverage, idleness, cost, etc. Machine learning methods for the offline coordination of path planning include multi-objective, combinatorial optimization techniques such as evolutionary algorithms that can effectively search waypoint permutations and take into account constraints such as proximity to cell tower for communication purposes or safe distance from targets to escape detection [32]. Differential evolution [33] is an efficient technique for the evolution of waypoints as continuous values such as latitude-longitude or degree coordinates that replaces the traditional crossover technique of evolutionary algorithms. Differential evolution climbs the search space of possible solutions by exploiting differences in the population while exploring new solutions.

Environmental factors affect the traverse time of UAVs and therefore any offline route optimization has to incorporate a reactive component for replanning in mission-level tasks. ADAPTIV is a pheromone, swarm-based approach that provides a dynamic approach for the coordination of UAVs in the battlespace environment [34]. Its approach is to embed a swarm of heterogeneous interacting agents on sensor platforms. Digital pheromones, deposited by *place agents* on unattended ground sensors (UGSs), act as potential fields for guiding UAVs toward their targets while avoiding collisions and threats. Place agents exchange information between themselves while UAVs, *walker agents*, dynamically interact with UGSs to plan a path in real time.

This chapter was contributed by Myriam Abramson of the US Naval Research Laboratory.

References

1. Toshiharu Sugawara and Victor Lesser, "Learning Coordination Plans in Distributed Problem-solving Environments", In Twelfth International Workshop on Distributed Artificial Intelligence, 1993.
2. Tom Mitchell, "The Discipline of Machine Learning", Technical Report CMU-ML-06-108, Carnegie Mellon University, 2006.
3. Anita Raja and Victor Lesser, "Reasoning about Coordination Costs in Resource-bounded Multi-agent Systems", In Proceedings of the American Association for Artificial Intelligence (AAAI), 2004.
4. Lynn Parker, "L-ALLIANCE: Task-oriented Multi-robot Learning in Behaviour-based Systems", In Advanced Robotics, Special Issue on Selected Papers from IROS'96, pp. 305-322 , 1997.
5. Thomas H. Labella, Marco Dorigo, and Jean- Louis Deneubourg, "Efficiency and Task Allocation in Prey Retrieval", In Proceedings of the First International Workshop on Biologically

Inspired Approaches to Advanced Information Technology (Bio-ADIT2004), Lecture Notes in Computer Science, Springer Verlag, pp. 32-47, 2004.

6. Myriam Abramson, William Chao, and Ranjeev Mittu, "Design and Evaluation of Distributed Role Allocation Algorithms in Open Environments", In International Conference on Artificial Intelligence, 2005.

7. Yoav Shoham, Rob Powers, and Trond Grenager, "If Multi-agent Learning is the Answer, What is the Question?", In Artificial Intelligence Journal, Vol. 171, No. 7, pp. 365-377, 2007.

8. Peter Stone, "Multiagent Learning is not the Answer. It is the Question", In Artificial Intelligence Journal, Vol. 171, No. 7, pp. 402-405, 2007.

9. Sandip Sen and Mahendra Sekaran, "Multiagent Coordination with Learning Classifier Systems", In Proceedings of the Workshop on Adaption and Learning in Multi-Agent Systems at AAMAS, Springer Verlag, pp. 218-233, 2005.

10. Marco Dorigo and Hugues Bersini, "A Comparison of Q-learning and Classifier Systems, In Proceedings of From Animals to Animats", In Third International Conference on Simulation of Adaptive Behavior, MIT Press, pp. 248-255, 1994.

11. Gerhard Weiss, "Learning to Coordinate Actions in Multi-agent Systems", In Readings in Agents, Morgan Kaufmann Publishers Inc. pp. 481-486, 1997.

12. Pragnesh J. Modi, "An Asynchronous Complete Method for Distributed Constraint Satisfaction", In Autonomous Agents and Multiagent Systems (AAMAS), pp. 161-168, 2001.

13. Claus Boutilier, "Learning Conventions in Multiagent Stochastic Domains using Likelihood Estimates", In Proceedings of the Twelfth Conference on Uncertainty in Artificial Intelligence, pp. 106-114, 1996.

14. Mitchell A. Potter, and Kenneth A. D Jong, "Cooperative Coevolution: An Architecture for Evolving Coadapted Subcomponents", In Evolutionary Computation, Vol. 8, pp. 1-29, 2000.

15. Eric Bonabeau, Marco Dorigo, and Guy Theraulaz, "Swarm Intelligence: From Natural to Artificial Systems", Oxford University Press, USA, 1999.

16. Thomas Haynes, Kit Lau, and Sandip Sen, "Learning Cases to Compliment Rules for Conflict Resolution in Multiagent Systems", In Working Notes for the AAAI Symposium on Adaptation, Co-evolution and Learning in Multiagent Systems, AAAI Press, pp. 51-56, 1996.

17. M. Benda, V. Jagannathan, and R. Dodhiawalla, "On Optimal Cooperation of Knowledge Sources", Technical Report BCS-G2010-28, Boeing AI Center, Boeing Computer Services, 1985.

18. Hiroaki Kitano, Milind Tambe, Peter Stone, Manuela Veloso, Silvia Coradeschi, Eiichi Osawa, Hitoshi Matsubara, Itsuki Noda, and Minoru Asada, "The RoboCup Synthetic Agent Challenge 97", In Fifteenth International Join Conference on Artificial Intelligence, San Francisco, CA, Morgan Kaufmann, pp. 24-29, 1997.

19. Peter Stone, and Manuela Veloso, "Layered Learning", In Proceedings of the Eleventh European Conference on Machine Learning, Springer Verlag, pp. 369-381, 2000.

20. Tom G. Dietterich, "The MAXQ Method for Hierarchical Reinforcement Learning", In Proceedings of the Fifteenth International Conference on Machine Learning, Morgan Kaufmann, pp. 118-126, 1998.

21. Martin L. Putterman, "Markov Decision Processes", 2nd edn.,Wiley-Interscience, 2005.

22. Robert Axelrod, "The Evolution of Cooperation", Basic Books, 1984.

23. Andreas Birk, "Boosting Cooperation by Evolving Trust", Applied Artificial Intelligence, Vol. 14, pp. 769-784, 2000.

24. Milind Tambe, Paul Scerri, and David V. Pynadath, "Adjustable Autonomy for the Real World", In Proceedings of AAAI Spring Symposium on Safe Learning Agents, pp. 43-53, 2002.

25. Paul Scerri, David V. Pynadath, Nathan Schurr, Alessandro Farinelli, Sudeep Gandhe, and Milind Tambe, "Team Oriented Programming and Proxy Agents: The Next Generation", In Workshop on Programming MultiAgent Systems at AAMAS, 2004.

26. Ronald Parr, and Stuart Russell, "Reinforcement learning with Hierarchies of Machines", In Neural Information Processing Systems, 1998.

27. Myriam Abramson, "Training Coordination Proxy Agents using Reinforcement Learning", Technical report, Fall Symposium of the American Association of Artificial Intelligence (AAAI), 2006.
28. Gianni D. Caro and Marco Dorigo, "AntNet: Distributed Stigmergetic Control for Communications Networks", In Journal of Artificial Intelligence Research, No. 9, pp. 317-365, 1998.
29. Avi Rosenfeld, Gal Kaminka, and Sarit Kraus, "Adaptive Robot Coordination Using Interference Metrics", In Proceedings of The Sixteenth European Conference on Artificial Intelligence, 2004.
30. Jumpol Polvichai, Paul Scerri, and Michael Lewis, "An Approach to Online Optimization of Heuristic Coordination Algorithms", In Proceedings of the 7th Int. Conf. on Autonomous Agents and Multiagent Systems (AAMAS), 2008.
31. Myriam Abramson, Ranjeev Mittu, and Jean Berger, "Coordination Challenges and Issues in Stability, Security, Transition and Reconstruction (SSTR) and Cooperative Unmanned Aerial Vehicles", In International Conference on Integration of Knowledge Intensive Multi-Agent Systems (KIMAS), pp. 428-433, 2007.
32. Ionnis K. Nikolos, and A.N. Brintaki, "Coordinated UAV Path Planning using Differential Evolution", In Proceedings of the 13th Mediterranean Conference on Control and Automation, 2005.
33. Rainier Storn, and Kenneth Price, "Differential Evolution: a Simple and Efficient Adaptive Scheme for Global Optimization over Continuous Spaces", Technical Report TR-95-012, Berkeley, 1995.
34. H. Van Dyke Parunak, Sven Brueckner, and John Sauter, "Digital Pheromones Mechanisms for Coordination of Unmanned Vehicles", In Proceedings of the 1st Int. Conf. on Autonomous Agents and Multiagent Systems (AAMAS), 2002.

Chapter 7 Applications of Multi-agent Coordination

Abstract The purpose of this chapter is to describe the broad range of application domains which implement many of the coordination strategies and techniques from the field of multi-agent systems. The domains include defense, transportation, health care, telecommunication and e-business. The objective of this chapter is to describe the diversity of the applications in which multi-agent coordination techniques have been applied to overcome the challenges or obstacles that have existed with regard to performance, interoperability and / or scalability. While the number of application domains is steadily increasing, the intent of this chapter is to provide a small sampling of domains which are applying coordination techniques to build intelligent systems. This chapter will also describe an emerging and important problem domain which can benefit from multi-agent coordination techniques.

7.1 Introduction

This chapter provides an overview of the application domains in which multi-agent systems have been developed. The inherent distributed nature of these application domains reveals that benefits in performance or efficiency can be derived through the coordination between multiple agents. In other words, the collective behaviour of the system is improved through the coordinated interaction of their parts. In this chapter, we will cover applications from defence, transportation, health care, telecommunication and e-business.

From the defence sector, we will describe how multi-agent systems have been deployed to support course of action analysis through their ability to monitor the battlefield environment as depicted in command and control systems, and additionally by tapping into simulations are able to reason about deviations occurring in the movement of entities that are represented in command and control systems. We also describe a large multinational experiment in which hundreds of agents were federated in a simulated coalition scenario. From the transportation industry, multi-agent coordination techniques have been applied to manage and improve the overall efficiency of incoming aircraft. From the health care industry, distributed multi-agent system coordination concepts are emerging to support the monitoring and treatment of diabetic patients. In the area of communication networks, coordination techniques are being applied to diagnose faults in such networks through agents that are able to communicate and exchange local information in order to

A. Bedrouni et al., *Distributed Intelligent Systems: A Coordination Perspective*,   141
DOI: 10.1007/978-0-387-77702-3_7, © Springer Science + Business Media, LLC 2009

understand non-local problems. In another setting, coordination techniques are being applied to more efficiently route information in a communication network, utilizing auction mechanisms to purchase or sell commodities such as bandwidth on links and paths (with paths comprised of multiple links from source to destination). Lastly, an e-business application is described in the area of supply chain management, which incorporates Coloured Petri nets as a coordination mechanism between agents.

The chapter will also describe an emerging problem domain requiring the coordination of large teams that span the civil-military boundary, specifically during stability, security, transition and reconstruction operations. These operations require the coordination of the military with the civilian sector and non-governmental organizations in response to either natural or man-made disasters. The goal of these operations is to bring stability, enable rebuilding and provide security in order to maintain order during crisis situations. We will describe how multi-agent coordination techniques can provide tremendous value in these situations.

7.2 Defense

7.2.1 Simulation-C4I interoperability

As the complexity of modern warfare increases, managing and interpreting operational data will continue to be one of the greatest challenges to commanders and their staffs. The wealth of data collected and distributed via Command, Control, Communications, Computers and Intelligence (C4I) systems during battlefield operations is staggering. The ability to effectively identify trends in such data, and make predictions on battlefield outcomes in order to affect planning is essential for mission success. Future commanders will need to rely upon new information technologies to support their decision making processes.

Simulations have been used by analysis and planning staffs for years during exercises and operations. Typically, combat simulations are used most heavily during the planning stages of an operation, prior to execution. However, simulations are increasingly being used during operations to perform course of action analysis (COAA) and forecast future conditions on the battlefield. Recent efforts by the Defense Modeling and Simulation Office (DMSO) to improve the interoperability of C4I systems with simulations have provided a powerful means for rapid initialization of simulations and analysis during exercises, and have made simulations more responsive and useable during the execution portion of an exercise. Real-time interfaces between C4I systems such as the Global Command and

Control System (GCCS) and the Integrated Theater Engagement Model (ITEM) simulation have provided command staffs with the capability to perform faster, more complete, COAA.

As can be seen in Figure 7.1, intelligent agents, coupled to C4I systems and simulations, offer another technology to help commanders manage information on the battlefield. The Defense Advanced Research Projects Agency (DARPA) has sponsored the development of the Control of Agent-Based Systems (CoABS) Grid. The Grid is middleware that enables the integration of heterogeneous agent-

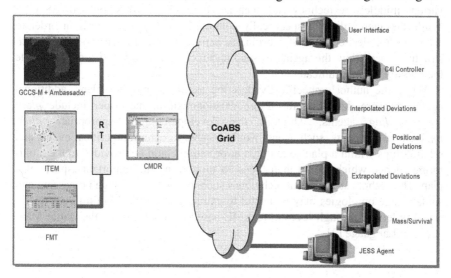

Figure 7.1: Federation of intelligent agents, C4I systems and simulations

based systems, object-based applications and legacy systems. The CoABS grid was used to develop the Critical Mission Data over Run-Time Infrastructure (CMDR) that allows dynamic discovery, integration and sharing of High Level Architecture (HLA) Run-Time Infrastructure (RTI) compliant simulation objects with legacy C4I systems and grid-aware software agents. The bridging of the CoABS grid and the HLA RTI using CMDR makes it possible to leverage the power of agent technology with the ability to tap into multiple C4I sources and simulation systems simultaneously. This synergy could lead to profound benefits in situation assessment and plan-execution monitoring using agents.

The key idea behind the capability as depicted in Figure 7.1 was to present the intelligent agents with real (notional) and simulated battlefield information, so that these agents can analyze both streams of data in order to understand and provide alerts when the notional battlefield information has changed as compared to the information contained in the data stream coming from the simulation [1]. Several types of agents were developed to check for positional deviations in the battlefield entities using the simulated data as ground truth, using extrapolation and interpolation techniques. Extrapolation techniques were needed to project the entity's real reported position when the entity's reported time was less than the reporting time of that entity in the simulation in order to compare any changes to position at the same instance of time. Similarly, interpolation techniques were used when the entity's real reported position time was greater than the reporting time of that entity in the simulation. An additional mass monitoring agent was responsible for detecting deviations in combat worth (number and value of assets) based on thresholds defined in the original plan in the simulation.

This example demonstrates end-to-end system level coordination, facilitated by various middleware technologies such as HLA RTI, CMDR and CoABS grid. While the agents did not specifically communicate with each other in order to achieve some desired level of coordinated activity within the federation, the infrastructure does allow the agents to send and receive messages in order to enable their ability to communicate.

While the author's specifically describe agents to monitor plans, additional agents that are described for future development in the paper include *plan-understanding* agents. Through the development of appropriate *plan-understanding* agents, such agents would be able to determine critical events and relationships within a plan so that this information could be provided to the monitoring agents, which would then focus on monitoring the important aspects of a plan. The authors suggest that techniques such as natural language processing and sublanguage ontologies may be useful to extract key events from military operational orders or through leveraging XML-based techniques such the Battle Management Language [2].

7.2.2 Coalition Interoperability

Coalition operations are characterized by data overload, concerns regarding with whom to share information, dealing with security issues and the need to overcome the stovepipe nature of systems -- all of which contribute to the challenges in achieving coalition interoperability. The goal of the Coalitions Agents Experiment (CoAX) was to demonstrate that coordination through multi-agent techniques could provide the mechanism to improve interoperability between systems. The CoAX [3] was an international effort between the Defense Advanced Research Projects Agency (DARPA), Defense Science Technology Office (DSTO), Defense Scientific Technical Laboratory (DSTL), and The Technical Cooperation Program (TTCP). The CoAX participants included defense laboratories from around the world, industry as well as academia, which were brought together under the CoAX to demonstrate the value of multi-agent systems to support the ability to rapidly construct and maintain a coalition Command and Control structure. The experiment leveraged investment from the DARPA Control of Agent-based Systems (CoABS) program, specifically the CoABS grid framework.

In the fictional CoAX scenario, two countries, Agadez and Gao, are in dispute over the territory of Binni, with Agadez becoming increasingly desperate over the territory. Because of this desperation, the country of Agadez launches a submarine-based missile strike against an Australian ship in the Red Sea. This strike injures many on board and damages critical capabilities on the ship, including the Magnetic Anomaly Detection systems (MAD detectors). As the coalition becomes aware of the strike and subsequent damage, mobile medical monitoring agents are dispatched to the ship to collect injury reports contained in medical databases. From these reports, agents are able to work cooperatively to schedule the evacuation of those critically injured. A neutral country on the eastern coast of the Red Sea, Arabello, agrees to offer its ASW (Anti-Submarine Warfare) capabilities to help track down and neutralize the Agadez submarines. These ASW capabilities are rapidly integrated with the coalition systems already in place via agent technology, and expeditiously begin to provide contact reports on possible positions of the Agadez submarines.

In the context of the scenario, the goals of CoAX were to demonstrate that stovepipe barriers could be overcome across systems. For instance, through techniques such as policy enforcement to bind the behavior of the agents in accordance with the coalition partner's requirements, some form of trust could be achieved. For instance, services provided through the Knowledgeable Agent-Oriented System (KaOS) [4] assured that the agents would follow certain operating policies. The CoABS grid infrastructure provided the agents with registry, communication and logging services. There were dozens of agents that were developed and integrated using the CoABS grid in support of the scenario. In one particular instance within the scenario, the agents must deconflict air plans, and this is accomplished through a multi-level coordination agent. This agent is built upon the notion of sharing plans that are represented hierarchically, and through the upward propagation of the conditions that hold true and the timing constraints between sub-plans, relationships between sub-plans at different levels of abstraction can be identified. Hence, agents can share these various subplans with each other at the appropriate level of detail in order to coordinate their activities. In summary, some of the goals of CoAX were to demonstrate that semantic web technologies could support interoperability between agents, an agent infrastructure (CoABS grid) could be used to rapidly integrate a diverse set of agents by providing support for communications and message logging, and that domain policies such as KaOS could lead to an ability to place a bound on the agents' behavior, which could eventually lead to trust relationships to be formed between the users and multi-agent system.

7.3 Transportation

7.3.1 Air Traffic Flow Management

Air traffic congestion is a world-wide problem leading to delays as well as sub-sequent monetary loss to the commercial flight industry. The ability to either manage the flow of traffic more efficiently or improve the infrastructure (e.g., adding more runways) to increase capacity are two available mechanisms to improve the efficiency of commercial aviation. Given the fact that increasing the capacity through improvements to the infrastructure is a costly and very time consuming solution, information technologies may be useful for efficiently managing the traffic flow.

The Optimal Aircraft Sequencing using Intelligent Scheduling (OASIS) [5] is an intelligent agent-based system which is able to ingest data from Sydney Airport at the rate of 65 aircraft arriving in 3.5 hours. It is designed to assist the Flow Director in arranging the sequencing of incoming aircraft through intelligent agents that represent the aircraft and supporting global agents. The aircraft agents are responsible for predicting aircraft trajectories, monitoring the actual movement versus predicted to understand discrepancies, and engaging in planning activities. The global agents consist of a coordinator agent, sequencer agent, trajectory manager agent, wind model agent and user interface agent. The coordinator agent is the central node for interacting with all of the other agents in the system. The sequencer agents uses search techniques based on the $A*$ search algorithm to determine the arrival sequence which minimizes delay and overall cost. The trajectory manager agent ensures that aircraft maneuvers do not violate statutory separation requirements. The wind model agent is responsible for computing and providing the forecast winds based on the reported wind by the aircraft agents. Lastly, the user interface agent is the mechanism by which the flow director receives information from the system.

The planner agents accept a schedule time from the sequencing agent and decide how to execute that plan to meet a given schedule, and these agents must monitor the actual movement against the plan and be able to predict the trajectory. If there are discrepancies, the aircraft agent must notify the global agents so that another sequence may be computed. The coordination between agents is facilitated through communication of their activities using the Procedural Reasoning System (PRS). The PRS system is an agent-based framework for agents to coordinate their activities with each other based on the Belief, Desires and Intention (BDI) model. The PRS framework is comprised of knowledge bases that contain agent beliefs as represented through first order logic, agent's goals or desires, a library of plans and a reasoning engine. Depending on the agent's beliefs and desires, the appropriate plans are triggered for execution, which in turn affect the environment.

The OASIS system is compared against COMPAS, MAESTRO and CTAS. The COMPAS system is developed for the German Civil Aviation Authority to provide flow control. It has been pointed out that the key difference between COMPAS and OASIS is that the former only handles single runway sequences and the aircraft's progress is not monitored. The MAESTRO system is developed for the French Civil Aviation Authority. Similarly to COMPAS, MAESTRO only considers a single runway, but does provide aircraft monitoring capabilities to provide a comparison of the progress against the plan. The CTAS is being developed by NASA-AMES for the US Federal Aviation Administration, and is described as more complex than either MAESTRO or COMPASS.

7.4 Healthcare

7.4.1 Monitoring Glucose Levels

The ability to carefully monitor blood sugar levels is critical in the essential care of diabetes, which can lead to serious health problems and even death if not treated in a timely manner. A prototype application called the Integrated Mobile Information System (IMIS) for diabetic healthcare is described in [6]. The IMIS demonstrates how multi-agent coordination can be leveraged to support critical collaboration between healthcare providers in the Swedish health care industry in support of monitoring diabetic patients.

Two types of problems are identified in [6] with regard to the proper care of diabetic patients, that of accessibility and interoperability. The accessibility problem is further categorized as physical service accessibility and information accessibility. The former implies that medical resources should be available to all healthcare providers while the latter implies that the appropriate information must be available from those resources. The key challenge identified in the diabetic healthcare system in one specific province, Blekinge, is due to a gap in information accessibility across the municipality and county council, each of which is responsible for various aspects of healthcare. For example, the municipality is responsible for the elderly, disabled or non-medical healthcare while the county council is responsible for medical and surgery related care. The various medical records cannot generally be shared between county council and municipality. The interoperability problem is one of overcoming the various forms in which the information is stored; in other words, there is a need for an information sharing standard to enable semantic interoperability.

The IMAS system is a multi-agent system that enables coordination between agents through acts of communication, in order to provide decision support to the human actors to support their collaborative activities. It was developed from the IMIS system and supports the collection and manipulation of healthcare information, and subsequent presentation of that information to the human actors based on their preferences in order to help them better collaborate. Three collaboration levels are identified in this specific problem domain: *Glucose management, Calendar arrangement* and *task delegation*. Glucose management involves providing the healthcare actors, perhaps through a centralized database, with the right information so that they can take the appropriate actions. Calendar arrangement includes the ability to schedule patient visits, while task delegation involves the ability of the healthcare providers or software agents to take certain actions (and the ability to report on the completion of those actions) based on the diagnosis.

There are four types of agents implemented in the IMAS system: *PatientAgent, ParentAgent, HospitalNurseAgent* and *SchoolNurseAgent*. These agents act on behalf of their user's preferences in order to better coordinate their activities through the communication of appropriate information (e.g., glucose levels). For example, in the scenario described in the paper [6], if a young boy (named Linus) has an elevated sugar level which is detected by the *PatientAgent* through readings from a database (which is updated by Linus via the IMAS patient control panel installed on his mobile device), then a message will be sent to the *ParentAgent* and *SchoolNurseAgent* to give Linus an insulin shot. When the alarm is received by the *ParentAgent,* this agent will search for additional information or charts to present to the mother, who will take the appropriate action. The IMAS system was implemented using the Java Agent Development Environment (JADE) and uses an ontology as well as the Foundation for Intelligent Physical Agents (FIPA) Agent Communication Language (ACL). The FIPA ACL is based on speech act theory.

Future areas for investigation include techniques to ensure the privacy of the information so that only the right individuals or agents have access, and also the necessity to properly deal with the security of the information that is being transmitted so that it cannot be altered by third parties.

7.5 Communication Networks

7.5.1 Fault Diagnosis

As with any communication network, telecommunications networks are inherently distributed with expertise and data residing throughout various nodes of the network, hence, the management of the network requires access to, and analysis of, data that resides in various parts of the network. Due to the distributed nature of these networks, monitoring and diagnosing faults can benefit from a distributed approach as can be offered through multi-agent system techniques. The Distributed Intelligent Monitoring and Analysis System (DIMAS) is described in [7], which builds upon the more centralized Intelligent Monitoring and Analysis System for monitoring and diagnosing faults. Specifically, the paper describes a distributed architecture based on a multi-agent approach for monitoring and detecting faults in cellular communication networks.

The problem which is described in the paper consists of monitoring and detecting faults across cellular base stations. Since multiple base stations may use the same frequency for communication due to the limited number of frequencies available, this has the effect of increasing the capacity of the network. Interference of frequencies across base stations is minimized by limiting the coverage and strength of the radio signal at each base station. However, in certain cases, natural phenomena such as winds or storms can cause the base station antenna to misalign. Such as misalignment can cause the frequencies to interfere, thereby affecting other nearby base stations by causing "noise" on the frequencies which overlap.

The DIMAS system is applied to monitoring this problem and diagnosing which base station is causing the frequency interference. The DIMAS system is comprised of a data store, data filter and expert system which is interfaced to a network simulator. The data store contains information obtained from the network, the data filter enables the processing of a large amount of information, and the expert system is the engine used to provide the diagnostic capabilities based on information obtained from the data store. The expert system in DIMAS is built on the AT&T C5 language, and its workflow processes through a series of steps: *monitor symptoms, reply to queries, do actions, analyze results, analyze evidence* and *decide next step*.

The authors also differentiate the DIMAS system with other related work. For example, they compare DIMAS to Distributed Big Brother (DBB). The DBB uses the Contract Net Protocol to distribute the monitoring task to Local Area network managers. However, within DIMAS, rather than offering tasks to potential bidders and then awarding the task to one bidder, the DIMAS agents are asked whether they can suggest possible actions to diagnose a problem. The suggested actions are then evaluated by the temporary owner of a problem and then contracted out to the agent that suggested the action. For example, each agent that detects a symptom of a problem may suggest further diagnostic tests, such as checking for changes to base station parameters or monitoring the signal strength of call attempts. However, for each action there is only one agent that can execute it. The decision that must be made by the coordinating agent is which action to choose, rather than which agent will execute that action. The subtle difference is that in DIMAS, the contracting is action-centric and not agent-centric, as a series of actions may be spread over multiple agents.

The Large-internetwork Observation and Diagnosis Expert System (LODES) is an expert system for diagnosing faults in a LAN that consists of multiple networks connected via routers. Each LAN has its own LODES system, which is used to detect remote faults based on local data. The primary difference between LODES and DIMAS is that the latter is a passive approach while the former is both passive as well as active (e.g., proactively sending test packets).

In DIMAS, the agents can only observe local symptoms and / or faults. Coordination between the agents is facilitated through the use of communication using KQML performatives such as *ask, tell* and *achieve* to gather non-local information. These performatives are used in various phases of the agent's process such as *assign-responsibility, gather-evidence* and *allocate-blame*. In the *assign-responsibility* phase, the problem is detected using the *ask* and *tell* performatives. The base station at which the symptom is detected uses the *ask* performative to query the other base station agents about possible causes for increase in calls with poor transmission quality (frequency interference), while the other base stations use the *tell* peformative to report back as to the fact that the cause may be due to a misaligned antenna or a frequency change. The affected base station agent then uses the *achieve* performative to ask the other base station agents to check for changes in frequency within their logs (*gather-evidence*). When this is ruled out, then more expensive requests are made such as checking for conditions which are indicative of a misaligned antenna. The *allocate-blame* phase assigns responsibility to the offending base station, and communicates its findings to other base stations.

7.5.2 Routing

A market-based approach to routing in telecommunication networks using a multi-agent system model is described in [8]. It is argued that a market-based approach requires no *a-priori* cooperation between agents and provides a robust mechanism for routing. Specifically, the approach relies on an adaptive price setting and inventory strategy based on bidding in order to reduce call blocking. The approach relies on several layers of agents, specifically, link agents that interact in link markets to purchase slices of bandwidth, path agents that interact in path markets to sell paths and on link markets to buy necessary links in order to offer paths on the path market, and lastly the call agents. Each of these agents buys or sells their commodity on the appropriate market.

The author compares the market based approach to routing with other approaches. For example, in a centralized scheme where traffic predictions are used to compute the paths there are issues with scalability particularly as the size of the network grows, the amount of information to monitor and process also increases and there is a single point of failure. Similarly, the authors argue that in optimal network flow algorithms there are performance issues in heavily loaded networks and unpredictable oscillations between solutions. Hence, the author suggests that a decentralized solution may be appropriate. However, the authors also describe a few challenges in decentralized solutions. For instance, they indicate that such solutions may have non-local effects on the entire network and it would be difficult to understand these effects due to the lack of complete information about the entire network. Complete information is infeasible since the network is dynamic and there is a delay in propagation and therefore the solution is prone to error and there may also be scaling issues.

As previously mentioned, the system architecture is comprised of link agents, path agents and call agents, each operating on one or several markets. A link agent and path agent is associated with each link and path, respectively, in the network. A call agent is associated with each source and destination pair in the network. Link and path markets are sealed bid double blind auctions in order to minimize any delays in the system, as callers will not want a delay in establishing a circuit in the network. The agents buy and sell the appropriate resource for which they are responsible, and depending on what they have sold and / or purchased, they use a simple function in order to either increase or decrease their buying / selling price. Similarly, path agents maintain an inventory that is profitable. Lastly, call agents trigger the auctions at the path and link agent level.

The authors present various results from their experiments. In the first experiment, they compare Vickery and First price auction strategies in their market-based approach to static routing on a 200 node network with link capacities for 200 channels. They show that they can do at least as well as static routing, but with the added advantage of achieving the performance level through an open architecture without the need to rely on static network policies. They demonstrate improved scalability through their approach, since the entire network topology need not be known in advance and, furthermore, using their approach are able to provide a quicker response as information is not needed about the broader network. The authors also provide results that demonstrate that about 61% of the time, the call was routed through the most efficient route and 46% of the time the call was routed through the least congested route. Research areas that are left for future work include the ability of the callers to request different types of services, which might be routed differently through the network and the ability for market-based routing to support such activities.

7.6 E-Business

7.6.1 Supply Chain Management

A supply chain is described in [9] as "*a network of suppliers, factories, ware-houses, distribution centers and retailers through which raw materials are acquired, transformed, reproduced and delivered to the customer*". A Supply Chain Management System (SCMS) manages the interaction of these processes in order to achieve desired end goals.

The paper in [9] describes a SCMS based on the coordination of multi-agent systems, as represented through information agents and functional agents. The information agents are a source of information to the functional agents (for example, they provide a registry of other agents available in the system), while the functional agents are responsible for specific roles in the dynamic supply chain. The key notion behind these agents is that there is no assumption that a certain number of agents be available in the supply chain. The agents are assumed to enter and leave the system through a negotiation process based on the negotiation performatives that have been developed within the FIPA community. For example, *accept-proposal, CFP, proposal, reject-proposal* and *terminate* are used for pair-wise negotiation between agents while a third performative, *bid*, has also been included to capture third party negotiations as, for example, through an auctioneer.

The paper further describes the use of Colored Petri Nets (CPN) as a modeling tool for managing the negotiation process between agents. A simple example of the interaction between buyer and seller agents is described through the use of CPNs. The buyer agent initiates the negotiation process by sending a message indicating a *call-for-proposal* from the seller agent. The buyer agent then waits, while the seller agent receives the message for consideration. When the seller agent sends the reply (proposal, accept-proposal, reject-proposal or terminate) to the buyer agent, the buyer agent then enters the waiting or thinking / inactive state. If the thinking transition is triggered, the cycle repeats and it is up to the buyer agent to send the next round of message. The paper also describes the internal logic of the functional agents in making decisions by providing an example of an agent that represents a company's need for a certain quantity of supplies in a given time period. This company is represented through an agent that sends a CFP message to other agents. The other agents evaluate the CFP and provide the quantity of supplies that can be provided, their cost and lead time. After receiving the other agents offers the initiating agent constructs a search tree for evaluating the constraints. If a solution can be found, then the initiating agent will accept one or more offers. If a solution cannot be found, either the initiating agent will relax its constraints, or ask the other agents to relax their constraints.

Several key issues are described for future research, including understanding of the convergence behavior of the network and strategies for deciding how and when to relax the agent constraints.

7.7 Stability Operations and Disaster Relief

The emergence of new doctrine is enabling Security, Stabilization, Transition and Reconstruction (SSTR) operations to become a core U.S. military mission. These operations are now given equal priority to combat operations. The immediate goal in SSTR is to provide the local populace with security, restore essential services, and meet humanitarian needs. The long-term goal is to help develop indigenous capacity for securing and maintaining essential services. Therefore, many SSTR operations are best performed by indigenous groups with support from foreign agencies and professionals. Large scale disasters, however, are an example where military support can improve SSTR operations by providing a much needed boost to foreign governments and nongovernmental organizations which may already be under great stress to respond in a timely and effective manner. However, without the means to effectively coordinate the efforts between many diverse groups across the civil-military boundary during SSTR operations, basic assistance and relief operations may be severely impeded.

Many SSTR operational tasks are best performed by indigenous groups, with support from foreign or U.S. civilian professionals. Complex disasters are an example where military involvement and support for SSTR operations can provide significant value to foreign governments and non-governmental organizations (NGOs) which may already be under great stress to respond in a timely and effective manner. The command and control structure, resources and assets that the military can offer in such situations can shorten the response timeline. However, without the means to properly coordinate the efforts of such a large and diverse group which spans the civil-military boundary, basic assistance and relief operations may be severely impacted, leading to delays or waste in the overall response cycle.

There are many operational challenges in the ability to coordinate such a large group across the civil-military boundary during SSTR operations. Usually, in the civil sector, coordination is the result of voluntary effort; hence coordination by "directing" is rarely effective. Generally, relief agencies partly function within a framework of self-interest. In other words, they assist their beneficiaries in such a way that their good works are seen and valued by the donor community and the "profile" of their agency is enhanced. In many cases, farther down on the list is the goal of recognizing the contribution of others or admitting someone else can do the job better and therefore coordination with other agencies is not necessarily an agencies first priority. With regard to coordination across the civil-military boundary there are also a number of challenges. The military tends to be a highly structured organization with hierarchical command and control, while the civil sector in many cases is more loosely structured and tends to be less formal. These kinds of functional divisions can be confusing for each side involved in the coordination efforts. Furthermore, in the interest of national security, the military may be inclined to withhold certain information, while at the same time they may see it as the obligation of the civilian sector to provide as much information as possible. Hence, without adequate information exchange, coordination can become problematic.

With the signing of the Department of Defense Directive (DoDD) 3000.05, *Military Support for Security, Stabilization, Transition and Reconstruction (SSTR) Operations* into policy, SSTR operations have become a core U.S. military mission that the Department of Defense (DoD) must be prepared to conduct and support. These operations are now given equal priority to combat operations and there is now a greater opportunity to overcome these fundamental cultural barriers and issues in order to move in the direction of proactive coordination. Therefore, the scientific research community must help to identify the types of technologies that would be useful in order to provide decision support capabilities in order to enable better coordination within the civilian sector, as well as across the civil-military boundary. It is the view of the authors that there are several potential areas that are worthy of exploration.

Understanding emerging social networks and using the information that is provided through such networks is important for effective coordination. Social networks provide a visual cue as to the relationships between people or groups and can be used to identify "mutual" friends. This is particularly important when there is a requirement by one or more individual or groups to locate other individuals or groups that might be able to provide support in order to achieve a desired end result. Research and tools from the Social Network Analysis (SNA) community may allow users to understand who the experts are in the SSTR community and to whom and how they are linked. As a simple example, social maps that depict connectivity between users based on their discussion threads, and an ability to filter the content within a social map based on specific keywords are likely to provide the foundation to enable the community to identify service providers or those that may offer similar services or support capabilities. The ability to rate individuals within the social network may also be an important aspect in building trust within the community of users. This is particularly important during pre-disaster situations (i.e., prior to any crisis situation) so that some level of trust and common understanding can be achieved. Furthermore, pre-disaster interactions can help in the development of concept of operations or doctrine to provide guidance during real life situations by helping people or organizations form the bonds of working together. One of the challenges, however, will be to effectively visualize such a network or efficiently filter through the various dimensions of information contained in the social network.

There is also a lack of automated coordination tools to support the ability of people or groups to actively coordinate their activities. There are processes in place but most coordination is manual. The ability to manage tasks across the diverse actors involved in these operations has the opportunity to improve the overall efficiency of these operations. Due to the complexity of SSTR operations, multi-agent coordination techniques may provide benefits.

There is already ongoing research into developing information sharing environments to be used during SSTR operations within which automated coordination tools could be developed. These environments leverage content management systems and web 2.0 technologies to integrate various collaboration mechanisms such as weblogs, wiki's and forums. One of the key uses of such sites would be to enable service requestors to find service providers during crisis situations. As potential service providers are identified from the information sharing site's content, additional techniques could be developed and applied to transform and map the services that are being requested (again, from content posted on the site) into appropriate tasks. These tasks would be defined by appropriate users of the information sharing environment, and when executed, would enable the requested services to be fulfilled by the service providers (aka, task performers). The tasks may be hierarchical or peer-to-peer. For instance, hierarchical tasks may be appropriate for the military as protocols tend to be very structured and organized, while tasks for the civilian side may be peer-to-peer. However, the determination and selection of the appropriate task representation is best handled locally and there is no strict requirement that organizations use one representation or the other.

In order to automate task scheduling and assignment to a degree, the tasks and potential task performers might be organized into an assignment matrix, and the entries in the matrix would contain numerical values that represent the cost for doing each of the tasks across each of the performers (Figure 7.2). The costs may be monetary or may be based on a more complex cost function and it is up the participants to agree upon and choose the appropriate cost model. The computation of the cost functions across performers may vary, so some normalization techniques may need to be applied. Once these costs are determined, the goal of the matching algorithm would be to find a set of assignments between tasks and performers in the matrix that globally minimizes the total cost of doing the tasks across all of the performers. Alternatively, numerical values for preference could be included instead of cost in the assignment matrix, and the objective would be to find a set of assignments that globally maximize the preferences.

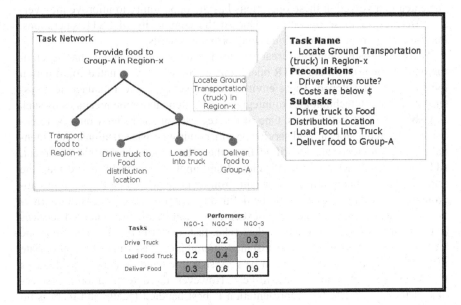

Figure 7.2: Task Assignment Concept

The task network would provide a visualization of the tasks and allow the user to modify the tasks or include new tasks, which would be subsequently reflected in the assignment matrix. The task network would also allow the specification of preconditions that need to be true before a task or subtask can be executed. The assignments that are calculated would update the task network to show which performers have been assigned to various tasks. Multi-agent coordination techniques could be employed to support a negotiation process to allow the performers to interact with each other to change their tasks assignments for various reasons that might not have been accurately reflected in the cost functions. The negotiation process could be facilitated, for example, through various coordination techniques that were described in earlier chapters. Such a negotiation would be pursued until task equilibrium is reached. Once equilibrium is reached, the passing of appropriate messages using any method chosen by the user (e.g., instant messaging, SMS, e-mail, etc.) would permit the transmission of the assignments to potential responders for action or renegotiation.

The conduct of SSTR operations may occur in critically damaged areas with degraded or no infrastructure (e.g., transportation, communication, etc) which presents a challenge in SSTR operations. We focus our discussion on the communications infrastructure. The ability to coordinate a large and diverse group of first responders begins with the ability to communicate guidance or orders, while receiving situation reports from those in the field. The lack of a stable communications infrastructure will negatively impact the efforts of those that need to coordinate and share information. Recent technological advances in Mobile Ad-Hoc

Networks (MANET) are key enablers in the deployment of net-centric cooperative multi-agent systems in disaster areas. MANET technology holds the promise of enabling communications between first responders when the local communications infrastructure is unusable. These networks support mobile entities, connected through a wireless network which supports discovery and self-organization through peer-to-peer message exchanges, leading to an increase in the robustness of the overall network. A comparison of MANET with the mainstream internet and high performance networks can be seen in the Table 7.1.

Table 7.1: Characteristics of Various Networks		
High Performance Networks	**The Mainstream internet**	**Mobile Ad-Hoc Networks**
Stable Infrastructure	Mixed range of assets	Ad-hoc assets
Fiber-optic/High speed RF/wireless optical	Mixed-media	Generally Wireless
Highest bandwidth	Tending to higher bandwidth	Design for degraded operation
Low latency	Over provisioned	Large variability in latency and bandwidth
Connection-oriented links	Low-to-high latency	Highly dynamic routing
Policy-based Quality of Service (QoS)	Table-based routing	More distributed network service models required
	Mixed policies in forwarding and QoS	Change is the norm

Although MANET technology is advancing to enable connectivity between mobile users, there still may be circumstances in which users get disconnected (examples such as distance between users or the affects of the environment on signal propagation). In order to improve the overall success of the deployment of MANET, new approaches and techniques that enable users to communicate to the maximum extent possible utilizing whatever network bandwidth is available will be needed.

The concept of "*NETwork-Aware*" Coordination and Adaptation is a potential area worthy of exploration. In such an approach, the users or applications are aware of the state of the network, thereby allowing the applications to adapt in order to "work around" network constraints, while the network is aware of the state of the applications or mission needs in order to better handle or prioritize traffic flows. Such cross-layer information exchange is important to enable a more robust communication strategy for the first responders in order to support their coordination activities. To the extent possible, coordination strategies also have to be robust against message loss and equipment failures.

A few of the research issues in network-aware coordination include defining measures for determining network congestion or other types of failures such as loss of connectivity within the network, in order to provide such measures and parameters to the multi-agent applications. The key challenges for the application layer include how to best utilize that information in order to adapt communication strategies (e.g., sharing images that are smaller in size, prioritizing certain information, or identifying certain nodes to act as communications relays).

7.8 Tiered Systems

A key enabler of a sustainable military force is the notion of a tiered system (Figure 7.3). A tiered system is an integrated, multi-tier intelligence system encompassing space and air-based sensors linked to close-in and intrusive lower tiers [10]. The lower tiers (e.g., UAVs) are not only the critical source of intelligence; they can also serve as a key cueing device for other sensors. There is active research and exploration within the US DoD to understand the technical challenges in building tiered systems. It should be noted that tiered-system components such as UAVs or space-based assets are not only useful for ISR activities supporting more traditional combat operations, but may also enable effective SSTR operations.

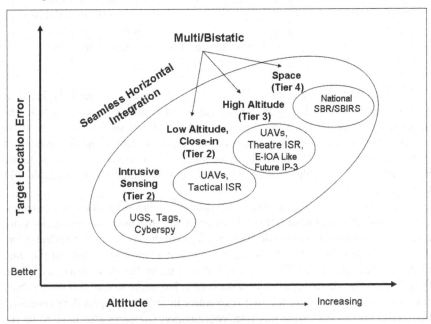

Figure 7.3: Future Tiered ISR system [10]

Given the diversity of the assets, and the fact that coordination must be achieved both in the horizontal and vertical planes, and the environments in which the components of a tiered system will operate; it is not likely that a single coordination approach or even a static family of coordination approaches would work in all scenarios. It is more reasonable to expect that systems should learn which approaches work well and under which circumstances, and adapt appropriately.

It is commonly recognized that many different disciplines can contribute to a better understanding of the coordination function as a way to build and provide appropriate tools and adequate approaches for designing complex organizations and systems. Agents incorporated into these self-regulating entities represent "communities of concurrent processes which, in their interactions, strategies, and competition for resources, behave like whole ecologies". This chapter has described a diverse set of application domains in which coordination of multi-agent systems has improved, or has the potential to improve, the behavior of the overall system. A common characteristic of these applications is their highly distributed nature.

References

1. Ranjeev Mittu, Myriam Abramson, Joshua Walters, Improving Simulation Analysis through Interfaces to Command Control Communications Computer and Intelligence (C4I) Systems and Use of Intelligent Agents. *Proceedings of the 2004 Spring Simulation Interoperability Workshop (SIW)*
2. Scott Carey, Martin Kleiner, Mike Heib, Richard Brown. Standardizing Battle Management Language – Facilitating Coalition Interoperability. Proceedings of the 2002 Euro Simulation Interoperability Workshop (SIW),
3. Ranjeev Mittu, Frank Segaria, Suleyman Guleyupoglu, Suzanne Barber,Tom Graser, Robert Ross. Supporting the Coalition Agents Experiment (CoAX) through the Technology Integration Experiment (TIE) Process", Proceedings of the 8th International Command and Control Research and Technology Symposium (ICCRTS), National Defense University, Washington, DC. 17-19 July 2003
4. P. Feltovich, J.M. Bradshaw, R. Jeffers, A. Uszok. Order and KAoS: Using policy to represent agent cultures. Proceedings of the AAMAS 03 Workshop on Humans and Multi-Agent Systems. Melbourne, Australia, 2003
5. Magnus Ljungberg and Andrew Lucas. The OASIS Air Traffic Management System. Proceedings of the Second Pacific Rim International Conference on Artificial Intelligence (PRICAI '92).
6. Peng Zhang, Guohua Bai, Bengt Carlsson, Stefan J. Johansson. The International Conference on Information & Communication Technologies: from Theory to Applications - ICTTA'08, Damascus, Syria, 2008.
7. Chris Leckie, Rye Senjen, Belinda Ward, Ming Zhao. "Communication and Coordination for Intelligent Fault Diagnosis Agents." In Proceedings of the Eighth IFIP/IEEE International Workshop for Distributed Systems Operations and Management (DSOM'97), Sydney, Australia, 21-23 October 1997, pp. 280-291.
8. M.A. Gibney, N.R. Jennings, N.J. Vriend, J.M. Griffiths. Intelligent Agents for Telecommunication Applications --- Proceedings of the Third International Workshop on Intelligent Agents for Telecommunication (IATA'99)
9. Ye Chen, Yun Peng. Tim Finin, Yannis Labrou. Scott Cost, Bill Chu, Jian Yao, Rongming Sun, Bob Wilhelm. A Negotiation-based Multi-agent System for Supply Chain Manage-

ment". In Working Notes of the Agents '99 Workshop on Agents for Electronic Commerce and Managing the Internet-Enabled Supply Chain., Seattle, WA, April 1999."
10. Jill Dahlburg. "Developing a Viable Approach for Effective Tiered Systems". NRL Memorandum Report 1001-07-9024. January 17, 2007

Chapter 8 Future Directions and Conclusion

Abstract Industrial applications and future commercial opportunities offer a useful perspective and provide the ability to identify key issues and future trends for multi-agent research in coordination. This chapter focuses on highlighting discrepancies between current and future needs and existing coordination technologies. In this context, it is organized to draw attention to potential directions and opportunities for future research, and discusses a wide range of open and emerging issues pertaining to multi-agent coordination.

8.1 Research Directions

Academic research has made substantive applied research contributions in varying degree to industry. Major technological opportunities and breakthroughs have resulted from bi-directional flow of ideas across boundaries between academia and industry. Indeed, industrial innovations and technological change in both economy and society have always been significantly influenced by academic research and development. With currently deployed agent-based applications featuring characteristics of prototypes developed through academic research, it is obviously clear that the area of research related to agent technologies is not an exception.

Insightful exploration of current industrial applications and future commercial opportunities offers a useful perspective and provides the ability to identify key issues and project trends for future multi-agent research. As already stated, despite intense and persistent efforts consented to building practical agent-oriented applications, the actual number of deployed systems is still surprisingly limited. Attempts to explore the obstacles preventing the development and consistent widespread use of such applications may offer the opportunity to better understand current progress, grasp current preoccupations of researchers and practitioners, dissect their priorities, and identify research issues in this area.

Indeed, current agent-oriented applications deployed in industry and other sectors can be described as classical systems driven by the need to solve practical problems, rather than test the possibility of existing technologies. Focusing on practical results, a project aiming to build and deploy an agent-based system is evaluated based on how well it addresses and solves a problem, instead of how sophisticated is the technology. Deployed real-world agent-oriented applications highlight the existing gap between theoretical research and practice.

A. Bedrouni et al., *Distributed Intelligent Systems: A Coordination Perspective*,
DOI: 10.1007/978-0-387-77702-3_8, © Springer Science + Business Media, LLC 2009

As noted, it is commonly acknowledged that building practical industrial-strength systems bringing together a large number of interacting agents is an inherently complex construction endeavor. However, practical applications in current deployment may indeed be characterized as *closed* agent-based systems featuring a set of systemic properties. Indeed, existing applications are each designed and developed by a *single team* to allow a group of *homogeneous* agents to interact within a *single corporate environment*. Only suited for a *single problem-domain*, each system incorporates an ensemble of participating agents that share common high-level goals. Hence, the design of such systems obeys to a traditional approach which consists in analyzing the task domain so as to impose upon participating entities pre-defined rules, languages, and typically in-house interaction protocols. Provided with ready-to-use knowledge, participating agents can thus interact effectively, share a common environment, and exhibit a set of desirable properties. On the other hand, despite considerable efforts to address scalability problems, current applications are scalable under "controlled or simulated conditions". Rather than implementing appropriate standard design methodologies, practical agent-oriented systems are thus currently conceived and developed using ad hoc design rationale inspired by the agent paradigm.

Indeed, a range of practical industrial and commercial problems can only be addressed through open, robust, secure, scalable, and multi-corporate agent-based approach. However, growing security concerns arising in open environments may obviously slow down the development and delay the introduction of open and large-scale agent-oriented applications. Thus, it is unlikely that the acknowledged commercial need for well-secured and closed agent-based applications will decline and suddenly cease as progress in the area of multi-agent research will promote and impose novel technologies.

In addition to this broad view on actual progress related to deploying commercial and industrial agent-oriented applications, current academic research interests and activities in this area have also been monitored so as to extract appropriate information for identifying trends for future research. Without any reference to a timescale, future developments in the area of multi-agent systems can thus be distinguished along the following dimensions:

1. Inter-corporate agent-based applications.
2. Heterogeneity of agents.
3. Scalability of emerging agent-oriented systems.
4. Openness of next generation systems.

8.1.1 Inter-corporate Agent-based Applications

AgentCities [1], *Grid computing* [2], and the *Universal Information Ecosystem* [3] are few examples of many on-going strategic research initiatives designed to create worldwide networks of agents (Figure 8.1). Though the end-objective is to produce truly open, robust, adaptive, self-organizing, and scalable environments, it is highly likely that the next phase will, in the *short-term*, lead to the development of systems that address the same domain *across corporate boundaries*.

Thus, while inter-agent interactions will obviously concern the same domain, emerging systems will, in contrast with actual applications, bring together a large diversity of agents having fewer goals in common. Despite this growing diversity, agents incorporated into a given system will, in the short term, still be designed by the same team in charge of designing a whole system. Based on current research to develop Grid applications and AgentCities, emerging agent-oriented technologies will thus provide the ability to integrate, handle, and federate a large number of distributed agents within *pre-determined environments*. Thus, *interaction protocols* required to implement such complex applications will, in the short term, still *remain non-standard*. However, agent-oriented systems' designers will, in the foreseeable future, increasingly rely on *standard communications languages*, such as the Foundation for Intelligent Physical Agents (FIPA) Agent Communication Language (ACL).

Figure 8.1 Agent platforms around the world registered in the AgentCities Network- February 2003 [1]

8.1.2 Heterogeneity of Agents

Substantial efforts to address real-world problems in areas such as e-Commerce and Bioinformatics will, in the *medium-term*, lead to agent-oriented systems that allow flexible integration of diverse *heterogeneous agents* conceived and developed by different designers. This step will give birth to open commercial and industrial agent-based applications. However, such systems will be specifically designed for *particular application domains*.

Available agent-oriented technologies will be such that participating agents will be designed to behave in accordance with *"publicly-stated requirements and standards"*. In this respect, systems' designers from different design team will, in the medium term, use either *pre-defined* and *agreed-upon* or *standardized interaction protocols*. Based on current research, it is likely that agents will, in the medium term, be allowed to evaluate and use *alternative coordination protocols* and *mechanisms* drawn from accessible *public libraries*.

On the other hand, while standardized communications languages will still be used, it is commonly acknowledged that language and terminological heterogeneity could greatly affect inter-agent communication. In this respect, problems associated with *semantic heterogeneity* will certainly be addressed particularly through the use of different *ontologies* about various topics. Since heterogeneous agents will use private ontologies, systems' designers will have to devise an approach designed to allow *merging* and *mapping* of individual ontologies.

8.1.3 Scalability of Emerging Agent-oriented Systems

Indeed, advances in networking technologies are paving the way towards building *large-scale* agent-oriented application systems. In the *medium-term*, it is expected that *large numbers* of autonomous and *heterogeneous* entities will be deployed in networks and the Web to pursue specific goals related to *different domains*. In this context, specific abstractions, methodologies and tools are greatly required to enable an engineered approach to building such complex applications.

Thus, a fundamental issue underlying the design of high-quality, large-scale, and complex agent-based systems lies in the need to adequately and effectively handle interactions between continuously active and heterogeneous agents involved in different domains. As mentioned in the literature, this decisive phase in the emergence of truly scalable agent-based systems is likely to witness the development of *bridge agents* designed to translate between separate domains. In a multi-agent application built to automate the design of a given product, bridge agents can be used to interact with other e-Commerce systems and engage in effective commercial negotiations for ensuring access to patent-protected information. On the other hand, standard agent-specific design methodologies, including design patterns and architectural patterns, are important vehicles for constructing reliable and high-quality large-scale systems.

8.1.4 Openness of Next Generation Systems

In the *long-term*, agent-oriented research is expected to result in unprecedented implementation of *open* and loosely coupled multi-agent systems. Incorporating *heterogeneous entities* developed by *different design teams*, an open system will be deployed across *multiple application domains*. Using agent-specific design methodologies, such systems will be developed to exhibit openness and thus a genuine scalability, in that no limit or restriction will be imposed on complexity and the number of autonomous agents and users.

In this respect, handling agent *behavior* in future open agent-based systems will present a special issue. It requires methodologies and tools to predict, control, and prevent undesirable behavior attributed to agents in open and large-scale applications. Consequently, agents may be designed to *learn appropriate behavior*, instead of having to adhere to a given code of conduct or behavior prior to joining the system.

As already discussed, standard communication languages and interaction protocols will have been developed before the emergence of open agent-oriented systems. Rather than defining and imposing communication languages and interaction protocols, inter-agent coordination will be tailored to particular contexts. Thus, in future open systems, agent communication and coordination will evolve from actual interactions of participating entities.

8.2 Technological Challenges

In summarizing present and future developments in the area of agent-oriented systems, the previous section shed light on a variety of new challenges in R&D over the next decade. Indeed, the area of agent-oriented systems is a rapidly expanding field of R&D. It represents an amalgam of disparate ideas, theories, and practices originating from such areas as distributed computing, software engineering, artificial intelligence, economics, sociology, organizational science, and biology.

Agent-oriented R&D will have a considerable impact in various application domains such as those described in the previous chapter. Agent concepts and paradigms will be used as an abstraction tool and a metaphor to design and build complex, distributed computational systems. While offering an appropriate way of considering complex systems as multiple, distinct, and independent entities, agent-based approaches will remain a source of technologies for building a number of challenging real-world applications.

As stated above, current deployed applications can be described as typically closed systems, designed through ad hoc methodologies, scalable in simulations, and incorporating pre-defined communication languages and interaction protocols.

However, current technology development such as Web Services, Grid computing, and peer-to-peer toolkits are rapidly changing the way systems deployed in public networks are integrated to interact. In this context, it is likely that real-world problems will, in the long-term, impose the emergence of truly-open, fully-scalable agent-oriented systems, spanning across different domains, and incorporating heterogeneous entities capable of learning and adopting adequate protocols of communication and interaction. With the perspective of deploying such open, dynamic, and unpredictable environments, the traditional critical issue regarding the coordination of participating agents will remain a fundamental challenge in multi-agent R&D.

Indeed, located at the heart of the area of agent-based systems is a central concept of intelligent and autonomous agents interacting with one another to achieve individual or collective goals. However, agent-oriented technology is breaking with current practices to undergo a transition from monolithic systems based on a single overall design philosophy to open architectures involving conglomerates of heterogeneous, and independently designed agents and agent-based systems. Among all the identified problems inherent in such dynamic environments, none is more complex than the fundamental and imperative need to appropriately control and coordinate the activities attributed to large number of disparate entities. Based on the practical issues discussed above, an attempt is thus made to objectively identify future academic and industrial research themes directly related to inter-agent interaction. Since short-term issues are already being addressed by the research community, this section is consequently dedicated to what is considered as strategic medium and long-term research objectives.

8.2.1 Appropriate Design Methodologies

As already noted, despite widely acknowledged advantages associated with agent-oriented technologies, the number of deployed agent-based applications is still limited. Thus, the discrepancy between the current state-of-the-art in agent-oriented research and the actual deployment of commercial and industrial agent-based systems should obviously deserve a greater attention. In this respect, researchers and practitioners often highlight the current use of ad-hoc design methodologies with limited specification of requirements in order to explain the gap between academic promises and reality.

The lack of widely-accepted development tools and methodologies is described as one of the major roadblocks to commercial and industrial deployment of such applications. In this context, the implementation of comprehensive *analysis* and *design methodologies* dealing with both the macro-level – *societal* - and micro-level – *agent* – aspects is commonly seen as appropriate to enhancing the quality of agent-based applications to industrial standard. These methodologies would provide the ability to model and specify agent-based systems and their corresponding requirements. However, attempts to develop appropriate analysis and design methodologies imply the need to identify characteristics of real-world applications, in relation to specific domains. In describing the semantics of agent-based systems – without any concern for implementation details, specifications of requirements will, on the other hand, provide a basis for verification, testing and validation of systems' functional and non-functional properties.

According to the *Foundation for Intelligent Physical Agents*[1] (FIPA), existing development methodologies - *AOR, Cassiopeia, Gaia, Mase, Message, PASSI, Tropos* – provide different advantages when applied to specific problems. It is thus argued that a developer of an agent-based system would prefer to use phases or models coming from different methodologies so as to generate a personalized approach suited for his own problem. Focusing on the identification of an appropriate analysis and design methodology, the FIPA Technical Committee proposes the adoption of the method engineering as the referring paradigm to allow developers to reuse contributions from existing methodologies. In other words, FIPA suggests that a developer can use coherent fragments from existing and future contributions the best analysis and design process for his or her needs and problems.

Anyway, a fundamental requirement associated with the process of analyzing, designing, and constructing large-scale, open, and loosely coupled agent-based systems lies in the ability to ensure certain properties and handle features, such as goals, mobility, adaptation, learning, autonomy, planning, coordination, etc. Thus, appropriate techniques will be developed and implemented to model and structure properly functional as well as non-functional properties in the suitable development stage. In this context, basic to the analysis of future open environments is the use of "*dedicated concepts and languages*":

- Concepts representing dynamic – e.g., *time* and *action* – and locality aspects – e.g., *position in a space* – as well as mental state – e.g., *belief* and *desire*.
- Concepts related to coordination, interaction, organization, and society – e.g., *organization forms, society norms, interaction protocols, joint goals*, and *joint plans*.

8.2.2 Standards

Emerging properties regarding ubiquity, openness and scalability of agent-oriented systems provide a framework to support future research in this area. A key to a successful transition from current applications to building complex systems exhibiting such properties lies in the need to formulate, establish, and implement effective and largely agreed-upon standards to support interoperability between heterogeneous agents.

---

[1] http://www.fipa.org/activities/methodology.html

Agent-oriented standardization efforts are currently conducted through different bodies and communities: the Knowledge Query Meta Language[2] (KQML), the Object Management Group[3] (OMG), the Mobile Agent System Interoperability Facility[4] (MASIF), and FIPA. However, FIPA has emerged as the leading and significant active organization. Relying on input from its members as well as the agent research community in general, this organization was formed to produce and promote standards for heterogeneous and interacting agents and agent-based systems.

Among other important activities, FIPA is currently addressing various issues directly related to agent communication and interaction:

- Develop a new semantic framework to reflect the need for verifiability and conformance. The objective is to particularly adopt or define a semantic framework that can give an account of FIPA's existing communication acts and interaction protocols as well as a number of additional constructs such as contracts, agreements, policies, trust, agent descriptions, etc.
- Establish a *roadmap* on how to develop a second generation of new interaction protocols. Indeed, the literature regarding agent-oriented systems has repeatedly outlined the importance of developing new interaction protocols in accordance with parallel efforts directed towards building open and scalable applications. In the medium-term, it is likely that future communication and interaction protocols will be largely agreed-upon and standardized.
- Standardize methods for knowledge sharing and filtering through ontological representation. Such an approach will allow interoperating systems to automate message processing with respect to cross-referenced semantic classification. These efforts will enable a structured, standardized approach designed to support multiple ontologies.

However, rather than specifying how agents process and reason about received information, FIPA focuses on specifying communication and interoperability between heterogeneous entities. In other words, this organization concentrates on agent interfaces or on specifying external communication rather than the internal processing of the communication at the receiver. In addition, a drawback associated with FIPA standards lies in the absence of tools offering the ability to certify FIPA compliant platforms. Obviously, this drawback comes from the difficulty to validate platform behavior through an interface designed to allow agents to exchange messages.

Furthermore, a crucial requirement of future ubiquitous, open, and scalable agent-based systems is to address the issue of having to use a large number of alternative protocols designed for specific interactions. To deal with more sophisticated interactions, future agent-oriented applications are likely to incorporate pub-

---

[2] http://www.cs.umbc.edu/kqml/
[3] http://www.objs.com/survey/omg.htm
[4] http://www.fokus.gmd.de/research/cc/ecco/masif/

lic libraries of specifically dedicated interaction protocols. Some protocols will likely use existing communication languages such as the Contract Net and other protocols based on the Dutch auction and the English auction which use FIPA ACL. On the other hand, other protocols may be implemented using in-house or ad-hoc communication languages like many dialogue game protocols designed for agent argumentation.

Based on current debate over future agent-oriented applications, it is likely that activities parallel to on-going standardization efforts will be conducted to develop approaches and tools that provide heterogeneous agents in open systems with the ability to collectively evolve communication languages and interaction protocols suited for an application domain and participating agents. Research addressing this particular issue is both complex and challenging, in that it is designed to allow a group of agents with no prior experience of each other to evolve a sophisticated communication language or interaction protocol. Such research is expected to draw from linguistics, social anthropology, biology, information theory, etc.

8.2.3 Incorporate Learning and Reasoning Capabilities

Coordinating heterogeneous interactions in open and scalable systems spanning across different real-world domains raises the challenging problem of uncertainty in terms of dynamism, observability, and non-determinism. In the absence of common pre-established protocols to deal with large numbers of agents, each with its own beliefs, goals and intentions, inter-agent coordination in open and scalable systems will, as already noted, rely on libraries of alternative standardized interaction protocols. In this context, designers will incorporate into future open systems learning and reasoning ability to allow heterogeneous agents to make rational decisions under uncertainty, update beliefs from information, determine new intentions, act on the basis of these intentions, and dynamically select an appropriate interaction protocol or mechanism.

8.2.4 Agent Organizations

In "*Agent-based computing: Promise and Perils*" [4], Jennings argues that the development of robust and scalable systems requires agents that can *complete* their *objectives* while situated in a dynamic and uncertain environment, engage in rich *high-level interactions*, and operate within *flexible organizational structures*. Moreover, he observes that the problem regarding scalability of agent-oriented systems is increasingly complex as the number of agents in a system will, at a given time, fluctuate significantly in open and dynamic environments [5].

Advocated by Foster et al. [6], the concept of *virtual organization* can be used to design adequate flexible organizational structures in future open and scalable agent-based applications. In the area of Grid computing, a virtual organization refers to dynamic collections of individuals, institutions, and resources. Thus, the specific problem that underlies the Grid concept is *coordinated resource sharing and problem solving in dynamic, multi-institutional virtual organizations*.

On the other hand, in addressing challenging organizational problems, researchers introduced various notions such as *self-organization* and *adaptation* to support the design and deployment of complex systems suitable for real-world application domains. In other words, open agent-oriented systems should be both *self-building* – agents are able to determine the most appropriate organizational structure for the system – and *adaptive* – agents change this structure as the environment changes. Thus, self-organization represents *"the process of generating social structure, adapting and changing organizational structure"* [7]. It is the result of individual choices by a set of agents to engage in interaction in certain organizational patterns, depending on their own resources and the environmental context, enabling agents to reason and have such kind of behavior.

On the other hand, existing agent organizations cannot handle adequately issues inherent in open agent-oriented systems, such as heterogeneity of agents, trust and accountability, failure and recovery, and societal change. Future research efforts may thus partly focus on developing appropriate representations of analogous computational concepts analogous to norms, rights, legislation, authorities, enforcement, etc. In this context, researchers may need to draw on political science and sociology to develop sophisticated agent societies.

8.2.5 Coalition Formation

Agent organizations in future open and scalable systems are likely to involve dynamic coalitions of small groups so as to provide better services than a single group. Through coalition formation, agents in large and open systems faced with a set of goals can thus partition themselves to maximize system performance [8]. Hence, self-organization can be achieved through coalition formation. While it provides better saving of time and labor, automating coalition formation may also lead to *"better coalitions than humans in complex settings"*.

In the past, coalition formation has been largely addressed in game theory to typically deal with centralized situations. Thus, computationally infeasible, the approach suffers from a number of serious drawbacks. Though, it generally favors grand coalitions, coalition formation is applicable for a small number of agents, thus limiting the scope of the application. However, research regarding the use of a dialect of modal propositional dynamic logic (PDL) to model games and interactions lead to appropriate representation of coalitions. This method may indeed prove efficient in introducing and formalizing reasoning about coalitions of agents.

8.2.6 Negotiation and Argumentation

Negotiation and argumentation strategies will certainly play an important role in designing and deploying future commercial and industrial agent-oriented applications. However, research regarding negotiation in agent-based systems can be described as disparate efforts and examples rather than a coherent negotiation science. Efforts devoted in this area have not yet provided a computational agent capable of effective negotiation in any arbitrary context. Strategies identified by economic or theoretic reasoning tend, for example, to be specific to the auction or game mechanism involved.

In addition, considered as more complex than auctions and game theoretic mechanisms, negotiation and deliberation mechanisms are not fully investigated. Parallel to enhancing research in negotiation mechanisms, appropriate argumentation strategies and mechanisms should also be investigated, developed and deployed.

Finally, future deployment of exiting negotiation and argumentation strategies and mechanisms requires the need to:

- Adequately evaluate existing algorithms to determine their strengths and weaknesses in more realistic environments.
- Identify the circumstances in which well-evaluated and adequate algorithms can be implemented.
- Design and develop negotiation algorithms adapted to more open, complex environments – e.g. argumentation.
- Develop adequate argumentation engines including more adapted argumentation strategies.
- Develop appropriate strategies and techniques to allow agents to identify, create, and dissolve coalitions in inter-agent negotiation and argumentation.
- Develop *domain-specific models of reasoning and argumentation.*
- Develop agent ability to adapt to changes in environment, etc.

8.3 Conclusion

A suitable coordination framework should be flexible enough to permit the detailed study of the challenging coordination issues that have been brought forth in this chapter. Furthermore, the framework should provide an ability to study and evaluate coordination under various resource constraints which may be imposed by the potential shortfall in the communications ability of the agents, as well as shortfalls in the agent's computational and temporal dimension. Communication constraints may include either complete lack of communication, or varying degrees of communication degradation. In these circumstances, can the agents share information with the network, and vice-versa, to enable a more robust coordination mechanism between the agents? This type of "cross-layer" information exchange would enable the agents to prioritize information so the network layer could give priority to more important coordination messages, and the network could provide information to the agents so the agents could "work around" network constraints. This mechanism would also lead to a more graceful degradation to the performance of the agent system as a whole. Nowhere is this more important than in Mobile Ad-Hoc Networks (MANET), where the nodes, or agents, are continuously moving, the routing topology may be continuously changing and hence the messages between agents may be delayed. Lastly, the framework should permit the study of issues such as security and privacy in information exchange and the impact to coordination.

With regard to the other types of constraints, agents may be bounded in the computational dimension due to lack of computing resources, or temporally such that decisions must be made in a relatively short time. The framework should allow the ability to study the tradeoffs between communications, computational and temporal bounds and their impacts to the quality of coordination, and subsequently to the quality of decisions that are made by the multi-agent system. The agent system should be adaptable under these constraints. Furthermore, coordination in the computational and temporal-bounded environments should include the costs and benefits associated with time needed for reasoning in a given context, compared with the set-up time and interaction "cycles" associated with the various coordination strategies and techniques.

The framework should provide flexibility for problem definition, and allow for studying different concepts, including models, algorithms, or agent-mediated decision support capabilities. Furthermore, the framework should permit basic simulation capabilities in order to validate advanced multi-agent coordination concepts in order to asses the value of coordination.

The framework should support the study of coordination in heterogeneous, uncertain and open environments where the numbers and capabilities of the agents are not fixed (but rather change over time), coordination models associated with the agents may be unknown to other agents, and there may be uncertainty in the agents understanding of the capability of other agents. Given the dynamic nature of this environment, issues might include the examination of the benefits and costs of using a mixture of implicit or explicit coordination metaphors such as stigmergy, organization structuring, market-based techniques, hybrid methods, etc based on the problem space complexity. Open environments will present uncertainties in many dimensions regarding the actions or intentions of friendly agents, and those that might be adversaries; hence, coordination must be studied under partially observable and non-deterministic environments. Furthermore, the ability to study the performance of a particular coordination mechanism or technique in dynamic and open environments should be provided, particularly in the context of modeling adversarial agents (e.g., adversarial intent and plan recognition). As a specific example, some deficiencies in surveillance and reconnaissance to enable persistence, penetration and identification, battle damage assessment, and data processing, exploitation, and dissemination are due to serious limits [*of sensor assets*] to penetrate foliage, track individuals, defeat camouflage, and identify decoys. Dealing with these surveillance and reconnaissance challenges will require better sensors, better cooperation, or better models of adversarial behaviors. However, even as users become more dependent on improved capabilities of networked sensors, additional capabilities can be gained by modeling adversarial behaviors and the ability to model deception. This is an area where game theory can play a significant role in understanding adversarial behaviors, which can be encoded in coordination techniques in order to enable the agents to react more efficiently.

Despite all proposed frameworks, a unified approach for coordination remains elusive as there is still no single best way to coordinate due to problem space properties, domain, system and state characteristic dependencies, required frequency of interaction and, respective intrinsic strengths and weaknesses of various approaches. Can a unified coordination framework be achieved, and under what circumstances? What are the conditions to dynamically switch between centralized and decentralized mechanisms? Agent-based coordination is limited, in part, by the fact that agent technologies are still primarily built within stove-piped architectures, in many cases causing duplication of efforts and barriers to coordination across large and diverse communities of interest.

In exploring the progress that has been achieved with regard to coordination of multi-agent systems, it is evident that many in the research community have acknowledged the need to develop "unifying" models and frameworks in order to better understand the coordination process, and indeed researchers are moving in that direction. However, it is apparent the community can gain tremendous knowledge through a formal and systematic documentation of the "best practices" for the use of pre-existing as well as new coordination models and techniques under realistic operational environments. This should lead to further opportunities to incorporate new approaches in multi-agent coordination within more mainstream application domains.

Lastly, here we devote a small discussion on a topic that has not been previously addressed in this book, in particular, the relationship between coordination and vulnerability / risk. With large scale agent systems, it may not always be clear which agents are malicious. Hence, coordination becomes a challenge as an agent may only wish to coordinate with the trusted agents, but in an open environment where agents may not provide all of their information to other agents, knowing which the trusted agents are and which are the malicious agents can be difficult. In many cases, it may not be possible to determine if an agent is malicious simply through the circulation of control messages. These situations require a more sophisticated method of detecting vulnerabilities posed by malicious agents. We briefly describe two notional approaches to dealing with this problem; one directed at agent self monitoring and the other at monitoring other agents.

Because the actions of malicious agents can have effects on the behavior of other, cooperative agents, it is important that agents be able to reason about their own behavior as well as the behavior of others. Many multi-agent algorithms require agents to sacrifice all or part of their autonomy in order to achieve team goals. While this can benefit the system, it also leaves the agents susceptible to exploitation by malicious agents. Under these circumstances, the first notional approach would involve technologies that would allow a cooperative agent to detect when it is involved in undesirable behavior which might be indicative of the presence of a malicious agent.

The second notional approach is based on the development of agent models describing normal behavior of other agents, and subsequently using these models to detect anomalies where agents behave differently than expected. Such anomalous behavior may indicate the presence of a malicious (or malfunctioning) agent and hence a vulnerability. Normalcy models have been used in computer network security applications, where system activity is monitored for anomalous behavior in order to detect network intrusions or misuse. The challenge from a distributed MAS perspective in building normalcy models of other agents is due to decentralized environments, where the propagation of information between agents is unreliable and, hence the environment is partially observable. This contrasts with current approaches found in other disciplines, which are primarily centralized, static, and depend on reliable communication. In a decentralized environment, all agents should construct and maintain normalcy models, while sharing information and / or models with neighbors.

Techniques that can lead to the development of multi-resolution models in order to recognize anomalous (i.e., malicious) agents would be potentially more robust as compared with those that employ a single model, Such a "layered" approach to anomaly detection, with the layers defined by the model resolution i.e., individual agent (instance) models, models of classes of agents and team behavior models, would help an agent overcome potential deficiencies in any one layer while being able to aggregate information from all layers in order to more intelligently reason about potential anomalies. For example, normalcy models of agents may have biases due to the fact that those models may have been developed by an agent with limited (or even incorrect) information, or being based on idiosyncratic behavior. However, by developing normalcy models for classes of agents, it may be possible to remove any biases that exist at the individual agent level model.

A key research question in the development of instance normalcy models is when to modify or update an instance level model of other agents (issue of model aging and refresh), and should it be based on information received from these other agents in question, or from third party agents? The concern for the agent that is updating the model is one of trust; if there is a mechanism that has enabled trust to be developed between agents, then it would be more advisable for the agent to update its models of other agents based on information it receives from trusted agents than perhaps less trusted agents.

Several key research questions arise in the development of class behavior models. For example, how to merge the output of much simpler individual agent models into aggregate models based on classes? Also, when and how often should the aggregate models be updated based on changes to the instance level models? Due to the possible explosion in the number of instance models in the system, can synchronizing fewer class models across the agents overcome the need to synchronize the many more individual agent models, and how well does the system of agents perform with respect to anomaly detection? Furthermore, can biases such as poor information in relation to the construction of instance models be overcome through the use and sharing of class models? A notional approach for developing aggregate i.e., class models, might be based on broker techniques that weight the output from the instance layer (based on model age, etc) in order to compute the aggregate models, with perhaps feedback mechanisms between the class and instance layers.

A key research question in the development of team behavior models, which may be composed of a mixture of instance and class models, concerns the development of scalable reasoning capabilities to understand potential anomalies within the context of the dynamic operating environment. Reasoning across each model layer within the context of the environment is also likely to produce a more accurate understanding that reduces false alarms regarding anomalies. For example, observing an unmanned aerial vehicle agent deviating (i.e., anomaly) from its expected flight path may be explained by high wind (environment). While it is impractical to enumerate all environmental contexts in a given setting, the key research challenge is how to develop scalable reasoning capabilities about anomalies when dealing with a large variety of models as envisioned through a mixture of instance and class models, as well as in the face of a complex operating environment. The development of scalable agent reasoning capabilities, specifically regarding the impact of context data on the behavior of the other autonomous agents may lead to an understanding of whether the resulting behaviors can be reasonably explained, or whether they are indeed anomalous and might present a vulnerability and risk in trying to coordinate activities with such agents.

Inherently cross-disciplinary in nature, the coordination concept is located right at the intersection of various disciplines, including computer science, sociology, psychology, biology, political science, managerial and organization sciences, and economics. While there is a broad consensus that the issue of coordination is highly interdisciplinary, the lack of a true trans-borders flow of information and knowledge between disciplines is however commonly acknowledged.

In the absence of a desirable systematic integration of ideas, concepts, and paradigms from different disciplines, trans-disciplinary exchange of knowledge pertaining to coordination, rather that being well-established, can only be described as sporadic. A strongly advocated solution thus lies on the need to bring the concerned research communities driven by common research goals around concerted actions designed to organize heterogeneous views, ideas, concepts, methods, and approaches from different disciplines within a common conceptual framework.

Common to this perspective is the idea that such actions would offer the prospect of gradually inducing cross-fertilization in the interdisciplinary research area of coordination. In this respect, designing a set of classification schemes to group a large diversity of concepts, models, and approaches is identified in this book as an attractive solution for making order out the chaos and mess characterizing research pertaining to coordination. It is thus highly recommended to focus on defining and establishing alternative sub-theme taxonomies that are stable, formal, and recognized across disciplines in order to bridge gaps, facilitate the integration of fragmented results, bring clusters of coordination experts together, establish a true collaboration across traditional disciplinary boundaries, and provide an effective transfer of coordination knowledge and technology to industry.

From a lack of a unitary view across disciplines, a global and unanimous consensus is forged on the common idea that the concept of coordination, though ill-defined, is inherently vital to building complex systems and organizations. However, the disparate area of research pertaining to coordination is still characterized by very serious and frustrating inconsistencies in terminology related to vital corresponding objects, attributes, or features. Indeed, a key recommendation of the present book is to bring a panel of experts from various disciplines in order to establish and incorporate a specific standard terminology relative to coordination. Such standard vocabulary would be used as a foundation for defining concepts, expressing models and frameworks, and specifying protocols and mechanisms.

Characterizing the state-of-the-art research in the area of coordination is a particularly complex endeavour, as the space of available approaches is indeed considerable, and research is independently conducted in a great number of domains. While existing surveys deal with specific aspects of coordination, the major contribution of this book lies in the attempt to provide an in-depth review covering a wide range of issues regarding multi-agent coordination in DAI. In addition to reporting various sources of confusion, this book outlines the existence of a plethora of protocols and mechanisms adapted to different problems, agent-oriented systems, environments, and domains. In short, the current study identifies the absence of a single unified approach to address multi-agent coordination problems arising in any system or organization.

In the presence of multiple coordination strategies and a corresponding wide range of protocols and mechanisms, developing adequate performance-based measurement procedures represents an important cornerstone of the area of DAI for building robust agent-oriented systems and applications. While reporting about only few studies dedicated to this issue, the present book outlines the absence of a commonly accepted standard and highlights the need for additional efforts to address the specific need for developing coordination performance measurement criteria and metrics.

Based on the examination of current status and future opportunities, the present book identifies major challenges in the area of multi-agent coordination over the next decade. Indeed, currently deployed agent-oriented applications can be typically characterized as closed systems incorporating predefined communication and interaction protocols. In the long-term, current research efforts will however lead to the emergence of ubiquitous, truly-open, fully-scalable agent-based systems, spanning across multiple domains, and integrating arbitrary numbers of heterogeneous agents capable of reasoning and learning appropriate communication and interaction protocols.

Over the next decade, research in the area of multi-agent systems is likely to be directed towards bridging the gap between academic promises and reality. In this respect, particular efforts will focus on enhancing the quality of agent-based systems to industrial standards. In the mid-term, the research community will thus concentrate on providing widely-accepted analysis and design tools and methodologies in order to remove a major obstacle to future deployment of highly sophisticated, open and scalable systems. On the other hand, similar collective efforts will trigger the use of libraries of standardized communication and interaction protocols. In addition, more complex approaches are likely to be developed to allow future open and scalable agent-oriented systems to evolve communication languages and interaction protocols specific to application domains and agents involved.

Finally, the emergence of various concepts such as virtual organizations and self-organization will result in the use of dynamic coalitions – coalitions that automatically form and disband – of small groups of agents equipped with learning and reasoning abilities. Related to this challenge, various issues that will be similarly addressed to devise novel concepts, approaches, and techniques include domain-specific models of reasoning, negotiation and argumentation. Future research associated with open and scalable systems will also be devoted to other issues related to inter-agent coordination: reusability, mobility, emergent behaviour, and fault-tolerance.

References

1. Jonathan Dale, Bernard Burg, and Steven Willmott, "The Agentcities Initiative: Connecting Agents Across the World", In WRAC 2002, LNAI 2564, W. Truszkowski, C. Rouff, M. Hinchey, Editors, pp. 453-457, Springer-Verlag, 2003.
2. Soumen Mukherjee, Joy Mustafi, and Abhik Chaudhuri, "Grid Computing: The Future of Distributed Computing for High Performance Scientific and Business Applications", In IWDC 2002, LNCS 2571, S.K. Das and S. Bhattacharya, Editors, pp. 339–342, Springer-Verlag, 2002.
3. P Marrow, E Bonsma, F Wang and C Hoile, "DIET — a Scalable, Robust and Adaptable Multi-agent Platform for Information Management", In BT Technology Journal, Vol. 21, No 4, October 2003.
4. Jennings, N, "Agent-based computing: Promise and Perils", In Proceedings of the 16th International Joint Conference on Artificial Intelligence (IJCAI-99), pp. 1429–1436, 1999.
5. P. J. Turner and N. R. Jennings, "Improving the Scalability of Multi-Agent Systems", Proceedings of the 1st International Workshop on Infrastructure for Scalable Multi-Agent Systems, Barcelona, 2000.
6. Ian Foster, Carl Kesselman, and Steven Tuecke, "The Anatomy of the Grid: Enabling Scalable Virtual Organizations", In International Journal of Supercomputer Applications, 2001.

7. M. Schillo, Klaus Fischer, Bettina Fley, Michael Florian, Frank Hillebrandt, and Daniela Spresny, "FORM – A Sociologically Founded Framework for Designing Self-Organization of Multiagent Systems", In RASTA 2002, LNAI 2934, G. Lindemann et al., Editors, pp. 156–175, Springer-Verlag, 2004.
8. Mark Sims, Claudia V. Goldman, and Victor Lesser, "Self-Organization through Bottom-up Coalition Formation", In Proceedings of the second international joint conference on Autonomous Agents and Multiagent Systems, pp. 867-874, 2003.

Index